Budget Deficits and Debt

Budget Deficits and Debt

A GLOBAL PERSPECTIVE

EDITED BY
Siamack Shojai

Westport, Connecticut
London

Library of Congress Cataloging-in-Publication Data

Budget deficits and debt : a global perspective / edited by Siamack
  Shojai.
     p. cm.
   Includes bibliographical references and index.
   ISBN 0–275–95712–8 (alk. paper)
   1. Budget deficits.   2. Debts, Public.   I. Shojai, Siamack.
  HJ2005.B797   1999
  339.5'23—dc21   98–15653

British Library Cataloguing in Publication Data is available.

Library of Congress Catalog Card Number: 98–15653
ISBN: 0–275–95712–8

First published in 1999

Praeger Publishers, 88 Post Road West, Westport, CT 06881
An imprint of Greenwood Publishing Group, Inc.

Printed in the United States of America

The paper used in this book complies with the
Permanent Paper Standard issued by the National
Information Standards Organization (Z39.48–1984).

10 9 8 7 6 5 4 3 2 1

To my sons,
Saman, Sohrob, and Soheil,
and to my parents

Contents

Preface

Since World War II, many economies of different sizes and states of development have experienced unprecedented fiscal imbalances. The Cold War and the economic rivalry between the Western and Eastern bloc countries overwhelmed the socioeconomic and political life of the United States and many European countries as well as many developing nations, leading to the creation of a welfare state in many parts of the world and accompanying huge fiscal deficits. Many researchers and politicians are still debating and alarming the public about the potential adverse effects of these deficits on the global economy.

This volume deals with the challenges and new developments in the global economy concerning the fiscal actions of various nations. Part I provides a discussion of technical issues related to budget deficits. In particular, it provides a good analysis of measures of a deficit, the politics of the budget process, and the size of deficits in the U.S. and Organization for Economic Cooperation and Development (OECD) economies. Part II deals with the economic consequences of budget deficits. A comprehensive survey of the issues and theoretical as well as empirical studies of fiscal imbalances is provided in this section. Part III addresses the political economy of deficits in European, U.S., and developing economies. A major effort has been made to include a thorough discussion of all aspects and issues related to fiscal imbalances in this volume. However, a comprehensive and exhaustive presentation would require at least two additional volumes of this nature.

The views presented in this volume are those of the authors and do not represent the views of their corresponding institutions. Eileen Casey of Manhattan College deserves recognition for her dedication and assistance in the preparation of the manuscript. Professors Kudret Topyan, James M. Suarez, and two other anonymous colleagues deserve special thanks for agreeing to serve on the board of referees for this volume. Preparation of this volume has been supported by a generous grant from the Capalbo Endowed Fund at Manhattan College during the 1995–1996 academic year. The late Louis F. Capalbo, his wife, Mrs. Ruth Capalbo, and his entire family deserve my gratitude for their support of this book and two previous volumes on oil markets. Finally, my wife and children have my special thanks for understanding the many times I missed family occasions and for providing a peaceful and loving home to complete this task.

Introduction

SIAMACK SHOJAI

The controversial nature of fiscal policy and budget deficits has puzzled many students of economics. On the one hand, some argue that budget deficits do not matter. On the other hand, many politicians and policy makers across the globe are overly concerned about the existence of huge and persistent fiscal imbalances in many countries across the business cycles. This volume attempts to shed more light on these controversial public policy issues by gathering the expertise of a group of recognized scholars in this field. Addressing such diverse and specialized issues is beyond the ability and expertise of one individual scholar. Thus, the task is accomplished by a diverse group of scholars with expertise in finance and economics. This volume deals with the size, measurement, causes, consequences, and political economy of fiscal deficits.

In Chapter 1, Siamack Shojai introduces different measures of government budget deficits and debt. He cautions the reader about the potential impact of different measures of a deficit on the conclusions reached by the experts.

A brief discussion of the budget process in the United States and the interplay of politics and economics in the process is provided in Chapter 2 by James M. Suarez. The author addresses some major differences between the federal budgeting institutions and the states' budget institutions in the United States. He concludes that the checks and balances in the U.S. fiscal system are intended to reach a consensus and to protect the freedom of American people. Economic efficiency is not a consideration in this elaborate system.

In Chapter 3, James L. Chan distinguishes process-oriented laws and outcome-oriented budget laws that intend to reduce the federal budget deficit in the United States. After an overview of the major federal budget acts, Chan concludes that the budget laws are an effective tool for the budgetary process but are inadequate instruments for controlling the federal budget.

In Chapter 4, Anthony D. Apostolides examines the fiscal records of the countries of the Organization for Economic Cooperation and Development (OECD) and demonstrates that the ratio of national debt to gross domestic product increased enormously in all OECD nations because of dramatic increases in government spending rather than because of lower revenues. He carefully analyzes several factors that have contributed to higher spending.

In Chapter 5, James R. Barth and John M. Wells study alternative views and associated empirical evidence regarding federal budget deficits and economic activity in the United States. They suggest that the budget deficit may have negative effects on economic activity.

A succinct review of the literature on the impact of fiscal imbalances on exchange rates is presented by Siamack Shojai in Chapter 6. He argues that the ambiguous pictures presented by the theoretical models are not elucidated by the empirical work done in this area.

A succinct overview of the impact of budget deficits on the inflation rate in Canada is presented by Sohrab Abizadeh and Mahmood Yousefi in Chapter 7. Their econometric model seems to indicate that deficits have not been inflationary in Canada.

In Chapter 8, Bruce Collins discusses a Wall Street view of the link between the U.S. federal budget deficits and the financial markets. He concludes that there is little evidence of budget deficits explicitly influencing financial markets and financial asset returns over most of the postwar period.

Major theoretical and empirical studies of the relationship between budget and trade deficits are presented in Chapter 9 by Hassan Mohammadi and Neil T. Skaggs. They demonstrate that the findings of econometric models are sensitive to measures of budget and trade deficits and the form in which the variables are entered into the model.

In Chapter 10, Siamack Shojai deals with the issue of economic growth and fiscal imbalances. Despite the theoretical arguments of standard growth models, government deficit financing may stimulate investments in research and development and other capital-forming activities.

In Chapter 11, Robert C. A. Sorensen studies the historical, philosophical, and political roots of the welfare state (system) in various European countries and in the United States. He argues that there are broad parallels in the entitlement programs developed in the United States and other advanced industrial societies. In addition, pressures to roll back or eliminate these programs were similar in these countries in the late 1970s and 1980s. More recent events demonstrate popular resistance to cutbacks in the welfare systems all across the industrial world.

In Chapter 12, Herschel I. Grossman presents the traditional normative theory of public debt. He argues that the history of fiscal policy in the United States and Great Britain from the 1930s until the 1970s is explicable without any reference to Keynesian economics.

In Chapter 13, James Alm and Raul A. Barreto examine the size, nature, and causes of budget deficits during the 1971–1985 period in a select group of developing countries from Africa, Asia, and Latin America. The economic and political causes of deficit spending in the context of Public Choice Theory are discussed and examined empirically. They argue that countries with more political corruption and hierarchical budget institutions tend to have a larger budget deficit.

In Chapter 14, Ismail Adams studies the new fiscal federalism in the New South Africa since 1994. He reviews recent fiscal developments and attempts to reduce the fiscal imbalances to 3 percent of the gross domestic product by the year 2000. The new decentralized fiscal system and its impact on budgetary discipline are discussed.

Finally, John C. Gormley, in his ''Bibliographical Essay,'' provides a succinct guide to printed and electronic sources of information concerning government fiscal data. While Gormley does not exhaust all of the sources of information in this field, he does provide the reader with an overview of the types of materials available.

In conclusion, this volume provides a diverse view of the causes and impact of fiscal imbalances and deals with the most significant theoretical, empirical, and public policy issues surrounding global fiscal activities. However, while the ambiguity surrounding these issues has been brought to the fore, no attempt has been made to resolve them. We leave that to future studies.

Part I

Technical Aspects of Budget Deficits

Chapter 1

Measures of Budget Deficits and National Debt

SIAMACK SHOJAI

In the following chapters, a group of well-known scholars provide an engaging discussion of issues related to global fiscal imbalances and their implications. It is interesting to realize that budget deficit is measured in different economies based on the legislative, accounting, and economic peculiarities of the respective countries' institutions. In addition, many authors utilize various measures of deficit and debt that suit their intellectual, analytical, and political aspirations and often provide excellent scientific justifications for their choices. This chapter provides a brief discussion of the different measures of budget deficits and debt that have been employed in economics and business research. The intention is to highlight, from the beginning, the significance of the choice of a deficit measure and its possible bearing on the conclusions reached by researchers.

THE U.S. BUDGET LANGUAGE

Providing a comparative analysis of budgetary measures across the countries is beyond the scope of this book. However, a discussion of U.S. budget language can shed light on similar issues for other nations. The U.S. federal budget consists of general, special, and trust funds. General funds are not linked to any specific government program. They receive all income taxes, excise taxes, borrowing, and other receipts. The operating expenses of most government entities, national defense, and interest on national debt are paid out of the general budget.

Special funds are used for specific government activities and are designated as trust funds. Their activities are financed by user fees and special collections. The National Wildlife Refugee Fund is an example of special funds (Schick, 1995).

Social Security and Medicare are examples of government activities that are kept separate from the general budget and are designated as trust funds. Contributions made to these funds are kept in their separate, designated accounts to protect the integrity of the programs and to keep them safe from the general fiscal imbalances of the federal government. Currently, they show a surplus, which is lent to the federal government; they receive interest from the general funds.

Since 1968, the federal government has adopted the principle of a unified budget. Accordingly, the general and trust funds are combined in the budget. However, the U.S. Congress has mandated the exclusion of Social Security and the U.S. Postal Service from the measurement of the federal deficit. Thus, the budget provides two deficits: the on-budget deficit and the consolidated, or unified, deficit, which includes the off-budget items. Many authors argue that for analytical reasons the off-budget items should be included in the measures of the deficit. Arthur Laffer (1993) demonstrates that inclusion of these items in the budget would have reduced the federal budget deficit in 1992 from a reported on-budget deficit of $449.125 billion to $399.733 billion.

Unlike corporations and state and local governments, the federal government does not differentiate between capital expenditures and current spending. All federal investments in physical assets such as buildings, bridges, roads, and weapons are treated like current expenses and are not depreciated over their useful life. According to Laffer (1993), these amounted to $198.2 billion in the fiscal year of 1992, which overstated the unified budget deficit dollar for dollar. It must be noted that these adjustments provide alternative figures for analytical purposes; however, the reduction in officially stated budget deficits does not alleviate the real cash flow problem of the government when its total outlays are more than its total receipts.

The federal government owns and sponsors many corporations that provide services in pursuit of government social programs in education, housing, and farming. Government-sponsored entities such as the Federal National Mortgage Association (Fannie Mae) are considered private enterprises and are excluded from the budget. Federally owned agencies like the Government National Mortgage Association keep their books on an accrual basis and cannot be included in the budget. However, two statements are provided for most government-owned corporations and present the revenue and expenses as well as the financial conditions of those entities.

The federal government is also involved in providing direct loans or loan guarantees to special groups in the economy. The Federal Credit Reform Act of 1990 requires that these be included in the budget on a subsidized cost basis as opposed to a cash basis. Various measures of deficits may or may not include these obligations.

In summary, four measures of federal budget deficits are provided by the government: the consolidated deficit, the on-budget deficit, the federal funds deficit, and the operating deficit. The consolidated deficit recognizes outlays and receipts on a cash basis and includes the off-budget items, operating and capital accounts, and trust funds. Social Security and U.S. Postal Service expenditures are taken out of the consolidated deficit to calculate the on-budget deficit. The federal funds deficit excludes Social Security and all other trust funds. Finally, the operating deficit measures the difference between receipts and expenditures, excluding capital investments.

ANALYTICAL MEASURES

Many researchers utilize the current absolute level of deficit in their econometrics work. Like all other economic variables, the current levels incorporate the inflationary pressures of the economy. Thus, an appropriate price index (deflator) is generally used to calculate the real or constant dollar deficits. The current figures are effective tools for politicians to catch the eye of the general public, but they are misleading. In chapters that follow, the reader will see that some analysts scale the absolute deficits to a measure of national income, generally, the gross domestic product (GDP). This will make comparisons across nations of different sizes more meaningful. However, some researchers have employed the absolute deficit in recognition of the hypothesis that the level of public debt affects real interest rates, exchange rates, and trade balances differently. A nonscaled deficit measure is employed to capture the size effect of the deficit (Humpage, 1992). Deficits as a percentage of total government spending or receipts are also other ways of scaling those measures.

The International Monetary Fund (IMF), in its *World Economic Outlook* (May 1996), employs the actual deficit, the output gap deficit, and the structural deficit. In 1995, as a group, the major industrial countries, had an actual deficit of 3.3 percent of GDP, an output gap of 1.5 percent of GDP, and a structural deficit of 2.5 percent of their gross domestic product. It is obvious that each measure shows a different picture of fiscal imbalances. These measures are based on an estimate of the potential output. The potential output (GDP) is that level of output when full employment is reached at nonaccelerating inflation. Once this output is estimated, the fiscal imbalances are calculated as a percentage of the potential output to reach the structural deficit. In addition, the output gap is calculated as the difference between the actual and the potential deficit expressed as a percentage of GDP. The IMF also provides measures of net debt and gross debt. Net debt is the difference between the gross government debt and the assets held by the Social Security insurance systems.

In what follows, various measures of debt and deficit, as provided by the IMF *World Economic Outlook* of 1996, are employed to calculate the standard deviation of these measures. The results for the United States, Japan, Germany, France, Italy, the United Kingdom, and Canada during 1990–1995 are reported in Table 1.1. When these variables are included as an explanatory variable in econometrics studies, spurious conclusions can be made rather easily. The data demonstrate that except for the United Kingdom the output gap measure of a deficit has a higher standard deviation than other measures of the deficit. In all

Table 1.1
Variation in Different Measures of Deficits and Debt, 1990–1995

Country	Actual Deficit	Output Gap	Structural Deficit	Net Debt	Gross Debt
Canada	1.49 (-0.26)	1.85 (-0.19)	0.80 (-0.83)	8.89 (0.16)	9.77 (0.11)
France	1.99 (-0.49)	2.37 (-1.89)	0.53 (-0.17)	7.23 (0.29)	6.95 (0.17)
Germany	0.59 (-0.20)	2.61 (1.50)	1.54 (-0.50)	10.90 (0.34)	6.05 (0.13)
Italy	1.26 (-0.13)	2.74 (2.48)	2.40 (0.27)	10.11 (0.10)	11.66 (0.10)
Japan	2.65 (3.80)	3.43 (-7.15)	1.41 (5.20)	2.50 (0.38)	7.80 (0.10)
U.K.	2.59 (-0.52)	2.39 (-0.99)	0.62 (-0.17)	5.94 (0.18)	6.50 (0.16)
U.S.	0.89 (-0.29)	1.33 (3.80)	0.75 (0.22)	4.50 (0.09)	3.61 (0.06)

Note: Numbers in parentheses are standard deviation divided by the mean.
Source: Raw data for computation of this table are extracted from International Monetary Fund, May 1996, pp. 18–19.

but Germany, the standard deviation of the actual deficit is greater than the standard deviation of the structural deficit. The numbers in parentheses are the ratios of standard deviation to the mean of the variable. This statistic indicates that output gap shows a greater relative variation than other measures of deficits in all countries under consideration except Japan and Canada.

This simple statistical exercise demonstrates that regardless of economic theory, when different measures of deficits are employed as an explanatory variable, conflicting statistical results may be produced. The choice of the deficit measure should not be made without a careful analysis of the statistical properties of the variable. The net and gross measures of debt show similar variation. Thus, exclusion of the assets of the Social Security insurance system from government debt should not have a significant impact on the statistical results.

GENERATIONAL ACCOUNTING

More recently, some researchers (Auerbach, Gokhale, and Kotlikoff, 1991) have attempted to provide an alternative measure of deficits and a computational methodology based on the intergenerational distribution of the burden of financing government budget deficits. According to this approach, members of each generation receive payments and make contributions to the government budget at different times. The generational accounting system computes the net present value of these cash flows based on a given fiscal policy regime. Changes in the fiscal policy that alter the current budget deficit will affect the intergenerational fiscal burden. Auerbach, Gokhale, and Kotlikoff (1991) have computed the generational accounts of the United States as of 1989 and conclude that, given the current fiscal deficit, future newborns will bear a 20.5 percent greater burden than current newborns. The authors consider the consequences of reducing the current budget deficits through higher taxes or reduction in government spending. They conclude that the generational imbalances would be eliminated if government spending were permanently reduced by 3.3 percent annually.

Those readers familiar with the concept of time value of money are quite aware of the great impact of a capitalization rate on the net present value of a stream of cash flows. A lower discount rate can understate the burden to future generations, while a higher capitalization rate can understate the fiscal burden differentials. It must be noted that any generational redistributions of fiscal imbalances are only due to the potential effect of budget deficits on the rate of return to capital and economic growth. If current deficits lead to more consumption and less capital investments, the productive capacity of future generations may be undermined. Otherwise, each generation can only consume its current gross domestic product, and shifting fiscal payments can only affect the distribution of concurrently produced output among the living generations at the time. Current generations cannot consume output that has not been produced yet. Only the heirs of current generations may benefit or lose in the future as a

result of current fiscal decisions that make them either net lenders or net borrowers in the future.

REFERENCES

Auerbach, Alan, Jagadeesh Gokhale, and Laurence Kotlikoff. 1991. ''Generational Ac-
    counts: A Meaningful Alternative to Deficit Accounting.'' In David Brandford,
    ed., *Tax Policy and the Economy*. Cambridge, Mass.: MIT Press.
Humpage, Owen F. 1992. ''An Introduction to the International Implications of U.S.
    Fiscal Policy.'' *Economic Review* (Federal Reserve Bank of Cleveland), Vol. 28,
    No. 3, pp. 27–39.
International Monetary Fund (IMF). May 1996. *World Economic Outlook*. Washington,
    D.C.: International Monetary Fund.
Laffer, Arthur. March 1993. ''Deficits Don't Matter.'' *The World and I*, pp. 415–439.
Schick, Allen. 1995. *The Federal Budget: Politics, Policy, Process*. Washington, D.C.:
    Brookings Institution.

Chapter 2

The Federal Budget Process in the United States

JAMES M. SUAREZ

Political economy was the name originally given to the study of the impact of governmental taxation, expenditures, and other activities on a nation's economy.[1] Although the economics profession has moved away from the early name for this field (today it is commonly called *public finance* or *public sector economics*),[2] governmental budgeting in the United States is conducted in the context of the traditional concept of political economy. Economic factors do not dominate the budget process. Budgeting is a political process that may be influenced by economic considerations.[3]

Budget procedures attempt to pose for governmental decision makers the central question of economics: how to allocate scarce resources among alternative uses. In government budgeting the decisions are twofold. How many resources should the public sector take from the private sector? How should the government sector allocate its revenues among its expenditure programs?

The desire for lower taxes and more funds for the private sector clearly conflicts with the demands for new or expanded government programs. A consensus on economic, political, and social priorities is difficult to reach. Well-organized special interest groups exert tremendous pressure to continue or extend particular tax preferences or expenditure programs.

The proposed budgets that federal administrative agencies submit to the Office of Management and Budget (OMB) and in turn that the president submits to Congress may serve different functions. A budget may represent the amount of money an agency or an executive branch expects to see enacted into law and actually spent. Agency and executive requests may also represent the funds they hope to receive and spend. Since the amounts requested often determine the amounts received, budget proposals are usually strategies. The total amount of money and its allocation among various programs are designed to build support for the agency's budgetary and policy goals. As each direct participant—the agency, executive office, House of Representatives, and Senate—acts on the proposed budget, the budget eventually emerges as the end result of the preferences and desires of the different participants. The agency's clientele, special interest groups, and other affected constituencies try to influence each direct participant to incorporate their specific concerns into the budget.

After the budget has been enacted, it becomes a benchmark. Once something has been approved, it is likely to continue in the baseline budget. The baseline budget is a financial plan that estimates future receipts assuming no tax changes and future spending assuming that current services continue. Only substantial changes from the previous year's budget are normally given close scrutiny. An item that is not changed or little changed will probably continue year after year. For these reasons, budgets tend to be incremental. The largest determining factor of the size and content of this year's budget is last year's budget. Most spending under any new budget is on legislative programs that have existed for years. The current tax treatment or level of expenditures is considered to be the base from which any change is generally made in a manner consistent with other changes.

Any new initiatives on spending or taxation are just the tip of the total budget iceberg. However, new initiatives can affect future budgets significantly. Many government programs start out small but quickly grow to considerable size.

Two pivotal events in federal government budgeting will illustrate the interplay of politics and economics in the budgeting process and outcome: the Congressional Budget and Impoundment Control Act of 1974 and the revolutionary changes made by President Ronald Reagan early in his term.

As the size of the federal budget increased in the late 1960s with the growth of President Lyndon Johnson's Great Society programs and the rising outlays for the Vietnam War, a general dissatisfaction with the federal budget process became apparent. When President Richard Nixon in 1972, and again in 1973, cut, rescinded, and failed to spend money authorized by Congress for domestic programs, he technically "impounded" these funds; as a response, Congress finally acted to strengthen itself and reform the budget process.

Before the 1974 legislation the budget process in Congress was fragmented.[4] There was no satisfactory congressional control over total federal spending. Congress had no committees charged with consolidating the various pieces of budget legislation into a meaningful whole. The president's executive budget was torn into different parts to be reviewed by different committees and never seen as a whole budget proposal again. Congress did not have a staff that could provide an independent overview of the president's budget or its economic assumptions.

The Congressional Budget and Impoundment Control Act of 1974 established budget committees in both the House and Senate to coordinate budget policy. The act established the Congressional Budget Office (CBO) to provide Congress information and analysis comparable to that supplied by the Office of Management and Budget and the Council of Economic Advisers to the president.

The 1974 Budget Reform Act set up a new timetable and procedure for the congressional budget process. By setting specific dates when various actions should be completed, the timetable was intended to ensure that all appropriation bills for a new fiscal year were completed before the current fiscal year ends. The act integrated the previously existing executive and congressional budget schedules so that Congress could better control spending and taxation and assess the impact of the emerging budget on the economy.

Congress attempted in the 1974 budget reform legislation to discipline itself and to retrieve power from the president. The act imposed rules for efficiency and economic rationality in budgeting. It set up a procedure for Congress to regain control over the budget. The 1974 act was the most significant budget legislation since the 1921 Budget and Accounting Act when Congress delegated the power over the budget to the president.[5]

The revised budget process worked smoothly until the 1980 election of Ronald Reagan as president of the United States.[6] Candidate Reagan campaigned against inflation, unemployment, federal deficits, high taxes, and debt and promised a balanced budget in two years. President Reagan's landslide victory brought Republican control of the Senate and a working majority coalition of Republican and conservative southern Democrats in the House that supported his important budget and tax proposals during his first two years in office.

President Reagan used the budget to enhance his power and discipline Congress. He radically reduced the resources going to the federal government and changed the government's spending priorities. He enacted the biggest tax cuts in the nation's history. He slashed spending on social welfare programs and increased expenditures on military programs. The combination of unprecedented tax reductions, rising spending on entitlement programs such as Medicare and Medicaid, and increased military outlays created enormous budget deficits.

For the first time tax policy became as important as spending programs in the budget process. President Reagan broke with the tradition of initiating tax legislation in the House of Representatives. Instead of going through the House Ways and Means Committee—led by Democrats—President Reagan's tax proposals went to the Senate Finance Committee—controlled by Republicans.

The president's tax plans involved three major tax reduction measures. Two proposals concerned individual income taxes and one dealt with corporate taxes. The highest marginal tax rate would be lowered from 70 percent to 50 percent. Since the capital gains tax rate was 40 percent of the top personal income tax rate, this reduction cut the maximum tax on capital gains from 28 percent to 20 percent. In addition, personal income tax rates would be reduced for all taxpayers. These and other proposals, such as greatly expanded Individual Retirement Accounts, substantially reduced personal income taxes for middle- and upper-income taxpayers to provide incentives for greater work effort, savings, and investment.

The third tax proposal concerned reducing the depreciation life of corporate assets for tax purposes. Depreciation, an estimated measure of the wearing down of productive assets, is an unusual item in corporate accounting. It is a cost of doing business; so with steady receipts, an increase in depreciation means less taxable income and correspondingly less income taxes paid to the government. But depreciation is not a cash expense. A business in effect pays itself the depreciation charged on its assets by making an entry in its accounts. Taxes, in contrast, are paid in cash. By shortening depreciation lives and increasing depreciation charges, a firm can enhance its internal cash flow available for business purposes and reduce its cash outflow for taxes. Special interest lobby groups fought fiercely for drastically shorter depreciation lives for machinery, plants, equipment, and other deductions for various industries.[7]

President Reagan revolutionized the budget process. He reduced federal government revenues. He lowered the tax burdens on upper-income individuals and corporations. The Reagan revolution shifted government spending priorities from civilian to military uses. It reduced the revenue state and local government received from the federal government. It slowed the growth of social welfare spending by government. The combination of tax cuts and military spending increases led to massive deficits.

President Reagan achieved in the early years of his term what President Nixon failed to accomplish a decade earlier. President Nixon also tried to cut social programs and increase military outlays. He failed because he used confrontation, impoundment, and imperial policies. President Reagan accomplished his goals legally and constitutionally within the existing budget laws, by majority vote after majority vote in Congress and with the initial support of the public.

After the passage of the Economic Recovery Act of 1981 with its large tax reductions and the likelihood that huge budget deficits would continue into the future, the budget battles for the bulk of President Reagan's remaining term pitted the president against Congress over the size of the deficit. President Reagan wanted to pursue his economic and political agendas without regard to the deficit. Congress worried about the deficits, which had jumped from less than 2 percent of gross domestic product (GDP) in 1980 to more than 5 percent of GDP in 1983.

Concern over the growing size of the budget deficits stimulated Congress to pass the Gramm-Rudman-Hollings Act, officially the Balanced Budget and Emergency Deficit Control Act of 1985. This act listed a schedule for maximum annual deficits, with a balanced budget by 1991, an automatic procedure to cut budget outlays if Congress and the president failed to meet the mandated goals, and still another new timetable for budget actions.

The Gramm-Rudman-Hollings Act is notable for a few reasons. Congress and the president first devised imaginative and creative ways to get around the budget deficit constraints. When the deficit targets became too large to be handled by budgetary chicanery, the targets were raised. Finally, when it was obvious that the law was ineffective, it was essentially treated as irrelevant and ignored.

The Gramm-Rudman-Hollings Act gave the president, through the comptroller general, the power to impound or ''sequester'' funds. When President Nixon exercised this power in 1973, Congress proposed Articles of Impeachment for this and other acts.

Although Presidents Ronald Reagan and George Bush used the Gramm-Rudman-Hollings provision to sequester funds, no sequestration has yet been as dramatic as President Bill Clinton's sequester of funds during the 1996 budget. Lack of authorized funds caused a few government offices to shut down completely for weeks and many others to operate for months with a reduced staff. Some federal agencies went seven months into their fiscal year before the budgets were approved. The sequestration stemmed from policy disagreements between President Clinton and Congress, especially House Speaker Newt Gingrich.

The failure of the Gramm-Rudman-Hollings Act to eliminate federal deficits stimulated the movement for a balanced budget amendment to the Constitution.[8] Most economists view a balanced budget rule as unsound fiscal policy.[9] Keynesian stabilization theory indicates that a rigid regulation prohibiting deficit spending would mandate perverse governmental actions during business cycle downturns by requiring tax increases and spending reductions. A balanced budget rule would impose heavy tax burdens during transitory spending episodes such as wars or natural disasters. Dynamic optimal taxation theory holds that deficits and surpluses should be used to smooth temporary fluctuations in government expenditures and revenues. Both fiscal policy theories argue against a balanced budget regulation.

In the United States, most states—the number varies from two or three dozen to all states except Vermont, depending on how the laws are read—officially bar deficit spending.[10] These strictures are far less binding than the proposed federal balanced budget amendment.

Unlike the federal government, states make a distinction between ''operating'' and ''capital'' budgets. States' operating budgets are almost always subject to a balanced budget rule. However, the substantial portion of state expenditure that goes for construction of schools, prisons, highways, roads, bridges, airports, and other capital projects can be funded by debt. States often use flexible definitions for capital projects that qualify for financing by the sale of long-term bonds.

When faced with budget constraints, states have resorted to fiscal gimmicks to avoid the restrictions. New York sold a prison to a public authority, leased the prison back, and used the cash from the sale to help cover the state's operating budget. Many states, including New Jersey, have changed the accounting rules for employee pension plans in order to generate more net cash flow into current years and push spending obligations into future years.

A third widely used tactic to reduce state budget problems is to pass fiscal responsibilities on to local governments. Many localities have had to increase local tax revenue to make up for reductions in state aid. States impose mandates requiring local governments to provide services without supplying state funds to pay for these services.

State budgets are fundamentally different from the federal budget. State revenues and expenditures are less sensitive to economic recessions than the federal budget. The federal government has the responsibility to combat recessions by suffering a larger loss of tax revenues and picking up a greater share of the obligations to maintain the social safety net.

Just as the experiences of the states with constitutional limits on deficit finance provide little guidance for the federal government, Congress cannot look to Europe for examples of fiscal discipline.[11] Europe has adopted rules that limit the size of the government deficit to 3 percent of GDP and overall government debt to 60 percent of GDP. The United States has a current fiscal surplus and a general government debt-to-GDP ratio around 50 percent. The United States presently meets the more flexible European budgetary goals. The United States has reduced the federal deficit from $300 billion a few years ago to a small surplus today. Not many foreign nations can match that improvement.

The lessons from the recent history of budgeting in the United States seem clear. In the American governmental system, a political consensus is necessary to take major substantive actions. The system of checks and balances of power among the executive, legislative, and judicial branches, the shared powers among these bodies, the bicameral legislature where the House and Senate often conflict with each other, and the federal system itself with power divided between the states and federal government were all designed to protect the freedom of the American people. Economic efficiency was not a consideration in this elaborate political structure. When there is a consensus on major policy issues, the system functions well and can be efficient. If there is no general agreement on policy, the budget process at least provides a mechanism to ultimately reach a compromise solution.

NOTES

1. David Ricardo's classic book, published in 1817, was *The Principles of Political Economy and Taxation* (London: Everyman's Library, 1965). The first endowed professorial chair in an economics department in an American university was the McVickar Professor of Political Economy, established in the late nineteenth century at Columbia University. Such distinguished economists as E. R. A. Seligmann, Robert Murray Haig, Carl Shoup, William Vickrey, and Edmund Phelps have held the McVickar Professorship.

2. For example, Richard A. Musgrave's major work is titled *The Theory of Public Finance* (New York: McGraw-Hill, 1959), while Anthony B. Atkinson and Joseph E. Stiglitz's book is called *Lectures in Public Economics* (New York: McGraw-Hill, 1980).

3. The most notable recent analysts of budgeting in the United States have been such distinguished political scientists as Allen Schick, *The Federal Budget* (Washington, D.C.: Brookings Institution, 1997), and Aaron Wildavsky, *Budgeting* (Boston: Little, Brown, 1975). As economists have developed the field of public choice with its examination of the problems between principals and agents, economists have almost ceased to study the actual governmental budgeting process in the United States. The last significant book on

budgeting by a prominent economist may have been Jesse Burkhead, *Government Budgeting* (New York: McGraw-Hill, 1955). Such popular undergraduate public finance textbooks as David Hyman, *Public Finance* (Orlando, Fla.: Dryden, 1993), Harvey Rosen, *Public Finance* (Chicago: Irwin, 1995), and Joseph E. Stiglitz, *Economics of the Public Sector* (New York: Norton, 1993) do not include a specific chapter or section on budgeting.

4. For a full discussion of the 1974 budget reform legislation, see Joel Havemann, *Congress and the Budget* (Bloomington: Indiana University Press, 1978), and Allen Schick, *Congress and Money* (Washington, D.C.: Urban Institute, 1980).

5. See Louis Fisher, *Presidential Spending Power* (Princeton, N.J.: Princeton University Press, 1975).

6. See Howard E. Shuman, *Politics and the Budget* (Englewood Cliffs, N.J.: Prentice-Hall, 1988).

7. For a lively account of the difficulty of reforming the tax changes in the Economic Recovery Act of 1981 just a few years later, see the report on the making of the Tax Reform Act of 1986 in Jeffrey H. Birnbaum and Alan S. Murray, *Showdown at Gucci Gulch* (New York: Random House, 1987).

8. For a summary evaluation of the economic effects of balanced budget rules, see James M. Poterba, "Budget Institutions and Fiscal Policy in the U.S. States," *American Economic Review*, May 1996, pp. 395–400; Alberto Alesina and Roberto Perotti, "Fiscal Discipline and the Budget Process," *American Economic Review*, May 1996, pp. 401–407; and Giancarlo Corsetti and Nouriel Roubini, "European versus American Perspectives on Balanced Budget Rules," *American Economic Review*, May 1996, pp. 408–413.

9. Alesina and Perotti, "Fiscal Discipline and the Budget Process."

10. Poterba, "Budget Institutions and Fiscal Policy in the U.S. States."

11. Corsetti and Roubini, "European versus American Perspectives on Balanced Budget Rules."

REFERENCES

Alesina, Alberto, and Roberto Perotti. May 1996. "Fiscal Discipline and the Budget Process." *American Economic Review*, pp. 401–407.

Atkinson, Anthony B., and Joseph E. Stiglitz. 1980. *Lectures in Public Economics*. New York: McGraw-Hill.

Birnbaum, Jeffrey H., and Alan S. Murray. 1987. *Showdown at Gucci Gulch*. New York: Random House.

Burkhead, Jesse. 1955. *Government Budgeting*. New York: McGraw-Hill.

Corsetti, Giancarlo, and Nouriel Roubini. May 1996. "European versus American Perspectives on Balanced Budget Rules." *American Economic Review*, pp. 408–413.

Fisher, Louis. 1975. *Presidential Spending Power*. Princeton, N.J.: Princeton University Press.

Havemann, Joel. 1978. *Congress and the Budget*. Bloomington: Indiana University Press.

Hyman, David. 1993. *Public Finance*. Orlando: Dryden.

Musgrave, Richard A. 1959. *The Theory of Public Finance*. New York: McGraw-Hill.

Poterba, James M. May 1996. "Budget Institutions and Fiscal Policy in the U.S. States." *American Economic Review*, pp. 408–413.

Ricardo, David. 1965. *The Principles of Political Economy and Taxation*. London: Everyman's Library.

Rosen, Harvey. 1995. *Public Finance*. Chicago: Irwin.
Schick, Allen. 1980. *Congress and the Budget*. Washington, D.C.: Urban Institute.
Schick, Allen. 1997. *The Federal Budget*. Washington, D.C.: Brookings Institution.
Shuman, Howard E. 1988. *Politics and the Budget*. Englewood Cliffs, N.J.: Prentice-Hall.
Stiglitz, Joseph E. 1993. *Economics of the Public Sector*. New York: Norton.
Wildavsky, Aaron. 1975. *Budgeting*. Boston: Little, Brown.

Chapter 3

Major Federal Budget Laws of the United States

JAMES L. CHAN

The federal budget, accounting for almost one quarter of the gross domestic product (GDP) of the United States, is heavily influenced by both politics (Wildavsky and Caiden, 1997) and economics (Stein, 1996). More directly, it is governed by a number of public laws that formally designate the decision makers, prescribe their roles, and in recent years, specify its targets. The purpose of this chapter is to describe the legal foundation of the federal budget in terms of the major budget laws that shape the size of the budget and direct the behavior of the participants in the budgetary process.[1]

THE CONSTITUTION AND EARLY PRACTICES

The U.S. Constitution is rather parsimonious when it comes to the nation's finances. It gives Congress the power to levy taxes and requires appropriations made by law before funds may be drawn from the Treasury. However, it does not provide a blueprint on how to exercise this legislative power, nor does it assign a formal role to the president.

With its power of the purse, Congress created a committee structure and devised rules to carry out its financial responsibilities. In the first half of the 1800s, these were handled mainly by the House Ways and Means Committee and the Senate Finance Committee. After the Civil War, both houses of Congress set up Appropriation Committees to assume jurisdiction over spending measures. That arrangement left the House Ways and Means Committee and the Senate Finance Committee to concentrate on the revenue side of federal finances, a practice that continues to the present day.

Congress enacted the Antideficiency Act in 1905–1906 to regulate budget execution. The law requires apportionment, or allocation of appropriation by time period (such as by quarter), to prevent overspending. It also prohibits government officials from incurring obligations in advance of appropriations. It is also illegal to spend in excess of appropriations or for purposes unintended by the appropriations. These injunctions remain the cardinal rule for fiscal conduct by federal government officials and employees on a daily basis.

It would not be accurate to state that the federal government did not have a budgeting system in the early days. But it was a system that allowed executive agencies to ask for funding from congressional committees. These agencies were free from the president's control or even policy guidance. This state of affairs persisted until the early 1900s, prompting President William Howard Taft to appoint a Commission on Economy and Efficiency. The Taft Commission produced a report entitled "The Need for a National Budget," which the president endorsed in a message to Congress in 1912. As we will see next, this precipitated an almost decade-long debate that eventually led to the passage of a comprehensive budget law for the federal government.[2]

LAWS CREATING THE FEDERAL BUDGET SYSTEM

Laws, including budget laws, are not made in a vacuum. That certainly was the case with the two sets of laws that largely created the budget system of the United States. Enacted some 50 years apart, they were both designed to remedy a real or perceived imbalance of power between Congress and the president. The president for over 100 years labored under a constitutional handicap: The power of the purse was clearly vested in the legislative branch. The tide turned with the passage of the Budget and Accounting Act of 1921, which tipped the balance in the president's favor so much so that Fisher (1975) characterized the 1921–1975 period as "presidential budgeting." However, it would be an exaggeration to say that an executive budget system emerged as a result of the 1921 Act, for Congress has not merely rubber-stamped the president's budget. Fundamentally, to this day the system has always worked in the manner of "the president proposes; Congress disposes."

The system created by the 1921 Act, although amended in 1950, certainly stood the test of time over the following five decades. The institutional framework was sufficiently sturdy to support the ever weightier federal budget to meet ever-expanding U.S. commitments at home and abroad. It financed President Franklin Roosevelt's New Deal programs in the wake of the Great Depression as well as the massive military expenditures for World War II, the Cold War, and the Vietnam War. Crises such as these tended to increase presidential powers. Eventually, rebelling against what historian Arthur Schlesinger, Jr. (1973) calls the "imperial presidency," Congress in 1974 passed two laws that clipped the budgetary wings of the president: one creating a congressional budget process and the other curtailing the presidential power of impoundment of funds. This section describes how the pendulum of power swung, first in the direction of the president and then to Congress.

Budget and Accounting Act (1921)

Viewed from the vantage point of its seventy-seventh anniversary, the Budget and Accounting Act of 1921 retains almost a contemporary outlook. This may be due to the fact that the system and institutions it established are still functioning.[3] In essence, the act requires the president to submit a budget on behalf of the entire executive branch and provides him with the staff, the Bureau of the Budget, to carry out these responsibilities. No longer could agencies bypass the president and submit their budget requests to Congress. The president as head of the executive branch was finally given a necessary tool—the budget—to set policy priorities, coordinate actions, and enforce compliance. President Franklin Roosevelt, recognizing the value of the Bureau of the Budget, moved it from the Treasury Department to become part of the Executive Office of the President. Thirty years later, President Richard Nixon expanded the agency's scope and renamed it the Office of Management and Budget (OMB) (Fisher, 1975, pp. 36–58).

Congress was quite specific as to the information content of the budget "in summary and in detail": appropriations requested and proposed revenues; estimates of expenditures and receipts for the budget year and the current year; the current year's appropriations; levels of indebtedness; the past, current, and projected financial condition of the Treasury; and other information about the financial condition of the government. The president is further required to explain how he intends to handle any budget surpluses or deficits and is permitted to request supplemental appropriations. Agencies are required to comply with the president's information requests issued through the newly created Bureau of the Budget (U.S. Congress, 1921).

The act's prescription for submission of the president's budget and the information contained therein are codified in Chapter 11 of Title 31 of the United States Code. While the dates and some details have changed, the essence of the system has remained intact with some subsequent augmentations (U.S. Senate, 1993). It is remarkable that the act envisioned an integrated budget (prospective) and accounting (retrospective) information system that the federal government's principal finance agencies—Treasury, OMB, and General Accounting Office (GAO)—are still working on (Chan, 1994).

During the intervening 50 years between the 1921 and 1974 budget acts, the federal budget grew enormously as the federal government expanded functions domestically and assumed global military responsibility. It also became a major fiscal policy tool of the Keynesian revolution in economic thinking about the government's role in managing the economy. At the practical level, it would be hard to imagine how President Franklin Roosevelt could successfully undertake New Deal programs and lead the Allies to victory in World War II, had he not been able to commit the necessary budgetary as well as political resources to those tasks. The same applies to President Lyndon Johnson's execution of the figurative War on Poverty and the real war in Vietnam. By the time President

Richard Nixon assumed office, the power of the modern presidency had reached its historical heights. It is therefore not surprising that Congress, frustrated by having to fund an undeclared and unpopular war and by large presidential impoundment of funds over policy differences, decided to reassert itself. It did so by passing the Congressional Budget and Impoundment Control Act of 1974 (Public Law 93–344), which comprises the Congressional Budget Act and the Impoundment Control Act.

Congressional Budget Act (1974)

The Congressional Budget Act of 1974 strengthened the legislature's role in the federal budget process by enabling it to produce a master budget and equipping itself with the necessary analytical capability for the task. To the existing revenue and appropriation committees, each house of Congress added a Budget Committee, and Congress as a whole gained a Congressional Budget Office (CBO). As a consequence, no longer was the presidential budget (proposal) the only game in town and the OMB the only keeper of technical expertise on the budget. If necessary, a Congress dominated by the opposition party could produce a counterbudget. Now Congress can both propose and dispose budgets.

The centerpiece of the congressional budget process is the budget resolution, which sets ceilings for budget aggregates. Procedurally, the act requires each standing committee of the House and Senate to review the president's budget proposal and recommend budget levels and legislative plans to the Budget Committee in each house. The Budget Committee then initiates the concurrent resolution on the budget (or budget resolution in short), which specifies desired levels for total receipts and for budget authority and outlays, both in total and by functional category (such as national defense, agriculture). As a direct consequence, the level of budget deficit is also set; so is debt level. The budget resolution allocates amounts of budget authority and outlays within each functional category to the committees having jurisdiction over the programs in the functions. The Appropriation Committees are required to allocate the amounts to their constituent subcommittees. Other committees may, but are not required to, make allocations to their subcommittees. The budget resolution often contains reconciliation directives instructing authorizing committees to change the permanent laws affecting taxes and other receipts as well as entitlement programs in order to meet the goals contained in the budget resolution (Schick, 1995).

Analysts differ in their assessment of the success of the 1974 Congressional Budget Act, in part because they use different criteria to judge it (e.g., Schick, 1980; Fisher, 1991, pp. 198–203). Nevertheless, there is agreement on one point: The law was not designed to reduce the federal budget deficit—and it did not. It would take a different law ten years later to address this issue explicitly. But in the early 1970s there was a more urgent matter requiring congressional action: presidential impoundment of funds.

Impoundment Control Act (1974)

Upon the completion of congressional action and the president's signature, the administration is charged with the faithful execution of the budget. To prevent overspending, the Anti-deficiency Act of 1870 requires funds to be apportioned and requires government officials to adhere closely to the provisions of appropriations. Due to the lengthy period of time between the budget proposal and actual implementation, changes in circumstances may require deviations from the budget through the impoundment of funds already appropriated by Congress.

Impoundment of funds refers to the administration's rescissions (i.e., cancellation) or deferral (i.e., temporary withholding within the fiscal year) of funds also appropriated by Congress. Presidents may impound funds only under limited circumstances, such as to provide for emergencies or to achieve savings. The Nixon administration impounded funds on a massive scale and in order not to carry out policy objectives sanctioned by Congress. In response, Congress passed the Impound Control Act of 1974. The act requires the president to send special messages to Congress whenever he wishes to rescind or defer appropriated funds. For a proposed rescission to be effective, both the House and Senate must approve it within 45 days of continuous session. A presidential deferral takes effect and remains so unless it is overturned by an act of Congress.[4]

In summary, the federal budget system is presently characterized by an approximate balance of power between the executive and the legislative, with each branch of government being relatively more powerful at certain stages of the process. The president enjoys the advantage of initiative afforded by the 1921 Act. This advantage, however, is countered by Congress's constitutional primacy, buttressed with its own process and staff, of having the last word on money matters. As Schick (1995, p. 32) points out, budgeting is not optional because the alternative, under the Constitution, is government shutdown. The political price of public wrath over shutdown is high enough to encourage genuine cooperation or pragmatic compromises. The 1921 and 1974 budget process statutes provide a workable institutional framework within which the executive and legislators share budget powers.[5] No matter how sound the process might be, it did not deliver the outcome some people expected: hard choices that reduced the federal budget deficits. This became the agenda for budget laws in the next decade.

LAWS TO REDUCE DEFICITS

From 1969 to 1997 the federal government has been continuously running budget deficits. By the 1970s there was already considerable concern over the effects of "uncontrollable" entitlement expenditures. However, the amounts of deficits remained relatively small until the early 1980s. By that time President Ronald Reagan's twin successes in securing tax cuts and dramatic increases in military spending pushed federal budget deficits to unprecedented high levels. Congress reacted by making deficit reduction an explicit goal of budget laws, beginning with the Balanced Budget and Emergency Deficit Control Act of 1985.

Balanced Budget and Emergency Deficit Control Act (1985)

The Balanced Budget and Emergency Deficit Control Act of 1985, popularly known as the Gramm-Rudman-Hollings (GRH) Act, set out to balance the federal budget by 1991 by proposing fixed and progressively smaller deficit targets for each fiscal year from 1986 to 1990. If the projected budget deficit exceeded the specified target by more than the amount permitted, the cancellation of budget resources, called *sequestration*, is triggered. The law was amended in 1987 to extend the zero deficit target to 1993 and to transfer the responsibility of determining the sequestration trigger from the comptroller general to the director of the Office of Management and Budget. History shows, notwithstanding the threat of sequestration, the federal government continued to run budget deficits in each of the fiscal years covered by the law (Schick, 1995, pp. 37–39).

Budget Enforcement Act (1990)

The lack of success of the 1985 and 1987 GRH laws in achieving their stated deficit reduction objective led Congress to try a different process through the Budget Enforcement Act (BEA) of 1990 (Schick, 1995, pp. 39–41). Initially set to be effective through fiscal year 1993, the effectiveness of the BEA rules has been extended several times. The chief innovation of the BEA lies in its recognition of the different nature of programs subject to annual appropriations and those sanctioned by permanent laws (Schick, 1995, p. 191). The law refers to these, respectively, as discretionary spending and direct (or mandatory) spending and uses different methods for constraining them.

Discretionary spending requires prior program authorization by legislative committees and is subject to the annual appropriation process. The operating budget of federal agencies, including employee salaries, is typically discretionary spending. The BEA sets dollar limits or "caps" on total budget and authority for discretionary programs. The caps are adjustable annually (1) for the difference between the actual inflation rates and the rates used in setting the discretionary caps and (2) for emergency appropriations. Budget resolutions allocate budget authority and outlay amounts for discretionary spending. These amounts, as explained earlier, are further subdivided by appropriation committees for their subcommittees. If the appropriations for a year provide an amount for budget authority greater than the cap on budget authority, or if the amount of outlays associated with the budget authority is greater than the caps on outlays, the BEA calls for sequestration, or across-the-board cuts by a uniform percentage of most discretionary programs.

Unlike discretionary spending, spending for most entitlement programs is direct or mandatory in the sense that it is provided for in the substantive laws authorizing the benefits to individuals or organizations meeting specified criteria. Examples include unemployment insurance payments, Medicare payments to the elderly, and Medicaid payments to the poor. By design, Congress exempts these programs from the scrutiny of the annual appropriation process. The BEA does not prohibit spending increases for any program; it does, however, insist that such increases be deficit neutral. That is, the increases must be "paid for" by decreases in some other program or by raising revenues. This compensatory mechanism is described as pay-as-you-go (PAYGO). Similar trade-off requirements apply to revenues: Legislation decreasing one type of revenue must be fully offset by increases in other revenue sources.

It appears that the BEA, reinforced by political leadership and facilitated by favorable economic conditions, has had a measure of success in reducing the federal budget deficit. The experience with GRH and BEA shows that budget deficits are reduced by political will, not by setting unrealistic goals. The threat of sequestration was not credible because Congress could—and did—undo the GRH Act's fixed deficit reduction targets. These were replaced by BEA's discretionary caps and PAYGO procedures. The more flexible and discerning approach of the BEA probably contributed to its successful implementation. The larger explanation may lie in the public's heightened sense of the approaching day of reckoning. When the electorate elevated deficit reduction to a priority, both Democrats and Republicans found the incentive to reach agreement to aim for zero deficit by the year 2002. However, a budget surplus was achieved in 1997, and the debate has shifted to how to use the surplus.

CONCLUSION

There are two types of federal budget laws. The Budget and Accounting Act of 1921 and the Congressional Budget Act of 1974 are examples of *process-oriented* budget laws. These laws designate the players, assign their roles, and specify the rules of the budgetary game so that the president and Congress can reach compromises more or less in time to keep the government functioning each fiscal year. Their specific provisions reflect the political consensus regarding the proper sharing of the power of the purse. By and large, these laws have succeeded in erecting a relatively stable institutional framework for proposing and approving the federal budget. When disputes arise, the federal judiciary stands ready to settle them. The *outcome-oriented* laws, designed to achieve deficit reduction, have had less predictable and successful results. In view of the complex interactive relationship between the federal budget and the economy, lower budget deficits could not be preordained by law. Even if foresight were possible, a budget law that built on political consensus, as in the case of the Budget Enforcement Act of 1990, would stand a greater chance of success than one—like the Gramm-Rudman-Hollings Act—that tried to dictate numerical outcomes.

In view of legislators' specialty in lawmaking, it is hardly surprising that Congress has attempted to solve the nation's budget problems by stocking the government's legal arsenal with more statutes. An "anomaly of controls without control" has arisen, observes Schick (1995, p. 189). This chapter has argued that the pre-1980 laws sought *budgetary control*, while the post-1980 laws aimed at *controlling the budget*. Budgetary control is an intragovernmental compliance issue susceptible to legal resolution. Controlling the budget in a mixed economy, on the other hand, is much more difficult and complex. Much depends on favorable economic conditions and a conducive political climate. For, in the final analysis, the federal budget is not merely a legal constraint; it is the nation's blueprint for resolving conflicting values.

NOTES

1. Budget laws are to be distinguished from laws containing budgets, such as appropriation acts and laws that, by providing for entitlements, have budgetary implications. Furthermore, to some extent, what is considered a major budget law is a matter of judgment. I have sought guidance from two authoritative sources—see U.S. Office of Management and Budget (OMB), *The Budget System and Concepts* (1996); and U.S. Senate, Committee on the Budget, *Budget Process Law Annotated* (1993). The OMB's listing of principal budget laws, interestingly, omits the 1921 Budget and Accounting Act, which I regard as fundamental; and it includes the Federal Credit Reform Act of 1990, which seems to be too topical to warrant the designation "major" in the historical context. Parliamentary rules of the House and Senate that govern congressional budgetary deliberations are outside the purview of this chapter; so are presidential executive orders and OMB circulars on budget matters.

2. This section has drawn from Schick (1995, pp. 33–36). Fisher (1975) is a valuable reference source for this period, especially on the events leading to the 1921 Budget and Accounting Act.

3. Besides the Bureau of the Budget (later renamed Office of Budget and Management), the act also created the General Accounting Office, headed by the comptroller general of the United States (Trask, 1996). Given their positions in the system, it was inevitable that these agencies would be involved in the constitutional conflicts between Congress and the president in budgetary matters discussed by Fisher (1975, 1991).

4. For a detailed analysis of presidential impoundment and other issues surrounding budget execution, read Fisher (1991, pp. 196–198; 1975).

5. Refer to Fisher (1991, ch. 7) on the politics of sharing budget power.

REFERENCES

Chan, James L. 1994. "Accounting and Financial Management Reform in the United States Government: An Application of Professor Luder's Contingency Model." In Ernst Buschor and Kuno Schedler, eds., *Perspectives on Performance Measurement and Public Sector Accounting*. Berne, Switzerland: Haupt, pp. 17–41.

Fisher, Louis. 1975. *Presidential Spending Power*. Princeton, N.J.: Princeton University Press.

————. 1991. *Constitutional Conflicts between Congress and the President*, 3rd ed. Lawrence: University Press of Kansas, pp. 186–215.

————. 1993. *The Politics of Shared Power: Congress and the Executive*, 3rd ed. Washington, D.C.: CQ Press.

Schick, Allen. 1980. *Congress and Money: Budgeting, Spending and Taxing*. Washington, D.C.: Urban Institute.

————. 1995. *The Federal Budget: Politics, Policy, Process*. Washington, D.C.: Brookings Institution.

Schlesinger, Arthur M., Jr. 1973. *The Imperial Presidency*. Boston: Houghton Mifflin Company.

Stein, Herbert. 1996. *The Fiscal Revolution in America: Policy in Pursuit of Reality*, 2nd ed. Washington, D.C.: AEI Press.

Taft Commission [on Economy and Efficiency]. 1912. "The Need for a National Budget." U.S. House of Representatives Document No. 854 (June 27). Reprinted in Albert C. Hyde and Jay M. Shafritz eds., *Government Budgeting: Theory, Process, Politics*. Oak Park, Ill.: Monroe Publishing Company, pp. 4–11.

Trask, Roger R. 1996. *Defender of the Public Interest: The General Accounting Office, 1921–1966*. Washington, D.C.: GAO.

U.S. Congress. 1921. *Budget and Accounting Act of 1921*. 42 Stat. 18. Reprinted in Albert C. Hyde and Jay M. Shafritz eds., *Government Budgeting: Theory, Process, Politics*. Oak Park, Ill.: Monroe Publishing Company, pp. 12–19.

U.S. Office of Management and Budget. 1996. *Budget of the United States Government— The Budget System and Concepts, Fiscal Year 1997*. Washington, D.C.: GPO.

U.S. Senate. Committee on the Budget. 1993. *Budget Process Law Annotated*. Washington, D.C.: GPO.

Wildavsky, Aaron, and Naomi Caiden. 1997. *The New Politics of the Budgetary Process*, 3rd ed. New York: Longman.

Chapter 4

A Historical Perspective on the Size of Deficits and Debts in OECD Countries

ANTHONY D. APOSTOLIDES

This chapter examines the fiscal record of the countries of the Organization for Economic Cooperation and Development (OECD). The countries that belong to the OECD include the G-7 and a number of other countries. The G-7 group consists of the United States, Japan, Germany, France, Italy, the United Kingdom, and Canada. The OECD countries, in sum, are the industrialized group of countries in the world and account, by far, for the main portion of the world's output and foreign trade. First, there is an examination of the historical record of these countries with respect to annual budget performance (i.e., deficit or surplus). This is followed by a rather detailed appraisal of the factors that have contributed to the deficits over time; these include essentially factors that have affected increases in government spending. Next, there is an evaluation of the results of these increasing deficits and includes debt and the impact on interest payments. This is followed by a discussion of what these trends portend for the future of the global economic system.

THE HISTORICAL RECORD ON DEFICITS

A deficit is one outcome of the budget process of a country and results when annual government expenditures are greater than the revenues. A deficit is not a necessary result of the budget process; a surplus can also be the outcome, whereby annual government revenues are greater than expenditures. In assessing budget performance of OECD countries, use is made of two budget measurements: the general government budget and the central government budget. The general government budget includes activities of the central government at lower levels of government, such as local government (but excludes state-owned enterprises, which are important in some countries). The central government is by far the dominant factor in the overall budget.[1]

The magnitude of government spending can be related to the economy's output in order to gauge its relative importance, and this becomes the spending ratio. From 1830 to 1930, the spending ratios of the central governments of industrialized countries rarely exceeded 10 to 15 percent of gross domestic product (GDP). In the United States, federal spending was under 5 percent of GDP for the entire 1868–1914 period. Since 1930, however, there have been increases in the shares of both expenditures and revenues in output—leaving aside the war years (Masson, 1995).

In the period from the end of World War II until about 1970, expenditures and revenues increased more or less in parallel, and governments' fiscal positions were kept close enough to balance to ensure that public debt ratios were flat or declining. Until the early 1970s, there was a rather balanced picture in the fiscal developments of these countries. However, since that period, government expenditures have begun to diverge and grow faster than revenues, resulting in increasing deficits on the average. There was a narrowing of the divergence (gap) by the late 1980s; however, it thereafter began to again experience dramatic increases. No OECD country appears to have escaped the trend toward fiscal deterioration, although some countries have experienced it far more than others. The reasons for this deterioration deserve a serious analysis, and such an evaluation is presented below.

FACTORS CONTRIBUTING TO INCREASES IN DEFICITS

The basic reason for the rising government deficits in OECD countries has been the increasingly unbalanced relationship between *expenditures* and *revenues*; that is, both increased over time, but expenditures grew significantly faster than revenues (essentially through taxes). With respect to the *revenue side*, revenue collections do not seem to have been the problem. The ratio of revenue to GDP has increased for nearly every industrial country over the past couple of decades. For these countries taken together, revenues increased from a simple average of 28 percent of GDP in 1960 to 44 percent in 1994. Some countries, including Denmark, Finland, and Sweden, currently have revenue-to-GDP ratios which exceed 50 percent. Even "low-revenue" countries, such as Japan and the United States, have seen their ratios of revenue to GDP rise from the 18 to 25 percent range in 1960 to the 30 to 35 percent range today. For the most part, these higher revenues have been generated through higher direct taxes—often via high marginal tax rates—and through higher social security contributions. The result is that effective tax rates on income have become so high in some countries that they discourage work and create other distortions in labor markets and in the economy (International Monetary Fund, 1996).

Rather than being a revenue problem, modern fiscal imbalances stem from dramatic increases in government expenditures. They jumped from an average of 28 percent of GDP in 1960 to 50 percent in 1994—a year in which the ratio hit 69 percent of GDP in Sweden and roughly 55 percent of GDP in Belgium, France, Italy, and the Netherlands. Several factors have contributed to increased government spending. These include the role of government in the economy and functional finance, social spending, demographic factors, a slowdown of economic activity in various countries (affected by oil shocks, for one), structural unemployment, and inflation. These factors are examined below in some detail.

Over time, the public's mentality changed toward a more receptive view concerning the role of government in the economy. This change was partly the result of the widespread unemployment and hardship experienced during the Great Depression, which led many to look for greater government intervention in the form of stimulative fiscal policies to maintain employment and transfer payments in order to alleviate the distress of those who were poor or unemployed. Moreover, the increase of government authority and intervention in the economy, which took place during World War II, including care for the welfare of millions of men and women in the armed forces, prepared the framework for large-scale government social programs after the war. The norm of fiscal conservatism that prevailed until the middle of the twentieth century in most countries demanded that government budgets be balanced except in exceptional circumstances. And they were balanced except during the Great Depression and the two world wars. Furthermore, the wartime accumulation of government debt was repaid in subsequent years. Public opinion was strongly in favor of avoiding deficits, and one notes, for example, that Franklin Roosevelt was elected in 1932 after a campaign that attacked the Hoover administration for reckless spending, since it had run deficits for three years in a row (Masson, 1995).

Moreover, there was eventually a change in the view that government deficits were to be run only during exceptional occurrences. Influenced by Keynes's writings, countries began to apply functional finance in order to smooth out cyclical fluctuations in their economies. The use of functional finance meant that when the economy was in a recession and aggregate demand was declining, the central government would run deficits, by increasing its spending, thereby increasing aggregate demand, and thus help get the country out of the recession. Functional finance, however, need not produce government deficits, on average. When the economy is in a period of prosperity, government spending can slow down, while the tax revenues continue to grow in proportion to the economy—thereby resulting in a budget surplus.

The fiscal situation of OECD countries was adversely affected by the substantial and abrupt boost in oil prices brought about by the Organization of Petroleum Exporting Countries (OPEC) in 1973–1974. This oil shock adversely affected output levels (through increased prices of crude oil and its various derivatives) and resulted in a recession in 1975. In Keynesian fashion, governments tried to fight the recession and the fall in real income with a fiscal expansion. The result was that government expenditures increased (while revenues fell) and fiscal deficits widened.

A most important factor that affected increases in government spending was the introduction or expansion of social programs, including public pensions (Social Security), disability benefits, welfare benefits, unemployment benefits, and health care spending. Public sector budgets show that social transfers, as a percentage of GDP in OECD countries, jumped on average from 8.1 percent during 1960–1973 to 12 percent during 1974–1979. In most cases, governments found it easier to increase revenues in order to cover the spending increases, or to allow deficits to widen, than to tackle underlying problems. In some cases, the spending growth has been affected by the expansion of targeted social safety nets into universal benefits; in other cases, benefits became ''entitlements,'' and their administration became increasingly divorced from the normal budgetary process (Masson, 1995). As the public became accustomed to the social transfers, it became very difficult for governments to resist maintaining, and even increasing, social spending benefiting various portions of the population. As well-intentioned social programs became more generous and widely available, the number of beneficiaries increased sharply.

With regard to Social Security, spending on this program over the 1975–1993 period rose in all countries, as ratios to GDP, by amounts ranging from 1.5 percentage points (United States) to 6 percentage points (France). The average increase in this ratio was about 3.5 percentage points of GDP (Masson, 1995). Spending increases have also been affected by rises in the cost and quantity of publicly supported health care since 1980. For most OECD countries, the government finances and provides health care services for the vast majority of the population. Health care costs have been rising constantly in these countries, faster than GDP, so that the health costs to GDP ratio has been increasing significantly over time. Consequently, there has been an intensification of efforts to slow down the growth of health care costs by limiting the growth in the supply of health care as well as limiting demand for health care—for example, by imposing ceilings on the overall spending for specific health services. The results, as of yet, have not been very encouraging, as public health care expenditures have continued to grow rapidly.

Increases in social transfer spending were also affected by deteriorating labor market conditions, which resulted in increasing unemployment in the early 1970s. During the 1950s and 1960s, unemployment rates in the countries of Western Europe generally ran in the range of 2 percent to 3 percent, which was distinctly below the average unemployment rate of about 5 percent in the United States. However, the unemployment picture deteriorated substantially since the mid-1970s. In the United States, deep recessions in the mid-1970s and the early 1980s increased the unemployment rate to 6.5 percent, while most estimates indicated a natural rate of unemployment of about 6 percent. In most Western European countries and in Canada and Australia, the increases in unemployment rates were even higher, in the range of 8 to 10 percent (Masson, 1995). A related development since the early 1970s has been the large and persistent increase in structural unemployment that occurred in most industrial countries.

Furthermore, relatively high unemployment benefits can undermine incentives of unemployed workers to find and accept new employment, and this contributes to a higher rate of recorded unemployment. European countries, in particular, face difficult budget challenges because a large and growing share of their populations are not participating in economic production. Moreover, social programs can contribute to labor market rigidities. The incentive to hire workers is undermined when the employer knows that if employment termination occurs, a lump-sum payment to laid-off workers must be paid, possibly related to the number of years worked in the company. In that case, employers may well hold off hiring new workers and instead rely on the existing labor force to work more (e.g., overtime). Thus, new workers are not hired, and this contributes to higher government spending on unemployment benefits.

Demographic factors involved in increased government spending include increased life expectancy and reduction in the retirement age. Increases in life expectancy have been affected by improvements in health care, including health care technology and other programs. Increased longevity results in higher levels of retirement benefits and increased health care costs, as the older population tends to get sicker more often and more severely than other demographic groups. In a number of OECD countries, incentives for early retirement were implemented, undertaken partly in the belief (whose correctness has since been doubted) that this would expand job opportunities for younger workers and thereby diminish unemployment (Masson, 1995). The resulting reduction in the age of retirement also contributed to the higher costs of public benefits by the government.

Government budget deficits were also affected by the significant slowdown in economic growth and productivity after the early 1970s, which followed the high levels of postwar growth in the 1950s and 1960s. In the early 1970s, output growth started to fall significantly in virtually all OECD countries, and unemployment rates began to rise. Consequently, there was an adverse impact on government revenues and an increase in government spending. In addition, inflation has distorted the perceptions and effects of government debt. Governments in OECD countries have used progressive taxes, and when the rates or the taxpayers' incomes were not indexed to correct for price-level changes, higher nominal incomes affected by inflation pushed taxpayers into higher tax-rate brackets. This bracket creep has resulted in government taking a larger portion out of the extra nominal income while leaving taxpayers with a smaller fraction; and this has reduced the apparent deficit. Unanticipated inflation can also distort the size of the budget deficit for another reason—erosion of the real value of the outstanding government debt. This happened in OECD countries early in the postwar period; while price stability was generally the expected norm, inflation rates began to increase. A consequence was to reduce the real value of government indebtedness, although this effect was eventually weakened as expectations of inflation caught up with actual inflation.

Public Choice Theory has been rather predictive on the point of increasing deficits and debt. According to this theory, the voters tend to be rationally ignorant of most issues except a narrow range of those in which they are especially interested, and many of them do not vote. Moreover, the voters do not wish to pay higher taxes, although they do not mind higher government spending, especially when it benefits them. Also, the politicians have incentives that relate to getting elected and reelected, which means that they pay much attention to the vote-getting and vote-losing outcome of each of their votes for legislation. The government bureaucrats—particularly at high levels—like to see increased budgets for their programs, and that means increased government spending. In addition, the special interest groups—like trade associations and labor unions— are interested in obtaining higher incomes for their members, for example, higher subsidies for milk price supports. They use their clout—which includes political contributions to election campaigns—to help elect politicians who will support their agendas. The upshot is that there are powerful incentives at the government level that push for increased spending, while tax rates do not increase in the same proportion, and the final outcome is increased budget deficits. In such a framework, it is very difficult for politicians to vote for either revenue increases (by raising taxes) or spending cuts and thus risk losing votes in future elections. So while politicians bemoan the fact that deficits and debt are a bad thing for the country, they actually do very little to curtail them.

CONSEQUENCES OF DEFICITS: DEBT, INTEREST RATES

National debt is the result of borrowing by the government to finance accumulated deficits over time; accompanying this debt is the subsequent need to repay the principal as well as the interest on the debt. In order to derive an indication of the relative magnitude of national debts over time, one can relate them to the size of the economy, that is, the ratio of debt to GDP. Table 4.1 presents such ratios from 1970 to 1994, and this rather substantial time frame shows the evolution of government debt ratios for selected OECD countries. All countries shown experienced significant increases in the debt ratio and by amounts unprecedented in peacetime. A number of countries had debt ratios in the teens in 1970, but by 1994, these ratios had risen to well over 50 percent of GDP. By 1994, Norway was the only country that had a debt ratio less than 50 percent of GDP. The accelerating debt ratios are indicated for almost all countries irrespective of size or the relative structure of their economy. For example, the big and industrialized economy of the United States experienced a significant rise in the ratio from 45 percent of GDP in 1970 to 64 percent in 1994; in contrast, Germany's debt ratio rose at an even higher rate over the same period, from 18 to 60 percent.

Three countries have unusually high debt ratios—where the amount of government debt exceeds GDP: Belgium, Greece, and Italy. Taking Greece as an

Table 4.1
Industrial Countries: General Government Gross Debt (percent of GDP)

	1970	1975	1980	1985	1990	1994
Austria	19.4	23.9	37.2	49.6	56.2	59.0
Belgium	67.5	61.1	81.6	122.6	128.4	136.0
Canada	51.9	43.1	44.6	64.9	72.5	95.7
Denmark	11.3	11.9	33.5	64.1	59.7	68.7
Finland	15.2	8.6	14.1	18.9	16.6	71.1
France	53.1	41.1	30.9	38.6	40.2	55.9
Germany	18.4	25.1	32.8	42.5	44.0	60.4
Greece	21.3	22.4	27.7	57.9	89.0	120.7
Ireland	67.4	62.2	72.5	104.3	96.8	88.1
Italy	41.7	60.4	59.0	84.3	100.5	123.1
Japan	12.1	22.1	52.0	68.7	69.8	78.8
Netherlands	50.6	40.1	45.1	68.4	76.5	79.0
Norway	47.0	44.7	52.2	40.7	39.2	47.0
Portugal	21.8	26.3	37.5	66.5	66.6	61.8
Spain	14.2	12.1	18.3	50.8	48.7	64.1
Sweden	30.5	29.5	44.3	67.6	44.4	92.9
U.K.	81.8	63.7	54.1	52.7	34.6	51.8
U.S.	45.4	42.6	37.7	48.1	55.4	64.5

Source: Tanzi and Fanizza, 1995.

illustrative case (Apostolides, 1992), tax revenue as a proportion of GDP grew significantly over time, from 20.6 percent of GDP in 1965 to 37.4 percent in 1987. On the revenue side, a major problem with tax revenues in Greece has been low tax compliance (or tax fraud). On the spending side, the relative importance of government spending rose from 26.4 percent of GDP in 1970 to a significant 51.5 percent in 1989, with a substantially faster increase after 1981. Thus, the increasing deficit was affected more by increasing government expenditures than by lack of growth in tax revenues. And this is consistent with other OECD countries. All types of government spending increased—except investment—with some programs having grown particularly rapidly. These include public pensions (i.e., social security), transfers and subsidies, general government administration, and interest payments on the national debt. With regard to public pensions, the share of this item more than doubled over time, from 7.0

percent to 15.1 percent of GDP over 1970–1989. With respect to the cost of administering the government sector itself, this item grew substantially over time, so that its share in GDP rose from 2.9 percent in 1970 to 4.6 percent in 1987. Its growth seems to have been mainly affected by two factors: overstaffing of people working for the government and increases in wages paid by government. The justification for such increases, particularly on the employment side, has been questioned, and the growth of government employment has been criticized for exceeding the real demand for new positions.

Table 4.1 also shows that from 1970 to 1975 there was relatively little change in the public debt to GDP ratio in a sizable number of these countries. In fact, for a number of large economies—including the United States, the United Kingdom, France, and Canada—a decline occurred in the debt ratio over this time period; and for the United States, United Kingdom, and France, the decline of the ratio continued into 1980. From that year on, one observes two important phenomena: first, a reversal of the decreasing debt to GDP ratio (e.g., United States, France) or significant increases in the ratio, which can be observed for virtually all industrialized countries. In this regard, one notes the increase in the debt ratio of Portugal by over 25 percentage points, of Germany by 10 percentage points, of Greece by 30 percentage points, and of Italy by a marked 25 percentage points.

A major consequence of the rapid growth of national debt has been the significant increases in the payments of interest needed to finance the debt. Higher interest payments, in turn, become incorporated into the country's budget as an expenditure item and exacerbate the situation. In fact, interest payments grew considerably faster than the economy's output (GDP). For the G-7, as a group, the ratio of gross interest payments as a percentage of GDP grew from 1.9 of GDP in 1970 to 3.3 in 1980 and to 5.0 in 1994 (Tanzi and Fanizza, 1995). For some countries, this ratio has risen by even larger percentages. For example, interest payments for Italy in 1994 accounted for more than 10 percent of GDP, while the 10 percent ratio was reached by Belgium in 1985 and Greece in 1991 (Tanzi and Fanizza, 1995).

In the United States, interest payments reached over $100 billion annually in the mid-1980s and $150 billion in the late 1980s. They were still growing toward the $200 billion mark in the early 1990s. Thus, in recent years, the magnitudes of the annual interest payments on the national debt in the United States were equal to the size of the annual budget deficit. Moreover, the annual interest payments on the debt increased in the 1990s to become almost as large as the entire national debt in the 1950s (Apostolides, 1996). These are quite disturbing trends. These interest payments have also grown in comparison to the federal outlays, so that the share of interest payments has been at 13 to 14 percent of federal outlays since the mid-1980s. This was the highest ratio observed up to that time. The serious consequence of this is that the increasing funds absorbed by interest payments have not been available to go into other uses or programs.

The fiscal problems of OECD countries are actually considerably worse than they appear from looking at figures of "visible" government debt. There are also very large and growing liabilities that are implicit government commitments to provide social benefits—that is, public pensions and health care—for citizens in the future. These benefits must be paid out of future tax revenues, and at present, these liabilities do not show up in measured government deficits or public debt. However, if drastic policy adjustments are not made, the implicit liabilities will gradually materialize as excesses of public expenditure over revenue and will eventually turn into very large increases in the visible public debt.

With respect to these liabilities, demographic projections estimate a large increase in the proportion of people over the age of 60 in the total population of OECD countries and in relation to those at work. These trends imply a large deterioration in the financial balance of public pension plans, which are largely pay-as-you-go arrangements, starting around the second decade of the next century in most countries. OECD estimates of these public pension liabilities for the United States amounted (in present value terms) to 167 percent of 1994 U.S. GDP (Shigehara, 1995). Assets in the Social Security trust fund provide a small offset to these liabilities, as they are equal to 6 percent of 1994 GDP. For all of the other G-7 countries, except the United Kingdom, the future fiscal implications of public pensions schemes look much worse than for the United States. With more generous (and hence expensive) systems, the present value of pensions for these countries ranges between 195 percent of GDP for Canada and 351 percent of GDP for Germany. The situation looks even worse when account is taken of commitments to provide future health care benefits for retirees (Heller et al., 1986). It is estimated that for the United States net public debt as a percentage of GDP will rise from about 40 percent in 2000 to some 50 percent in 2015 and 120 percent in 2030. This result largely reflects increases in public expenditures on health care.[2]

INITIATIVES IN OECD COUNTRIES TO REDUCE DEFICITS

The importance of reducing fiscal deficits has increasingly been recognized by the OECD countries, and programs have been initiated to achieve that goal. The objectives aim mainly to stabilize the debt-to-GDP ratios (rather than reduce them). For example, the medium-term fiscal objectives of the G-7 countries included the following: for Canada, to reduce the federal budget deficit to 3 percent of GDP in 1996–1997; for Germany, to limit the general government budget deficit to 2 percent of GDP by 1996 and to reach near balance by 1998. Furthermore, Germany intended to reduce the budget deficit through expenditure restraint and allowing for a reduction in the tax burden. For the United States, the objectives include a fiscal policy that at the federal level was constrained by the Omnibus Budget Reconciliation Act of 1993, which places nominal limits extending to fiscal year 1998 on discretionary spending and required that legislation affecting entitlement programs or tax revenues not increase the deficit over a five-year horizon (International Monetary Fund, 1996).

In a recent letter to the *Wall Street Journal* (Barro, 1997), Barro points out that the success and permanence of fiscal adjustments depend on their form, especially on whether governments restrain the growth of outlays. He then points to the results of a recent International Monetary Fund (IMF) study (Alesina and Perotti) that examined the experience with budget deficit reduction in 20 major developed countries of the OECD from 1960 to 1994. The finding of the study was that the success or failure of a plan for fiscal adjustment depends on the composition of the reform. For one thing, the successful cases concentrated much more on spending reductions than on revenue increases. In the successes, 73 percent of the deficit reduction involved spending less, whereas for the failures, only 44 percent took this form. The composition of the spending cuts also differed markedly. In the successes, 51 percent of the spending decreases were in transfers and government wages, while 20 percent was in public investment.

CONCLUSION

There is increasing concern among policy makers that persistent government budget deficits and the resulting run-up in public debt in OECD countries will adversely affect economic performance by crowding out private sector investment. Also, when foreigners increase their ownership of domestic bonds, real estate, or equity, more of the income from production flows overseas in the form of interest, rent, and profit. Therefore, national income—the value of production that accrues to residents of a nation—falls when foreigners receive more of the return on domestic assets.

It would seem clear that current trends in fiscal performance are unsustainable. The debt to GDP ratios have been increasing rapidly, reaching 100 percent. Moreover, there are worrisome trends that will tend to widen deficits further if left unchecked. First, health care costs are growing faster than output, contributing to increased government spending. Second, public pension systems have typically not accumulated sufficient assets to provide existing benefit levels to the baby-boom generation when it retires without increases in the contribution rate. Major measures are needed to rein in the growth of government spending, since the high levels of taxation already provide disincentives to employment in a number of OECD countries. Moreover, if the interest costs continue to rise relative to government revenues, they will make it increasingly difficult for the government to cut spending; consequently, people will become more concerned that the government will resort to printing money in an effort to meet its loan obligations. The combination of heavy government borrowing to finance and refinance its debt and deep concern for rapid money growth and inflation can push interest rates up and make it even more difficult for the government to meet its debt obligations. And if the government did resort to printing money in order to pay off its debt, hyperinflation could occur, with a potential breakdown in the exchange system.

OECD governments have emphasized their concern over increasing deficits and debt and have initiated programs to reduce annual deficits. With regard to expected results, two possibilities may be noted. First, it would be rather difficult to achieve zero annual deficits—and thus start reducing debts—in the short term since it took a number of years for deficits to attain current levels. This implies a political will to stay with austerity programs over rather long time frames. Second, deficit reductions may be accompanied by economic hardships, particularly in the short run—although this is not necessary—and this will give rise to protests from various groups. Ultimately, the success of fiscal adjustments— or austerity programs—may depend on the credibility that governments have with their citizenry: faith that fiscal adjustment programs will be maintained as long as necessary (despite special group efforts, etc.) and that economic hardships would be borne equitably by the various groups in society.

NOTES

1. Local governments (e.g., municipalities and communities) tend to have little autonomy and obtain limited funds either from local tax collection or through borrowing from capital markets. The central government typically collects revenues for local authorities and subsequently transfers the proceeds to them. Still, another measurement is the general government primary balance, which removes from government expenditure the interest payments made to the holders of the public debt. Other measurements of budget balance are the general government structure balance, which attempts to remove the effect of the business cycle on the fiscal balance and is expressed as a share of potential GDP, and the general government inflation adjusted balance, which corrects the normal measure for the impact of inflation on the public debt (Tanzi and Fanizza, 1995).

2. For Germany and France, the ratio might remain broadly within a range of 40 to 50 percent between 2000 and 2015, then rise to reach around 100 percent in 2030. For Italy, the ratio might decline from 107 percent in 2000 to about 80 percent in 2015, then rise to 145 percent in 2030 (Shigehara, 1995).

REFERENCES

Alesina, Alberto, and Roberto Perotti. May 1996. "Fiscal Discipline and the Budget Process." *American Economic Review*, pp. 401–407.
———. 1997. "Fiscal Adjustment in OECD Countries: Composition and Macroeconomic Effects." *Wall Street Journal*, January 14.
Apostolides, Anthony D. Fall 1992. "An Analysis of the Budget of Greece in the 1980s." *Public Budgeting & Finance*, Vol. 12, No. 3, pp. 86–94.
———. 1996. "Deficits and Debt of the Federal Government in the United States Since 1950: Developments and Effects." Unpublished manuscript, Cincinnati, Ohio.
Atkinson, P. E., A. Blundell-Wignall, and J. C. Chouraqut. December 1981. "Budget Financing and Monetary Targets with Special References to the Seven Major OECD Countries." *Greek Economic Review*, Vol. 3, No. 3, p. 245.
Ball, Laurence, and Gregory N. Mankiw. 1995. "What Do Budget Deficits Do?" In *Budget Deficits and Debt: Issues and Options.* A symposium sponsored by the

Federal Reserve Bank of Kansas City, Jackson Hole, Wyo., August 31–September 2.

Barro, Robert J. 1997. "Serious and Nonserious Fiscal Reforms." *Wall Street Journal*, January 14.

Friedman, Benjamin M. 1986. "Increasing Indebtedness and Financial Stability in the United States." In *Debt, Financial Stability, and Public Policy*. A symposium sponsored by the Federal Reserve Bank of Kansas City, Jackson Hole, Wyo., August 27–29.

Hakkio, Craig S. 1996. "The Effects of Budget Deficit Reduction on the Exchange Rate." *Economic Review* (Federal Reserve Bank of Kansas City), Vol. 81, No. 3, pp. 21–38.

Heller, Peter, Richard Hemming, and Peter W. Kohnert. 1986. "Aging and Social Expenditure in the Major Industrial Countries, 1980–2025." IMF Occasional Paper 47, September.

International Monetary Fund. 1996. "Fiscal Challenges Facing Industrial Countries." *World Economic Outlook*, pp. 44–62.

Masson, Paul. 1995. "Long-Term Tendencies in Budget Deficits and Debt." In *Budget Deficits and Debt: Issues and Options*. A symposium sponsored by the Federal Reserve Bank of Kansas City, Jackson Hole, Wyo., August 31–September 2, pp. 5–55.

McDermott, John C., and Robert F. Wescott. 1996. "An Empirical Analysis of Fiscal Adjustments." IMF Working Papers WP/96/59. International Monetary Fund, Washington, D.C.

Organization for Economic Cooperation and Development. June 1996. *OECD Economic Outlook*.

Price, Robert W. R., and Patrice Muller. Autumn 1984. "Structural Budget Indicators and the Interpretation of Fiscal Policy Stance in OECD Countries." *OECD Economic Studies*, No. 3.

Rosen, Harvey S., ed. 1992. *Public Finance*, 3rd ed. Boston and Homewood, Ill.: Richard D. Irwin.

Shigehara, Kumiharu. 1995. "Commentary: Long-Term Tendencies in Budget Deficits and Debt." In *Budget Deficits and Debt: Issues and Options*. A symposium sponsored by the Federal Reserve Bank of Kansas City, Jackson Hole, Wyo., August 31–September 2, pp. 57–87.

Tanzi, Vito, and Domenico Fanizza. 1995. "Fiscal Deficits and Pubic Debt in Industrial Countries, 1970–1994." IMF Working Papers WP/95/49. International Monetary Fund, Washington, D.C.

Tanzi, Vito, and Ludger Schuknecht. 1995. "The Growth of Government and the Reform of the State in Industrial Countries." IMF Working Papers WP/95–130. International Monetary Fund, Washington, D.C.

Part II

The Economic Consequences
of Budget Deficits

Chapter 5

Budget Deficits and Economic Activity

JAMES R. BARTH AND JOHN M. WELLS

The state of the federal budget has been a continuing source of controversy in the United States. The long string of budget deficits in recent years has aroused particular concern. Indeed, some have argued in favor of a balanced budget amendment to the Constitution to resolve the deficit problem once and for all. Although such an amendment is unlikely to be enacted, the two major political parties were concerned enough about deficits in the mid-1990s that each proposed a budget that reduced the deficit to zero over several years. Ironically, the recent decades' budgetary concern is in sharp contrast to the situation that existed roughly a hundred years ago, when the issue being addressed was what to do about a string of budget surpluses, not deficits.

The purpose of this chapter is to examine alternative views and associated empirical evidence regarding the effect of U.S. federal budget deficits on economic activity. More specifically, the next section provides information on the budgetary record over the more than 200 years since the first federal budget was prepared in 1789. The third section discusses the economic effects of budget deficits. The fourth section describes the government's budget constraint and alternative views of the relationship between spending and taxes. The fifth section examines the sustainability of deficits. And the last section contains the conclusions.

HISTORICAL BUDGETARY RECORD

There have been 208 federal budgets in the United States, which encompasses the time period 1789 through 1996. Whether these budgets resulted in deficits or surpluses is shown in Figure 5.1. The amount of federal debt outstanding, which results from the issuance of federal securities to finance deficits over time,

Figure 5.1
U.S. Deficits and Debts as a Percentage of GNP, 1789–1996

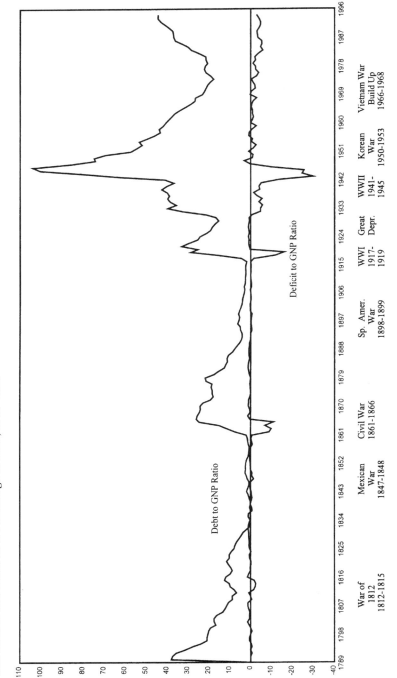

Source: U.S. Office of Management and Budget.

is also shown in this figure. Both of these variables are expressed as a percentage of gross national product (GNP).[1] Over the entire time period, there have been 105 deficits and 103 surpluses. Major war years account for 26 percent of the deficits, while recession years account for an additional 40 percent of the deficits over this period. Sixty-six percent of the deficits, in other words, have occurred during years in which there were either wars or recessions. Furthermore, the four largest deficits (as a percentage of GNP) occurred during the Civil War, World Wars I and II, and the Great Depression. During these periods the debt to GNP ratio also rose sharply. But in all these cases the large deficits and rapid growth in debt were temporary. The wars and the recessions were of relatively short duration, and the deficits during these periods were followed by surpluses. The sharp rise in the debt to GNP ratio associated with these events therefore converted to an equally sharp decline once the wars and recessions ended.

What is unusual, as Figure 5.1 shows, is the fact that the federal budget has been in deficit every year since 1969. The debt to GNP ratio has also trended upward during this period. Yet these particular budgetary developments largely occurred during a relatively peaceful, nonrecessionary period in U.S. history. Indeed, of the 42 deficits since 1950, only 7 are associated with wars and another 11 occurred during recessions. At the same time the average size of the nonwar, nonrecession deficit to GNP ratio has increased during the postwar period.[2] This recent situation represents a significant break from the past and portends dire economic consequences, should deficits and debt continue to grow relative to GNP for any sustained time period.[3] Possible adverse economic effects of budget deficits are discussed in the next section.

ECONOMIC EFFECTS OF BUDGET DEFICITS

The initial effect of a budget deficit is to lower national saving, consisting of both public and private saving. The specific way in which deficits lower saving can be best understood by examining the national income and product accounts. Private saving is the difference between disposable income and consumption, or $S = Y + Tr + Int - Tx - C$, where S is private saving, Y is gross national product, Tr and Int are government transfer and interest payments, respectively, Tx is tax revenue, and C is consumption. Substituting for Y based upon the income expenditure identity, $Y = C + I + G + NX$, yields the uses of private saving identity:

$$S = I + (G + Tr + Int - Tx) + Nx, \qquad (1)$$

where G is government spending, I is investment, and Nx is net exports. This fundamental relationship clearly points out that a deficit $(G + Tr + Int > Tx)$, with private saving held constant, lowers national saving $(S - G - Tr - Int + Tx)$ and thereby adversely affects investment or net exports or both.

The mechanism through which a decline in national saving reduces investment and/or net exports is the interest rate. When the government finances a deficit by borrowing in financial markets, the interest rate rises, thereby reducing investment spending and causing an appreciation in the U.S. dollar. The appreciation, in turn, retards exports and stimulates imports.

The preceding analysis depends crucially on the assumption that private saving does not respond to government deficits. Barro (1974), however, argues that private saving will not remain unchanged but instead will actually increase in response to the sale of government bonds to finance deficits. This argument is based upon the so-called Ricardian Equivalence theorem, which holds that the private sector fully anticipates higher future taxes to repay the borrowing undertaken to finance the deficit. In order to pay for the expected future increase in taxes the private sector will therefore simply increase saving accordingly. Bond-financed deficits in this case will have no adverse effect on investment or net exports because the budget deficit will be matched dollar for dollar by additional private saving, leaving the interest rate unchanged.

The view that deficits will have no effect on economic activity is disputed by both Keynesians and fiscal conservatives, who argue that it is based upon questionable assumptions (Bernheim, 1987). Regardless of the merit of the assumptions, substantial empirical evidence exists that fails to support the Ricardian Equivalence theorem.[4] Indeed, as Ball and Mankiw (1995) explain, investment, net exports, and private saving all declined over the period 1982 to 1994, despite the existence of large and persistent deficits.

Since there is persuasive evidence that U.S. deficits do appear to adversely affect both investment and net exports, it is important to trace out more fully their possible long-run consequences. In particular, the crowding out of investment translates into a smaller capital stock than otherwise. This implies a reduction in an economy's productive capacity and hence long-run growth.[5] A decline in net exports, on the other hand, means that more claims on domestic assets will flow overseas than otherwise to pay for those imports that are no longer financed by export earnings. As foreigners accordingly receive a greater share of the earnings on domestic assets, national income necessarily declines.

Since large and persistent budget deficits must eventually be offset by budget surpluses to prevent unbounded growth in debt or the monetization of deficits, future taxes must increase and/or spending must decrease in response to such deficits. Tax increases clearly reduce disposable income as well as create economic inefficiencies through additional compliance and avoidance costs.[6] Spending cuts also impose burdens on the public if transfer payments are reduced or government services are curtailed.

DEFICIT FINANCING AND THE GOVERNMENT BUDGET CONSTRAINT

The previous section indicated the way in which budget deficits can adversely affect economic activity. In this section, the implications of the government's budget constraint for the financing of deficits will be discussed. In particular, the constraint will be used to examine alternative views of the relationship between spending and taxes, thereby providing information about an appropriate fiscal policy for reversing budget deficits and thus limiting their adverse effects.

The government, like a household, is subject to an intertemporal budget constraint. The government's constraint states that any excess of spending over tax revenues must be financed by either money creation or selling bonds or a combination of the two. A simple form of this constraint can be expressed as

$$\Delta M + \Delta B = G + Tr + Int - Tx, \tag{2}$$

where M denotes the stock of base money, B is the value of one period government bonds, and Δ is the difference operator. The right-hand side of this equation is the government's budget position as determined by its current fiscal policy. The left-hand side indicates that the government is constrained to finance a deficit by a combination of printing money and selling bonds.

Expressed in present value form, this constraint implies that a current budget deficit must eventually lead to higher taxes, higher money growth, and/or lower spending. Historically, U.S. deficits have been mainly bond financed. Base-money financing, and the associated inflation tax, has played a relatively minor role.[7] With respect to the sources of budget imbalances, changes in both government spending and tax revenues have been important in producing deficits; changes in both have also been important in generating the subsequent budget surpluses necessary to reduce the debt incurred during wars and recessions.

The issue of whether the government should rely on spending or instead on taxes to correct budget imbalances is quite important. In this regard, there are at least three alternative views about the relationship between spending and revenues. Friedman (1978) maintains that all tax revenue will be spent by the government. He therefore argues that it is necessary to cut spending to reduce a deficit. In contrast, Barro (1979, 1986) and Ghosh (1995) contend that governments attempt to smooth tax rates over time. This means that it is the increase in spending associated with wars and recessions that causes a deficit. The spending increase occurs first and is only later followed by an increase in tax revenue. If so, a fiscal policy of setting the tax rate to generate the revenue sufficient to match desired spending would limit deficits to war and recessionary periods. Yet Buchanan and Wagner (1977, 1978) maintain that spending and revenue evolve independently of one another, perhaps in response to a common third variable (see also Hoover and Sheffrin, 1992; Alesina and Perotti, 1996). If this is true, eliminating budget imbalances requires reforming the budgetary process itself to assure that the necessary changes in spending and revenue will be made.

Each of these three views suggests a different causal relationship between spending and revenue. Friedman's view implies that taxes cause spending. Barro, however, contends the reverse is true. And Buchanan and Wagner simply argue that neither spending nor taxes respond systematically to one another when there are budget imbalances.

Empirical studies that have examined these views based on U.S. data typically use different econometric specifications, different sample periods, and different variable definitions and thus, not surprisingly, provide conflicting results concerning an appropriate fiscal policy for containing deficits.[8] Most studies indicate, however, that the time series for government spending and revenue are integrated stochastic processes (Campbell and Perron, 1991). To avoid misspecifying the long-run relationship between the two variables, one must therefore be sure to model their trends appropriately. More specifically, recent work indicates that the correct approach for making empirical inferences on the time series properties of deficits is a vector-error correction model (VECM) because it allows for a cointegrating relationship between spending and revenue (Engle and Granger, 1987). The cointegrating relationship itself describes the long-run equilibrium relationship between spending and revenue given by the right-hand side of equation (2). The entire VECM, on the other hand, enables one to examine the causal relationships and short-run responses of spending and revenue to budget disequilibria. Assuming that government spending and revenue are cointegrated, the VECM consists of the following two equations:

$$\Delta G_t = \gamma_1(G_{t-1} - \alpha TX_{t-1}) + \sum_{j=1}^{p1} \beta_{1j}\Delta G_{t-j} + \sum_{j=1}^{q1} \delta_{1j}\Delta TX_{t-j} + v_t$$

$$\Delta TX_t = \gamma_2(G_{t-1} - \alpha TX_{t-1}) + \sum_{j=1}^{p2} \beta_{2j}\Delta G_{t-j} + \sum_{j=1}^{q2} \delta_{2j}\Delta TX_{t-j} + \varepsilon_t \quad (3)$$

where Δ is the first difference operator, G_t is now total government outlays (i.e., $G + Tr + Int$), TX_t is tax revenue, γ, α, β, δ are parameters, and v_t and ε_t are residuals. The cointegrating relationship, $G_t - \alpha TX_t$, describes the long-run relationship between spending and revenue and thus provides a measure of budget disequilibria. The parameters γ_1 and γ_2 indicate how outlays and taxes respond to such disequilibria.[9]

The variables in equation (3) may be expressed in nominal or real terms or divided by nominal GNP. All these specifications are consistent with the government's budget constraint. In empirical work, however, each variable is typically deflated by nominal GNP, and logged values of the variables are employed to reduce heteroskedasticity in the error terms. Bohn (1991) provides one of the most comprehensive applications in this respect.[10] Based upon annual U.S. data from 1790 to 1988, he finds the spending to GNP and the revenue to GNP ratios to be cointegrated and the debt to GNP ratio to be stationary.

Bohn also uses his estimated VECM and impulse response functions to examine the causal relationship between spending and taxes. He concludes that 65 to 70 percent of all deficits due to higher government spending and 50 to 65 percent of all deficits due to tax cuts have been eliminated by subsequent cuts in spending. The remaining percentages have been eliminated by tax increases. Although this represents evidence of bidirectional causality, there is nonetheless more support for Friedman's (1978) view that spending adjusts to tax changes than Barro's (1979) spend-and-tax model.

Bohn's results, however, are silent with respect to Buchanan and Wagner's (1977, 1978) view that spending and taxes may be responding to some third variable and thus may evolve over time independently of one another. In particular, nothing in the U.S. budgetary process requires any coordination between the spending and taxation decisions made by the government. There is, for example, no requirement that the budget be balanced at the federal level and thus no legal reason to expect spending and taxes to adjust systematically to one another. This means that government spending could respond over time to secular economic growth, since such growth would likely increase the demand for public services. At the same time, changes in tax rates are generally quite controversial and hence less frequent than spending changes. Revenue may thus be driven more by cyclical movements in economic activity than by changes in fiscal policy. For these reasons, spending and revenue may respond over time to secular and cyclical factors rather than in a direct casual way to one another.

These possibilities are not explored by Bohn (1991), nor are they encompassed by equation (3). To test each of the three views about fiscal policy appropriately, it would seem necessary to include a macroeconomic control variable in the VECM. Indeed, Baghestani and McNown (1994) appear to be the first to do so by introducing GNP as the control variable. When testing for cointegration between the logs of nominal outlays, nominal revenues, and nominal GNP based upon quarterly data from 1955.1 to 1989.4, they find two cointegrating vectors. They interpret the first of these to be the long-run relationship between outlays and revenue. The second is interpreted to be either the long-run relationship between GNP and outlays in the error correction model (ECM) for outlays or between GNP and revenue in the ECM for revenue.

Based upon their estimation of the VECM, Baghestani and McNown find long-run evidence against both the tax-and-spend and the spend-and-tax views, as the cointegrating relationship between outlays and taxes is found to be insignificant in each equation. This indicates that neither outlays nor revenue respond significantly to budgetary disequilibria. However, both revenue and outlays adjust to the second cointegrating relationship as each corrects for disequilibria in its long-run relationship to GNP. These findings suggest that the supporting evidence for the first two views may be due to omitting the macroeconomic control variable considered to be important by Buchanan and Wagner. Indeed, once it is included, there is considerable support for the third view.

Of less importance are the short-run dynamics of the VECM suggested by the lagged differenced variables. In this case, the results tend to support both the tax-and-spend view and the Buchanan and Wagner view. Here, changes in GNP appear to cause changes in revenue but not changes in outlays. Lagged changes in revenue also cause outlays, but outlay changes do not significantly cause changes in revenue.

Overall, the findings of Baghestani and McNown (1994) indicate the importance of including a macroeconomic control variable in empirical tests of the relationship between spending and taxes. If their findings that neither outlays nor revenue appear to be responding to budget imbalances are correct, then they suggest that budgetary reform is required to eliminate large and persistent deficits. However, their results are based upon a relatively short time period in U.S. history and do not allow for the possibility that over different time periods each of the three competing views could have been operative.[11]

In view of this situation, Wells, Kondeas, and Wills (1996) adopt a more flexible approach to examining the budgetary issue by estimating rolling regressions on the Baghestani and McNown VECM over the longer period 1790–1996.[12] The rolling regressions enable one to examine regime changes, insofar as different models of the budgetary process may have been operative at different times, and to identify the dates at which any such regime changes occurred.

Over the longer time period, Wells, Kondeas, and Wills find cointegrating vectors that are quite similar to those found by Baghestani and McNown (1994). Using a 10 percent level of significance for the rolling regressions, the former find that outlays adjust to budget disequilibria and disequilibria between outlays and GNP before 1830. A regime shift occurs during the period 1830 to 1872, with revenue adjusting to disequilibria between it and GNP during the 1830s, to budget disequilibria during 1840–1870, and again to GNP disequilibria from 1845 to 1872. From 1872 onward, outlays once again adjust to both budget (1872–1922) and GNP (1872–1942) disequilibria. The period 1900 to 1950 is also characterized by revenue adjusting to its disequilibrium with GNP. Based upon a 20 percent level of significance, revenue adjusts to budget deficits from 1930 onward.

These more recent results would seem to indicate that no one view of the budgetary process explains the historical relationship between the variables. Indeed, none of the views is completely able to account for the long-run movements in the post–World War II period. However, these conclusions should be tempered by the fact that the data definitions used by Wells and coworkers (1996) differ somewhat from those used by Baghestani and McNown (1994) and by the fact that the same cointegrating relationships are assumed to hold over the entire sample period. Yet the cointegrating vectors may have changed over time as the link between the variables in the government's intertemporal budget constraint may have become unstable. This issue has received special attention in recent years and will therefore be discussed in the next section.

ARE CURRENT BUDGET DEFICITS SUSTAINABLE?

The large and persistent budget deficits that began in the early 1980s have raised questions about their sustainability. Intertemporal budget balance requires that current deficits be ultimately offset by future surpluses. This constraint rules out Ponzi schemes whereby the government simply pays off interest and maturing debt by perpetually issuing new debt. The government's budget constraint therefore restricts the present value of the budget balance to be zero, thereby assuming solvency or that growth in debt and base money will be bounded.

A sufficient condition for this restriction to be satisfied is that government spending, revenue, and interest payments all be cointegrated, with the cointegrating vector being $(1, -1, -1)$.[13] This means that sustainability of the government's fiscal policy requires a specific long-run relationship between these variables.

Several studies have examined the empirical implications of the present value requirement for the U.S. budget record. Of particular interest is the possible presence of a structural break in the cointegrating vectors signaling that the intertemporal budget constraint is not being satisfied. Although the evidence regarding whether this situation has actually occurred is somewhat mixed, it tends to indicate that the solvency requirement is being met. More specifically, based upon postwar data, Hamilton and Flavin (1986) and Kremers (1989) find that U.S. fiscal policy is consistent with the budget constraint. However, Wilcox (1989), in an extension of Hamilton and Flavin, finds that recent fiscal policy is unsustainable. Hakkio and Rush (1991), finding no evidence of cointegration over the period 1975 to 1988, reach a similar conclusion.

Tanner and Liu (1994) and Haug (1995) explicitly test for a possible structural break in the relationship between government outlays and revenue in the early 1980s. Each finds cointegration and hence fails to reject the hypothesis that there is present value budget balance over the postwar period. Trehan and Walsh (1988) and Ahmed and Rogers (1995), using data sets over a longer time period to test for cointegration, also find support for the existence of present value budget balance.

The most thorough of the above studies is Ahmed and Rogers (1995). They test whether both the intertemporal government budget constraint and the external borrowing constraint are satisfied. The latter constraint pertains to a condition on external solvency and implies that the current account deficit must be stationary. Combining these two constraints enables one to test jointly for both domestic and external balance. Based upon data for the United States for the years 1792–1992, they find that all the present value constraints are satisfied and that, thus far, the present course of fiscal policy can be viewed as being sustainable.

CONCLUSIONS

Evidence indicates that budget deficits may indeed have negative effects on economic activity. Furthermore, it appears that the relationship between government spending and revenue has undergone several different regime changes during U.S. history. At present, the current budget situation seems to be one in which neither outlays nor revenue are adjusting to reverse the deficit. Instead, each may be reacting to movements in overall economic activity and thus could significantly diverge from one another in the future and thereby cause the debt to GNP ratio to grow more rapidly. If so, a fiscal policy change that forces these variables to adjust to disequilibria would be necessary to reverse the upward trend. However, it is not clear what form such a policy change should take or whether the political will even exists to support a change.

Previous attempts to contain deficits, such as the Congressional Budget and Impoundment Control Act of 1974 and the Gramm-Rudman-Hollings Act of 1986, failed to coordinate spending and revenue decisions in a satisfactory manner. The more recent efforts (1995 and 1996) to add a balanced budget amendment to the Constitution were also unsuccessful. It is not obvious, moreover, that even if the amendment had become law, it would have been sufficient to prevent budget imbalances.

Since most of the studies examined here indicate that U.S. deficits are sustainable, it may seem appropriate to conclude that the current budget position does not represent a serious departure from earlier fiscal behavior and that reform is therefore not necessary. Before drawing such a conclusion, however, one should realize that the same studies generally point to a rising debt to GNP ratio and the low power of their econometric tests as reasons for skepticism regarding current policies.

Interestingly, Ball and Mankiw (1995) consider the possibility of a run of bad economic luck and the associated risk of a subsequent fiscal crisis as sufficient motivation to make difficult budget adjustments now while the overall economy is healthy.[14] Acting now, according to them, would certainly avoid a ''hard landing'' later. In this respect, history may be a guide. Fiscal crises preceded the French Revolution in 1789 as well as the hyperinflations in interwar Europe and Latin America in the 1970s and the 1980s. Although a collapse in the U.S. economy is unlikely, no one doubts that the adverse welfare effects would be enormous if one occurred. And even though one can doubt the probability of a hard landing if the present U.S. budget surplus continues, it is clear that such an event is not without historical precedent.

NOTES

1. The values for fiscal year 1996 are estimates of the U.S. Office of Management and Budget.

2. There are twelve years in which there were deficits not directly involving a war or recession during the period 1789–1949. The mean of the deficits was 1.55 percent of GNP. For the post-1950 period, there were 24 deficits unassociated with wars and recessions. They averaged 2.57 percent of GNP. The hypothesis that these two means are equal can be rejected at the 5 percent level of significance.

3. Whether there is a significant change in the process underlying deficits may be examined by performing a simple difference in proportions test. Wars and recessions explain 81 percent of deficits before 1950 but only 43 percent of the deficits from 1950

to 1996. The Z-statistic based on the null hypothesis that wars and recessions explain the same proportion of deficits over the pre- and postwar periods is equal to 4.03, which enables one to reject the null at the 1 percent significance level.

4. See Evans (1987, 1988, 1993) for statistical evidence based on direct tests of the Ricardian Equivalence theorem. The relationship between budget deficits and trade deficits is examined in Bernheim (1988), Abell (1990), and Rosenweig and Tallman (1993). Each of these studies finds that fiscal policy affects the trade balance.

5. Barth, Russek, and Wang (1986) examine the time series relationship between government debt and the capital stock.

6. The deadweight loss associated with compliance alone is estimated by the Joint Economic Committee to be $190 billion and 6 billion man-hours for 1996.

7. Joines (1985, 1988, 1990) finds that base money growth is not related to U.S. government deficits during peacetime periods.

8. See Baghestani and McNown (1994) for more detail.

9. For stability γ_1 should be negative, and γ_2 should be positive. See Hamilton (1994) for details concerning methods used to estimate a VECM.

10. Also, see Hoover and Sheffrin (1992), Jones and Joulfaian (1991), Miller and Russek (1990), and Trehan and Walsh (1988). Each of these studies relies on a shorter data set than Bohn.

11. Hoover and Sheffrin (1992) find two distinct regimes in their examination of postwar budgetary data.

12. See Thoma (1994) for an application of rolling regressions to an examination of money-income causality.

13. Sufficiency also requires rational expectations—that the marginal utility of consumption follows a random walk and that the conditional covariance between the marginal utility of consumption and g_t and tx_t be time invariant. See Ahmed and Rogers (1995) for a more complete discussion of these issues.

14. The probability of a fiscal crisis has been estimated to be between 10 and 20 percent, given the current debt situation and the historical behavior of interest rates and growth rates. See Ball, Mankiw, and Elmendorf (1995) for further discussion.

REFERENCES

Abell, John D. Winter 1990. "Twin Deficits during the 1980s: An Empirical Investigation." *Journal of Macroeconomics*, pp. 81–96.

Ahmed, Shaghil, and John H. Rogers. 1995. "Government Budget Deficits and Trade Deficits: Are Present Value Constraints Satisfied in Long-Term Data?" *Journal of Monetary Economics*, Vol. 36, pp. 351–374.

Alesina, Alberto, and Roberto Perotti. 1996. "Budget Deficits and Budget Institutions." NBER Working Paper 5556.

Baghestani, Hamid, and Robert McNown. 1994. "Do Revenues or Expenditures Respond to Budgetary Disequilibria?" *Southern Economic Journal*, Vol. 61, pp. 311–322.

Ball, Laurence, and N. Gregory Mankiw. 1995. "What Do Budget Deficits Do?" NBER Working Paper 5263.

Ball, Laurence, N. Gregory Mankiw, and Douglas W. Elmendorf. 1995. "The Deficit Gamble." NBER Working Paper 5015.

Barro, Robert J. 1974. "Are Government Bonds Net Wealth?" *Journal of Political Economy*, Vol. 82, pp. 1095–1117.

————. 1979. "On the Determination of Public Debt." *Journal of Political Economy*, Vol. 87, pp. 940–971.

————. 1986. "U.S. Deficits since World War I." *Scandinavian Journal of Economics*, Vol. 88, pp. 195–222.

Barth, James R., Frank S. Russek, and George H. K. Wang. 1986. "A Time Series Analysis of the Relationship between the Capital Stock and Federal Debt." *Journal of Money, Credit, and Banking*, Vol. 18, pp. 527–538.

Bernheim, B. Douglas. 1987. "Ricardian Equivalence: An Evaluation of Theory and Evidence." *NBER Macroeconomics Annual*, pp. 263–304.

————. 1988. "Budget Deficits and the Balance of Trade." In *Tax Policy and the Economy*. Cambridge: MIT Press, pp. 1–31.

Bohn, Henning. 1991. "Budget Balance through Revenue or Spending Adjustments? Some Historical Evidence for the United States." *Journal of Monetary Economics*, Vol. 27, pp. 333–359.

Buchanan, James M., and Richard E. Wagner. 1977. *Democracy in Deficit: The Political Legacy of Lord Keynes*. New York: Academic Press.

————. 1978. "Dialogues Concerning Fiscal Religion." *Journal of Monetary Economics*, Vol. 4, pp. 627–636.

Campbell, John Y., and Pierre Perron. 1991. "Pitfalls and Opportunities: What Macroeconomists Should Know about Unit Roots." *NBER Macroeconomics Annual*, pp. 141–201.

Engle, Robert F., and Clive W. J. Granger. 1987. "Cointegration and Error Correction: Representation, Estimation and Testing." *Econometrica*, Vol. 55, pp. 251–276.

Evans, Paul. 1987. "Interest Rates and Expected Future Budget Deficits in the United States." *Journal of Political Economy*, Vol. 95, pp. 35–58.

————. 1988. "Are Consumers Ricardian? Evidence for the United States." *Journal of Political Economy*, Vol. 96, pp. 983–1004.

————. 1993. "Consumers Are Not Ricardian: Evidence from Nineteen Countries." *Economic Inquiry*, Vol. 31, pp. 534–548.

Friedman, Milton. Summer 1978. "The Limitations of Tax Limitation." *Policy Review*, pp. 7–14.

Ghosh, Atish R. 1995. "Intertemporal Tax-Smoothing and the Government Budget Surplus: Canada and the United States." *Journal of Money, Credit, and Banking*, Vol. 27, pp. 1033–1045.

Hakkio, Craig S., and Mark Rush. 1991. "Is the Budget Deficit 'Too Large'?" *Economic Inquiry*, Vol. 29, pp. 429–445.

Hamilton, James D. 1994. *Time Series Analysis*. Princeton, N.J.: Princeton University Press.

Hamilton, James D., and Marjorie A. Flavin. 1986. "On the Limitations of Government Borrowing: A Framework for Empirical Testing." *American Economic Review*, Vol. 76, pp. 808–819.

Haug, Alfred A. 1995. "Has Federal Budget Deficit Policy Changed in Recent Years?" *Economic Inquiry*, Vol. 33, pp. 104–118.

Hoover, Kevin D., and Steven M. Sheffrin. 1992. "Causation, Spending, and Taxes: Sand in the Sandbox or Tax Collector for the Welfare State?" *American Economic Review*, Vol. 82, pp. 225–248.

Joines, Douglas H. 1985. "Deficits and Money Growth in the United States, 1872–1983." *Journal of Monetary Economics*, Vol. 16, pp. 329–351.

———. 1988. "Deficits and Money Growth in the United States: Reply." *Journal of Monetary Economics*, Vol. 21, pp. 155–160.

———. 1990. "Seasonality and the Monetization of Federal Budget Deficits."*Economic Inquiry*, Vol. 28, pp. 413–441.

Jones, Jonathan D., and David Joulfaian. Winter 1991. "Federal Government Expenditures and Revenues in the Early Years of the American Republic: Evidence from 1792 to 1860." *Journal of Macroeconomics*, pp. 133–155.

Kremers, Jeroen. 1989. "U.S. Federal Indebtedness and the Conduct of Fiscal Policy." *Journal of Monetary Economics*, Vol. 23, pp. 219–238.

Miller, Stephen M., and Frank S. Russek. 1990. "Co-Integration and Error-Correction Models: The Temporal Causality between Government Taxes and Spending." *Southern Economic Journal*, Vol. 57, pp. 221–229.

Rosenweig, Jeffrey A., and Ellis W. Tallman. 1993. "Fiscal Policy and Trade Adjustments: Are the Deficits Really Twins?" *Economic Inquiry*, Vol. 31, pp. 580–594.

Tanner, Evan, and Peter Liu. 1994. "Is the Budget Deficit 'Too Large'? Some Further Evidence." *Economic Inquiry*, Vol. 32, pp. 511–518.

Thoma, Mark A. 1994. "Subsample Instability and Asymmetries in Money-Income Causality." *Journal of Econometrics*, Vol. 64, pp. 279–306.

Trehan, Bharat, and Carl E. Walsh. 1988. "Common Trends, the Government's Budget Constraint, and Revenue Smoothing." *Journal of Economic Dynamics & Control*, Vol. 12, pp. 425–444.

Wells, John M., Alex Kondeas, and Douglas T. Wills. 1996. "Budgetary Regimes and Revenue-Expenditure Relationships in U.S. Data." Auburn University Working Paper.

Wilcox, David W. 1989. "The Sustainability of Government Deficits: Implications of the Present-Value Borrowing Constraint." *Journal of Money, Credit, and Banking*, Vol. 21, pp. 291–306.

Chapter 6

Fiscal Imbalances and the Exchange Rates

SIAMACK SHOJAI

In previous chapters, we looked at the size of relatively large budget deficits in the industrialized world since the late 1960s. The current public policy debate regarding the impact of budget deficits on the economy boils down to the issue of how a deficit reduction might affect interest rates and ultimately financial markets and real economic growth. Intergenerational impacts of deficit financing are also debated in the context of how a deficit reduction might affect real interest rates and the path of capital formation. Since the collapse of the Bretton Woods System, many economists have investigated the impact of deficit reductions on the real exchange rates and the value of a currency.

The issue is pivotal in terms of international transfer of real resources and export of unemployment across the nations. Under a flexible exchange rates system, a policy of beggar-thy-neighbor can be orchestrated via deficit spending. Feldstein (1986) highlights the political economy of the U.S. budget deficit and its connection to the European economies. He considers the reaction of the German economy to a historical increase in the U.S. deficits in the early to mid-1980s. Presenting a textbook discussion, he argues that the U.S. budget deficits caused higher real long-term interest rates in both the U.S. and German economies. However, higher real rates in the United States led to capital flights to the United States, which made the U.S. dollar stronger up to 1985. A weaker German mark led to imported inflation, lower investments, and slower economic growth in Germany. The decline in the German mark shifted the short-run Philips curve to the right and forced its monetary and fiscal authorities to adopt tight policies. Other countries in the European Monetary System had no choice but to follow the same monetary policy.

The profound impact of budget deficits on the political economy of creating a European Monetary Union is manifested in the convergence requirements.

Accordingly, members of the Union must reduce their respective budget deficits and national debt to 3 and 60 percent of their gross domestic product (GDP), respectively, before they can be admitted to the European Currency Union.

A casual observation of deficits and real exchange rates in the industrialized world provides a mixed picture as to the relationship between budget deficits and exchange rates. Hakkio (1996) demonstrates that in the early 1980s the U.S. dollar appreciated when the budget deficit was rising, while Finland, Italy, and Sweden experienced depreciation of their currency in the 1990s, during rising deficits. This chapter provides a discussion of the theory and the empirical findings of the impact of deficit reductions on the value of a convertible currency. The discussion is limited to cases of industrialized economies with a convertible currency and no capital movement restrictions.

DEFICITS AND EXCHANGE RATES: THE THEORY

A complete survey of the theories of exchange rate determination is beyond the intended scope of this chapter. In addition to the flow approach to modeling exchange rates, portfolio balance, monetary approach, and currency substitution approaches have been attempted by many researchers. Authors like Allen (1977), Penati (1983), Branson (1985), Bisignano and Hoover (1982), Hutchison and Pigott (1984), Hutchison and Throop (1985), Evans (1986), Frenkel and Razin (1987), Bundt and Solocha (1988), Abell (1990), and Hakkio (1996) have utilized alternative and complementary models of exchange rates to investigate whether budget deficits lead to currency appreciation or vice versa. Here, we limit our discussion to some recent developments.

Before direct and indirect impacts of a deficit reduction on exchange rates are discussed, we need to review three major theoretical tools of analysis: the Loanable Funds Theory (LFT), the foreign exchange markets, and the Fisher Effect.

THE LOANABLE FUNDS THEORY

According to LFT (Hoelscher, 1983, 1986), interest rates are determined as a result of interaction between supply and demand for loanable funds. Supply of loanable funds includes national saving and changes to the stock of money. Demand for loanable funds is composed of investments and changes in demand for money balances. An increase in supply or a reduction in demand for funds reduces interest rates. On the other hand, a decline in supply or an increase in demand for funds causes higher interest rates.

It is apparent that any deficit reduction that affects national saving, investments, monetary policy, or demand for cash balances would ultimately change the level of interest rates. In previous chapters, we addressed theoretical and empirical research on interest rates and fiscal imbalances. Here we focus on the ultimate reaction of exchange rates to a deficit reduction.

THE FOREIGN EXCHANGE MARKETS

Since 1973, under flexible exchange rate systems, the value of a foreign currency is set in the foreign exchange markets by market participants. A major component of demand for a foreign currency (supply of domestic currency) is net capital flows. With perfect capital mobility and globalization of the financial markets, changes in relative interest rates lead to changes in capital flows. An increase in domestic interest rates can make domestic securities more attractive and raise the demand for the domestic currency in the foreign exchange markets. In turn, higher demand would cause appreciation of the domestic currency relative to foreign currencies. Thus, reducing fiscal imbalances could lead to changes in interest rates and alter exchange rates.

THE REAL INTEREST RATE

Irving Fisher, in 1907, argued that in the long run nominal interest rates fully reflect the expected inflation rate. For example, a bondholder expects to earn a real rate of interest in addition to the expected inflation rate. Adding to this a risk premium for investing in risky securities provides a practical approximation for decomposing nominal interest rates into three components. Nominal or market interest rates (r) are composed of a real rate (R), an inflation premium (P), and a risk premium (S). Thus, we can write:

$$r = R + P + S.$$

Consider a real interest rate of 5 percent, an expected inflation rate of 7 percent, and a risk premium of 2 percent. This results in a nominal interest rate of 14 percent. A bond issuer who offers less than 14 percent for a bond with a 2 percent risk exposure will have a difficult time placing the bond in the market. Suppose that due to monetary policy or some other real shock, the actual inflation falls, unexpectedly, to 3 percent. Obviously, the existing bondholders will realize a sharp increase in real interest rate. The real rate for the existing bondholders is 9 percent.

An important issue in examining the effect of a deficit reduction on interest rates is whether nominal interest rates fully adjust to the new actual inflation rate. A full adjustment would bring nominal interest rates down, in the example above, to 10 percent. However, it is generally argued that nominal rates do not fully adjust to inflation premium changes, and the ultimate impact is smaller than the change in inflation premium. In such a case, if nominal rates adjust by only 70 percent, real interest rates would increase to 6.2 percent. In summary, unexpected changes in inflation rates can cause a change in real interest rates. A change in degree of riskiness can have similar impacts on the real interest rates.

It must be obvious by now that changes in budget deficits are transmitted to foreign exchange markets via changes in interest rates in the loanable funds market. Interest rate changes ultimately affect capital flows and the value of a currency in foreign exchange markets.

DIRECT IMPACT OF A DEFICIT REDUCTION

The direct impact of deficit reduction is analyzed within the framework of the crowding-out effect. Lower deficit financing by government reduces demand for loanable funds, which lowers interest rates and makes foreign portfolio assets more attractive. Demand for foreign currency rises, and as a result, domestic currency depreciates. For example, if the U.S. budget deficit and government borrowing were to decline, U.S. interest rates should fall and capital outflows from the United States would reduce the value of the dollar. Branson (1985) used a framework similar to this and argued that the dollar should decline to its pre-1980 level, should the U.S. deficit subside.

INDIRECT IMPACT OF A DEFICIT REDUCTION

The indirect influences of budget deficits are mainly related to the role of expectations in asset allocation. Market expectations of future deficits and exchange rates lead to immediate change in exchange rates and higher volatility in the market. Hakkio (1996) provides a summary of the indirect effects of deficits on exchange rates. He argues that a deficit reduction can cause a higher demand for loanable funds through three major channels: lower expected inflation, lower foreign exchange risk, and greater expected rate of return on domestic assets.

Large-size or out-of-control budget deficits that are financed by printing money lead to higher inflationary expectations. Even if the debt is not monetized, its large size could convince the markets that it eventually will be paid through an inflation tax. A credible attempt to control the deficit lowers inflationary expectations and the inflation premium in long-term interest rates. Based on the Fisher Effect, nominal long-term rates could decline by the same percentage and real rates would remain the same. However, if nominal long-term interest rates do not fall as much as the expected inflation premium has declined, then real long-term rates would increase. Thus, a deficit reduction makes domestic assets more attractive and causes the dollar to appreciate.

The real long-term interest rates could increase due to lower risk of domestic bonds. Reducing the deficit can lower the risk premium on domestic assets relative to foreign securities. Thus, given the same nominal rate, holders of domestic bonds realize a higher real long-term yield, and the dollar would appreciate.

The U.S. dollar could be indirectly supported by a deficit reduction if such an action results in a transfer of real resources from public consumption to private investments. Higher private investments and the associated higher growth and productivity could increase the real return to capital and hence push the dollar up.

THE OVERALL IMPACT

As noted in the discussion earlier, a deficit reduction can directly reduce the value of the dollar and appreciate it indirectly. The overall effect of a deficit reduction on the exchange rate is dependent on whether the deficit reduction is credible, long term, and sustainable (Hakkio, 1996). A credible deficit reduction plan can cause indirect factors to overwhelm and lead to a stronger currency. Sinai (1995) suggests:

A credible long-run deficit-reduction plan that had foreign investors believing as they should that inflation, on average, would be lower than it would have been otherwise, should then reduce the risk of holding U.S. assets in terms of an inflation-adjusted calculation. And then, because inflation is lower than it would otherwise be in the United States compared to other countries, the exchange rate should also do better, which would probably improve investors' perceptions of the currency and inflation-adjusted risk of holding U.S. securities relative to other securities. And, depending on the empirical significance of this, you could have something that was stronger than the effects of lower interest rates on the U.S. dollar from deficit reduction. (p. 147)

Sinai seems to believe that a deficit reduction lowers nominal interest rates and the value of the dollar. However, he acknowledges the dominance of lower risk and inflationary expectations when the fiscal authorities' attempt to lower deficits is perceived as credible and sustainable.

THE RICARDIAN EQUIVALENCE APPROACH

In a celebrated paper, Robert Barro (1974) argued that budget deficits and taxes are equivalent. The issue goes back to David Ricardo's argument about whether government bonds are wealth. Assuming that taxpayers realize that current deficits must be paid by future taxes, they will increase their saving by an amount equal to the present value of future tax liabilities due to current deficits. Thus, government deficit financing offset by higher saving does not affect interest rates or the exchange rate (Barro, 1989a, 1989b). In fact, Barro announced that deficits do not matter.

The Barro-Ricardo Equivalence theorem must be analyzed in the context of the literature on determinants of saving. For example, with taxes dependent on wages or income, a tax cut due to deficit reduction could change saving behavior in favor of a higher marginal consumption. A structural analysis of changes in marginal propensity to consume (save) due to a transfer of resources from government consumption to private investment is warranted.

DEFICIT AND EXCHANGE RATES: THE EMPIRICAL EVIDENCE

Ironically, empirical investigations of the impact of budget deficits on the exchange rates are as inconclusive as theoretical arguments. In this part, we discuss some of the major findings of some recent econometric studies.

Economic models of exchange rates that incorporate fundamental economic variables such as money measures, income, and prices have performed poorly compared to random walk models. Many researchers have concluded that there is no significant relation between exchange rates and fundamental economic variables (Meltzer, 1993). In 1983, Meese and Rogoff in a major study concluded that a random walk model of exchange rates performs as well as any structural model. More recent studies have concentrated on the stationarity of real and nominal exchange rates and whether exchange rates and fundamental economic variables are cointegrated (Chinn, 1991). These studies have attempted to establish the existence of a long-run relationship between exchange rates and economic aggregates. Many studies reject cointegration, suggesting that there is no long-run relationship between these variables. Earlier support of nonstationarity of exchange rates has been challenged by many more recent studies such as Huizinga (1987), Engel and Hamilton (1990), Hakkio and Joines (1990).

Meltzer (1993) provides evidence as to why trade-weighted nominal and real exchange rates move together. This had already been supported by studies done by Mussa (1986) and Edwards (1989) for developed and developing economies. Thus, we use real and nominal exchange rates interchangeably unless otherwise is specifically warranted.

Bundt and Solocha (1988) estimated a general two-country portfolio balance model of exchange rates with currency substitution over the period 1973–1987 for the United States, Canada, and Germany. Their study supports that increases in the U.S. debt stock caused an appreciation of the U.S. dollar against the German mark and the Canadian dollar.

Meltzer (1993) utilized a random walk model of exchange rates with a permanent and a temporary component to test whether the appreciation of the dollar in the early to mid-1980s was due to an increase in the U.S. defense spending or an increase in after-tax return to real capital. He found that changes in defense spending and the rate of after-tax return to real capital, as measured by the change in real GDP, had a significant impact on the appreciation of the dollar. He concluded that 44 percent of the appreciation of the U.S. dollar during the 1981–1985 period was due to changes in defense and real return to capital. Meltzer also used a change in real government debt as a measure of budget deficit and found that its impact on the value of the dollar was small and insignificant. In addition, Bohn's (1992) measure of government net worth, which includes principal government assets and liabilities as a measure of deficit, was utilized, and it was concluded that changes in the net worth have no significant effect on the exchange rate.

Humpage (1992) utilized the Engle-Granger Cointegration technique to test the existence of a long-run relationship between the level of the U.S. federal budget deficit and the exchange rates during the period 1973–1991. Unlike many other studies, Humpage used the level of deficit instead of deficit as a percentage of GDP. He argues that when the level of deficit is very large, it could have substantially different effects on the exchange rates. The Dickery-Fuller and Augmented Dickery-Fuller tests of the individual time series reject the null hypothesis of a unit root, and, therefore, cointegration is appropriate. However, the bivariate and multivariate cointegration tests indicate that the U.S. federal deficit, federal expenditures, or federal purchases are not cointegrated with the value of the U.S. dollar. As noticed by the author, the results of his study many not be robust with respect to different measures of deficit. Also, cointegration tests seek a long-run relationship between variables, and the existence of a short-run relationship cannot necessarily be rejected.

In the theoretical part of this chapter, we argued that a large deficit may convey that it cannot be sustained in the long run, and eventually the government will have to either monetize the debt or default. Thus, a deficit reduction in such cases should cause the dollar to appreciate. Many authors have studied the size of the federal budget deficit in order to examine the solvency of the U.S. government by applying cointegration tests to federal expenditures and revenues (Hamilton and Falvin, 1986; Trehan and Walsh, 1988; Bohn, 1991). Hakkio and Rush (1991) conclude that interest-inclusive government expenditures and revenues are not cointegrated one to one; therefore, the deficit is too large to be sustained in the long run. This suggests that the government has a tendency to default. If these results are reliable, then through the indirect impacts of deficits on the exchange rate one would expect that deficit reductions reduce the risk of domestic securities and cause the U.S. dollar to appreciate.

Tanner and Liu (1994) test the nonstationarity of the U.S. deficit and reject the null hypothesis of no integration for the periods 1950–1989, 1964–1989, and 1976–1989. They conclude that the U.S. deficit is sustainable and does not violate the intertemporal solvency of the government.

Hakkio (1996) uses pooled annual data during the period 1979–1994 for eighteen Organization for Economic Cooperation and Development (OECD) countries and regresses the real exchange rate on the budget deficit as a percentage of the GDP. To estimate the indirect impact of a deficit reduction on exchange rates, a country's inflation rate relative to the average OECD inflation rate, the stock of government debt (as a percentage of GDP) relative to the OECD average, and the change in government spending as a share of GDP are included in the regression line to proxy the impact of expected inflation, risk premium, and the expected rate of return effect on exchange rates.

The estimated results indicate that the direct impact of a deficit reduction in thirteen countries leads to a stronger currency, but in five countries, the currency weakens as the deficit is reduced. Also, in all cases the indirect impacts of deficit reduction have the correct sign and are statistically significant. The overall conclusions indicate that a deficit reduction leads to a stronger currency in the United States, Germany, France, Italy, and Canada. However, deficit reductions in Japan, England, and Australia weaken the currency. Interestingly, deficit reductions through tax increases and spending reductions have different effects on the currency of different countries. In general, in all countries under investigation, except Japan, England, and Australia, cutting the deficit by spending cuts causes the currency to appreciate more than when taxes are increased. In Italy, revenue increases have a small impact on the exchange rate, but spending cuts are more effective. In Portugal and Norway, deficit reduction through tax increases weakens the currency, but spending cuts strengthen the currency.

A multicountry structural and reduced form model was utilized by Taylor (1993) to stimulate the impact of an anticipated and an unanticipated change in fiscal policy on exchange rates. The simulation results indicate that anticipated and unanticipated fiscal expansion causes large exchange rate appreciations. The study indicates that in the United States an unanticipated permanent increase in the budget deficit by 1 percent of the gross national product (GNP) caused a 6 percent appreciation of the dollar in the 1980s. Taylor concludes that 30 percent of the U.S. dollar appreciation in the 1980s was caused by the budget deficit (Taylor, 1993, p. 216). One has to be cautious about accepting results of simulation models because many of them embody certain macroeconomic properties that may result in a bias in their conclusions.

CONCLUSION

This chapter provided a brief discussion of the relation between exchange rates and government deficits. The theoretical models provide an ambiguous picture of how a deficit reduction affects a currency. Direct impacts of such actions can lead to currency depreciation; however, the indirect impacts can easily overwhelm such exchange rate changes in the opposite direction. Many researchers have estimated the overall impact of fiscal imbalances on the value of a currency. Ironically, the empirical works do not shed any better light on the issue than the theoretical models. It seems that depending on the measures of the deficit, the econometric model, and the period of study, different conclusions can be reached.

More research in this area and consumer saving, consumption, and investment decision-making processes is needed before some of these issues can be settled. A structural analysis of consumers' behavior may shed more light on this issue.

REFERENCES

Abell, John D. 1990. ''The Role of the Budget Deficit during the Rise in the Dollar Exchange Rate from 1979–1985.'' *Southern Economic Journal*, Vol. 57, No. 1, pp. 66–74.

Allen, Polly R. 1977. "Financing Budget Deficits: The Effects on Income in Closed and Open Economies." *European Economic Review*, Vol. 10, pp. 345–373.

Barro, Robert J. 1974. "Are Government Bonds Net Wealth?" *Journal of Political Economy*, Vol. 82, pp. 1095–1117.

———. 1989a. "The Neoclassical Approach to Fiscal Policy." In R. Barro, ed., *Modern Business Cycle Theory*. Cambridge, Mass.: Harvard University Press.

———. 1989b. "The Ricardian Approach to Budget Deficits." *Journal of Economic Perspective*, Vol. 3, No. 2, pp. 37–54.

Bisignano, Joseph, and Kevin D. Hoover. Winter 1982. "Monetary and Fiscal Impacts on Exchange Rates." *Economic Review* (Federal Reserve Bank of San Francisco), pp. 19–33.

Bohn, Henning. 1991. "Budget Balance through Revenue or Spending Adjustments? Some Historical Evidence for the United States." *Journal of Monetary Economics*, Vol. 27, pp. 333–359.

———. December 1992. "Budget Deficits and Government Accounting." Conference Proceedings. Carnegie Rochester Conference Series on Public Policy, pp. 1–83.

Branson, William H. 1985. "Causes of Appreciation and Volatility of the Dollar." In *The U.S. Dollar—Recent Developments, Outlook, and Policy Options*. Kansas City: Federal Reserve Bank of Kansas City.

Bundt, Thomas, and Andrew Solocha. 1988. "Debt, Deficits, and Dollar." *Journal of Policy Modeling*, Vol. 10, No. 4, pp. 581–600.

Chinn, M. June 1991. "Some Linear and Nonlinear Thoughts on Exchange Rates." *Journal of International Money and Finance*, pp. 214–230.

Edwards, S. 1989. *Real Exchange Rates, Devaluation, and Adjustment: Exchange Rate Policy in Developing Countries*. Cambridge, Mass.: MIT Press.

Engel, C., and J. D. Hamilton. September 1990. "Long Swings in the Dollar: Are They in Data and Do Markets Know It?" *American Economic Review*, pp. 689–713.

Evans, Paul. 1986. "Is the Dollar High Because of Large Budget Deficits?" *Journal of Monetary Economics*, Vol. 18, No. 3, pp. 227–249.

Feldstein, Martin. May 1986. "U.S. Budget Deficits and the European Economies: Resolving the Political Economy Puzzle."*AEA Papers and Proceedings*, pp. 342–346.

Fisher, Irving. 1907. *The Theory of Interest*. New York: Macmillan.

Frenkel, Jacob A., and Assaf Razin. 1987. *Fiscal Policies and the World Economy: An Intertemporal Approach*. Cambridge, Mass.: MIT Press.

Hakkio, Craig S. 1996. "The Effects of Budget Deficit Reduction on the Exchange Rate." *Economic Review* (Federal Reserve Bank of Kansas City), Vol. 81, No. 3, pp. 21–38.

Hakkio, Craig S., and D. Joines. September 1990. "Real and Nominal Exchange Rates since 1919." Working Paper. Federal Reserve Bank of Kansas City.

Hakkio, Craig S., and Mark Rush. 1991. "Is the Budget Deficit 'Too Large'?" *Economic Inquiry*, Vol. 29, pp. 429–445.

Hamilton, James D., and Marjorie A. Falvin. 1986. "On the Limitations of Government Borrowing: A Framework for Empirical Testing." *American Economic Review*, Vol. 76, pp. 808–819.

Hoelscher, Gregory P. 1983. "Federal Borrowing and Short Term Interest Rates." *Southern Economic Journal*, Vol. 50, pp. 319–333.

————. 1986. ''New Evidence on Deficits and Interest Rates.'' *Journal of Money, Credit, and Banking*, Vol. 18, pp. 1–17.

Huizinga, J. Autumn 1987. ''An Empirical Investigation of the Long-run Behavior of Exchange Rates.'' Conference Proceedings. Carnegie Rochester Conference Series on Public Policy, pp. 149–214.

Humpage, Owen F. 1992. ''An Introduction to the International Implications of U.S. Fiscal Policy.'' *Economic Review* (Federal Reserve Bank of Cleveland), Vol. 28, No. 3, pp. 27–39.

Hutchison, Michael M., and Charles Pigott. Fall 1984. ''Budget Deficits, Exchange Rates, and the Current Account: Theory and U.S. Evidence.'' *Economic Review* (Federal Reserve Bank of San Francisco), pp. 5–25.

Hutchison, Michael M., and Adrian W. Throop. Fall 1985. ''U.S. Budget Deficits and the Real Value of the Dollar.'' *Economic Review* (Federal Reserve Bank of San Francisco), pp. 26–43.

Meese, R., and K. Rogoff. February 1983. ''Empirical Exchange Rate Models of the Seventies: Do They Fit Out of Sample?'' *Journal of International Economics*, pp. 3–24.

Meltzer, Allan H. March–April 1993. ''Real Exchange Rates: Some Evidence from the Postwar Years.'' *Economic Review* (Federal Reserve Bank of St. Louis), pp. 103–117.

Mussa, M. Autumn 1986. ''Nominal Exchange Rate Regimes and the Behavior of Real Exchange Rates: Evidence and Implications.'' Conference Proceedings. Carnegie Rochester Conference Series on Public Policy, pp. 117–213.

Penati, Alessandro. 1983. ''Expansionary Fiscal Policy and the Exchange Rate: A Review.'' International Monetary Fund Staff Papers No. 30.

Sinai, Allan. 1995. ''General Discussion: What Do Budget Deficits Do?'' In *Budget Deficits and Debt: Issues and Options*. A symposium sponsored by the Federal Reserve Bank of Kansas City, Jackson Hole, Wyo., August 31–September 2, pp. 139–149.

Tanner, Evan, and Peter Liu. 1994. ''Is the Budget Deficit 'Too Large'?: Some Further Evidence.''*Economic Inquiry*, Vol. 32, pp. 511–518.

Taylor, John B. 1993. *Macroeconomic Policy in a World Economy: From Econometric Design to Practical Operation*. New York: W.W. Norton.

Trehan, Bharat, and Carl E. Walsh. 1988. ''Common Trends, Intertemporal Budget Balance, and Revenue Smoothing.'' *Journal of Economic Dynamics and Control*, Vol. 12, pp. 425–444.

Chapter 7

Do Deficits Matter? A Review of the Deficit and Inflation Debate

SOHRAB ABIZADEH AND MAHMOOD YOUSEFI

Budget deficits are blamed for many economic ills of society by politicians and policy makers. Economically, the relevant question is, Do government deficits matter? Eisner (1986) argues to the affirmative since they add to the public debt and hence contribute to aggregate demand. (For qualifications and details, see Eisner 1986, pp. 71–73.) Others such as Barro (1974, 1978) and Kormendi (1983) contend that deficits do not matter. The eclectics in the deficit debate (e.g., Horrigan and Protopapadakis, 1982) contend that, contrary to popular belief, deficits and surpluses perform an important economic function. That is, they promote economic efficiency. Viewed as such, the debate should focus not on whether there should be deficits but instead on the optimal size of deficits in furthuring economic efficiency. Thus, frequent tampering with tax rates should be avoided in order to minimize the imposition of unnecessary costs on the economy. The advocates of supply-side economics dismiss deficit as an important issue in fiscal policy. They contend that deficits neither cause high interest rates nor lead to inflation.

It appears that controversy surrounds the deficit issue. The problem arises, in part, from failure to distinguish between active and passive deficits (Tatom, 1984). Also, failure to employ appropriate measures of deficit gives a distorted picture of true deficits. Horrigan and Protopapadakis (1982) and Eisner (1986), among others, address this problem.

Given the apparent controversy concerning the impact of deficits on the rate of inflation, the main thrust of this chapter is to examine the theoretical and empirical aspects of this debate. In order to provide further evidence, we will present a model, using an appropriate deficit measure, to empirically investigate the link between deficits and inflation using the Canadian data.

THEORETICAL AND EMPIRICAL ALTERNATIVES

Theoretically, two polar positions reflect the importance of deficits. The neoclassical paradigm holds that substituting debt for tax finance, *ceteris paribus*, increases current consumption and aggregate demand due to increases in the private sector's wealth. Since the increase in private saving is not matched by the amount of debt issue, interest rates rise and private capital accumulation is crowded out. The monetarists go one step further and argue that, in these circumstances, if the central bank, in its conduct of monetary policy, tries to smooth interest rates instead of controlling the money supply, the outcome would be inflationary.

According to the neoclassical paradigm, the method of financing government deficits affects the level of aggregate demand. For instance, bond-financed as opposed to tax-financed deficits causes real interest rates to rise at full employment. Thus, investment and/or net exports are crowded out. (For recent empirical evidence, see Cebula and Rhodd, 1993; Dua, 1993). The neoclassical paradigm, according to Yellen (1989), critically depends on three assumptions. First, it assumes that the economy's resources are fully employed. Second, the neoclassicals assume that official deficits are an economically meaningful measure of government dissaving. Finally, "the most critical assumption in the neoclassical argument is that the level of private consumption is higher when a given program of government spending is financed by deficits than by current taxes" (p. 19).

The full employment assumption has been challenged by the Keynesians. If markets do not clear and the economy suffers from a situation of Keynesian unemployment, then the negative trade-off between present and future consumption must be ruled out. Under these circumstances, deficits are likely to cause higher consumption as well as higher future output (Yellen, 1989). Eisner (1989) argues that under conditions of less than full employment increases in current consumption need not imply any borrowing from the future or a future generation of taxpayers. The otherwise unutilized resources finance the consumption, which, in turn, encourages more, not less, investment. The economy will be pushed to a higher growth path, and additional "taxes in the future, if there are to be any, may then readily be paid out of higher future incomes" (p. 74). Thus, deficits do matter, and their impact depends on the circumstances under which they occur. Eisner's position is shared by Domar (1993), who argues that certain economic conditions (e.g., an economic slowdown or a rise in unemployment) warrant deficit spending. What matters is the ratio of debt to gross national product (GNP), and a smaller, rather than a larger, ratio is preferable.

Bernheim (1989, p. 60) indicates that in addition to the possibility of unemployed resources the traditional Keynesian view of deficits "presupposes the existence of myopic or liquidity constrained individuals." This assumption secures the high level of sensitivity of aggregate consumption to changes in disposable income. Bernheim raises questions about the Keynesian theory of budget deficits and is skeptical about the benefits of using temporary deficits as an instrument of macroeconomic stabilization. (For details, see Bernheim, 1989.)

Perri and Shelley (1996) investigated the growth of federal expenditures and budget deficits, measured as a percentage of nominal GNP, in the United States over the period 1955–1993. They concluded that the growth in federal expenditures and budget deficits is due to three discrete increases in the means of these variables. "The timing of these increases is consistent with the government's use of expansionary fiscal policy to combat the recessions experienced in 1964–70, 1974–75, and 1981–82." They further argued that the reason government expenditures and deficits do not decrease after the end of these recessions is partly "due to two significant legislative changes in the Congress and budgetary process enacted during the first half of the 1970s" (p. 41). First came change in a series of bills that tempered "the power of committees in favor of subcommittees and relaxed seniority rules. This allowed previously less powerful members of the Congress to obtain additional federal spending within their home districts (and state) without offsetting increases in taxes. Secondly, the ICA effectively ended the President's ability to use impoundment as a check on deficit spending" (p. 41).

The challenge to the neoclassical paradigm comes from those who purportedly do not employ a set of symmetric assumptions about the private sector's perception of fiscal policies of the government. These challengers argue that the public perceives the implied future taxes of debt finance. If so, the value of future taxes offsets the current taxes avoided. Since the net wealth of the private sector is invariant with respect to debt or tax finance, the implications are neither changes in interest rates nor the level of prices. (For a counterargument, see Eisner, 1986, pp. 69–71.) Barro (1979), Kormendi (1983), Plosser (1982), and Evans (1985), among others, provide theoretical and empirical support for this position. The proponents of the Ricardian Equivalence theorem (e.g., Barro, 1974, 1978; Kormendi, 1983) posit the notion of the infinite-lived economic agent and hold that these agents treat the discounted present value of future taxes the same as the current taxes avoided. (For a counterargument, see Bernheim, 1989; and Gramlich, 1989, 1990.) Since the net worth of the private sector is invariant with respect to tax or debt financing, deficits imply neither inflation nor crowding-out effect.

Nicoletti (1992) found empirical support for the Ricardian Equivalence in Belgium. He found that the relationship between deficits, debt, and private consumption is not stable over time. Further, the stability of the relationship depends on the characteristics of the financing regime adopted by the government. Seater (1993) examined the empirical validity of the Ricardian Equivalence theorem for the United States. Based on his results, Seater concluded that his tests supported evidence of strong Ricardian Equivalence. However, his tests showed little power against the alternative of approximate equivalence. Mathis and Bastin (1992) conducted empirical tests to assess tax discounting versus crowding out and found no empirical support for tax discounting. They found, however, that government deficits do stimulate current consumption.

Bernheim (1989) dismisses the Ricardian Equivalence theorem on both theoretical and empirical grounds, by rejecting its crucial assumptions as unrealistic. Gramlich (1989) argues that for the Ricardian Equivalence theorem to hold, on average, each taxpaying family in the United States would need to save $1,500 annually in excess of what they otherwise would have to keep national saving unaffected. This would have meant that by 1989 "the average tax paying family would then have accumulated extra net worth of $10,000 solely to offset the deficits" (p. 28).

Essentially, the debate over government deficits hinges on whether or not federal debt is net wealth. As Barth, Iden, and Russak (1986) suggest, as long as the rate of growth of output (g) exceeds the rate of interest (i), then federal debt is unambiguously net wealth. The reason is that in such circumstances future taxes are not necessary to service the debt. Economic growth will accommodate indefinite deficits without jeopardizing the taxing capacity of the economy. If g is less than i, then the status of federal debt is ambiguous. Federal debt will be considered "net wealth only to the extent that current generations do not fully discount the increase in future tax liability to service the debt, which in this case cannot be serviced solely with revenues generated by economic growth" (p. 28). If i exceeds g and there are primary deficits (revenues less outlays net of interest payments), then federal debt will grow more rapidly than the economy.

DEFICITS AND INFLATION

Do deficits cause inflation? Government deficit spending as a primary cause of inflation has received serious attention in the last two decades. Buchanan and Wagner (1978), for instance, argue that deficit spending, in addition to being an ineffective means of stabilization policy, can cause inflationary pressures in the economy. Modigliani (1983) argues that current deficits are not a major cause of inflation; on the contrary, inflation is a major cause of deficits. Eisner and Pieper (1984) and Eisner (1986) concur with Modigliani's (1983) proposition.

Abizadeh, Yousefi, and Benarroch (1996) have developed a theoretical model that links deficits to inflation using two alternative macroeconomic scenarios. One is based on adaptive and the other on rational expectations. Using this model of a multilevel government, they have concluded that "when expectations are formed adaptively, the model confirms the positive link between deficits and the rate of inflation. However, with rational expectations, the model shows that inflation is, in part, explained by the forecast error" (p. 118). They propose that "only empirical testing of the theoretical models gives credence to such conclusions" (p. 118).

Conklin and Courchene (1983, p. 41) also argue that "since the alleged link between deficit and inflation is not a theoretical necessity, but rather an alleged probability, empirical evidence of such relationship would seem to be required.'' Even if one agrees with the foregoing assertion, an agreement on the causality issue would be difficult.

Abizadeh and Yousefi (1986) argue that one way of resolving the controversy over deficit and inflation is "to test for the possibility of a causal link between the growth of government and inflation. This should be done in light of the fact that governments can grow without necessarily generating deficits" (p. 394). These authors' study led them to conclude that "the hypothesis of direct link between the size of the deficit and the size of government is maintained" (p. 408). An implication was that large deficits are caused by increased government expenditures. (On the general issue of government spending, see Yousefi and Abizadeh, 1992.) If increased government expenditures result in higher deficits, and higher deficits in turn cause inflation, then increased government expenditure can cause inflation.

Economists have not reached a consensus on the possible relationship between the rate of inflation and deficits. The empirical evidence is fraught with contradictory results as well. Some studies do not find a positive link between the level of prices and government deficits, whereas others find a close link between government expenditures and a persistent drift toward higher prices (at least prior to the 1980s). Dwyer (1982), for example, tested the three leading explanations for the positive link between the level of prices and government deficits. He found no significant evidence to support the idea that inflation is caused by deficit spending. Crozier (1976) also concluded that there was not a causal relationship between deficits and the Canadian inflationary surge in the 1970s. Hamburger and Zwick (1981) examined the influence of deficits on monetary growth. They found that the effect of deficits on the growth of money was operative from 1961 to 1974 and again in 1977 and 1978. Hamburger and Zwick concluded that a combination of an expansionary fiscal policy and the Central Bank's attempts at moderating interest rate movement, begun in the mid-1960s, had principally caused a persistent drift toward higher U.S. inflation rates. McMillan and Beard (1982) in their reexamination of Hamburger and Zwick's study suggested that their results did not support the position that monetary policy is strongly influenced by the federal government's fiscal policy actions.

Darrat (1985) examined the link between deficits and inflation. He concluded that over the estimation period both monetary growth and federal deficits significantly influenced inflation. Additionally, he concluded that federal deficits bore a stronger and more reliable relationship to inflation than monetary growth. McCallum (1984) used a perfect foresight version of the competitive equilibrium model to investigate the theoretical validity of a "monetarist hypothesis"—one that asserts "that a constant, per capita budget deficit can be maintained without inflation if it is financed by the issue of bonds rather than money." He found the hypothesis to be valid under a conventional definition but invalid if deficit is defined to be exclusive of interest payments (McCallum, 1984, p. 134). Hafer and Hein (1988) investigated the temporal relationship between inflation and privately held federal debt. They discovered "that neither the par value nor the market value of debt measure Granger-cause inflation" (p. 239). Eisner (1989) examined the impact of deficits on inflationary pressure to see whether structural deficits contribute to inflation. He found "no support for the proposition that the federal budget deficit, by any measure, contributes to inflation. If anything the opposite appears to be true" (p. 87). Finally, Dua (1993) examined the relationship between long-term interest rates, government spending, and deficits within the context of a forward-looking model. He concluded that inflation uncertainty and the expected rate of growth of the money supply are important determinants of changes in long-term interest rates.

Giffen, McComber, and Berry, (1981–1982, pp. 66–67) conclude, "The data . . . offer little support for either the traditional Keynesian or current monetarist views on the cause of inflation." The authors proceed to suggest that the investigators might alternatively use some post-Keynesian approach (administered pricing or cost-push analysis) to determine the cause of inflation. Finally, Abizadeh and Yousefi (1988) reexamined the empirical evidence concerning the impact of deficits on inflation by using alternative measures of government deficits. They conclude that the empirical "results are highly sensitive to the type of deficit measure used" (p. 402).

DEFICIT MEASUREMENT

As discussed in Chapter 1, in order to assess the consequences of deficits, it is important to know how they are measured. As Eisner and Pieper (1984) and Eisner (1986, 1989) point out, a meaningful discussion of the impact of deficits requires an accurate measure of their size. For instance, it is important to know whether the deficit variable in question is the National Income Account (NIA) measure or the observed measure of deficits derived from the consolidated budget. Abizadeh and Yousefi (1988) posit that the empirical evidence on deficits appears to be highly sensitive to the type of deficit measure used in various studies. Deficits may or may not have a bearing on the economy, depending on how they are defined. We might fail, for example, to make a distinction between active and passive deficits. The former arise, *ceteris paribus*, from legislated changes in spending or taxes. Passive deficits, in contrast, come about as a result of changes in the level of economic activity, prices, and interest rates (Tatom, 1984). It is also important to know whether we are concerned with actual or full employment deficits. The former is the observed difference between actual expenditures and revenues, whereas the latter refers to deficits that would prevail if the economy were operating at full employment (Morely, 1984). In much of deficit debate, the distinction between actual and full employment deficits is either ignored or blurred. An appropriate indicator of fiscal policy is the full employment deficit. The surge in the U.S. deficits in the 1980s, stemming from the unusual cyclical economic experience, gives credence to the importance of the full employment deficits.

Some researchers (e.g., McMillan and Beard, 1982) use the absolute value of deficits as an independent variable in their analysis. As Domar (1993) points out, it is not the absolute level of deficits that matter but their relative size. Deficits per se, particularly under Keynesian conditions of unemployment, may not be harmful. But when they are too large, relative to national output, deficits could have undesirable economic consequences. As Eisner (1989, p. 73) states, "[B]udget deficits can . . . be too small as well as too large. To know which, you have to measure them right." As Eisner (1986) points out, a deficit per se should not be expected to contribute to inflation. Only a deficit that is too large relative to the size of national output would prove to be inflationary. This, according to Eisner, refers to a deficit that makes the debt grow more rapidly than the real value of output (Eisner, 1986, p. 74). Additionally, the inflationary impact of deficits is only felt when the economy operates at or near full employment. Under conditions of insufficient aggregate demand and unemployment, deficit-financed spending is not necessarily inflationary.

Other authors, namely, Horrigan and Protopapadakis (1982), Ott (1983), Eisner and Pieper (1984), and Eisner (1986, 1989), caution against the use of actual deficits, as they give a distorted picture of true deficits. Eisner and Pieper (1984, p. 15), for instance, point out that the conventional measure of budget deficits is particularly misleading during periods of significant inflation and high and fluctuating interest rates. Failure to allow for the effects of inflation on increased debts also gives a misleading picture of the impact of government borrowing. As Eisner (1986, p. 23) argues, "To secure a measure of the impact of the surplus or deficit on the financial wealth of all sectors other than the federal government, we would add to the surplus in national income accounts only the interest rate effects and the price effects." Moreover, failure to make proper adjustments for these changes may lead to overstating (or understating) deficits.

Ott (1983, p. 94) points out that the current deficits reported by the National Income and Product Accounts (NIPA) fail to take account of autonomous changes in government spending and income due to fluctuations in the level of employment and inflation rate. Niskanen (1983) links the 1980s surge in actual budget deficits to problems of adjusting to lower inflation. In periods of low inflation the revenue effect is immediate, whereas the reduction in outlays or growth in outlays occurs with a lag.

Boskin (1982) and Ott (1983) argue that federal deficits are not a reliable indicator of government drain on credit markets. The reason is that the borrowing of other governmental units and related agencies, such as off-budget federal agencies (e.g., the U.S. Postal Service or the Tennessee Valley Authority for the United States and similarly Canada Post and other crown corporations for Canada) and state/provinces and local government borrowings are not included in the federal deficits. Hamilton and Flavin (1986) propose a measure of deficits that excludes interest payments but incorporates revenues from monetization and capital gains on gold. Using such a measure, they contend that the apparent uninterrupted U.S. budget deficits from 1960 to 1981 grossly misstated the true fiscal posture of the government in the United States.

ASSESSMENT

The review of literature sketched above suggests that the deficit debate is still unresolved. Economists have genuine philosophical disagreements on the notion of crowding-out effect. Additionally, there is a mixed body of empirical evidence in regard to their philosophical positions. Our review of literature also suggests that there is not a commonly accepted measure of deficits. Finally, we cannot find an unequivocal body of evidence regarding the inflationary effects of deficits.

DEFICITS AND INFLATION IN CANADA

The Canadian federal (budget) deficits have been growing since the early 1970s when they were less than 1 percent of gross domestic product (GDP). Deficits assumed an upward trend in subsequent years, and the deficit-GDP ratio reached a peak of 7 percent in 1985. Streeter and Lemay (1993) indicate that Canada's deficits rose by 70 percent between the late 1980s and early 1990s. Much of the increase came about in the early 1990s due to an economic downturn that slowed revenue growth and generated upward pressure for government spending, particularly in social services. Concomitantly, there was a fundamental shift in the structure of the government deficits as provincial deficits became a more significant component of the overall deficits. Kneebone (1992) examined the effect of changes in the degree of centralization on the public sector's share of GDP. The impetus for the structural change in Canada's deficits, according to Kneebone, was citizen mobility. This phenomenon exerted a restraining influence on the growth of government and a corresponding pressure on nonfederal government sector deficits.

This part focuses on the inflationary effects of deficits in Canada. The small open economy model used here incorporates important features of the foreign sector. Rosensweig and Tallman (1993), Bahmani and Payesteh (1993), Macklem (1993), and Kawai and Maccini (1995), among others, have shown the impact of fiscal deficits on trade balance and exchange rate. Rosensweig and Tallman, for instance, concluded that fiscal policy appears to have played a significant role in the U.S. trade balance adjustment. Macklem, in his examination of the Canadian case, concluded that government deficits generate a real exchange appreciation that crowds out the export sector.

We use the consolidated (all levels of government) National Income Account measure of deficit in this study. As Gramlich (1990) points out, this measure is preferred to one that is used in the unified (U.S.) budget since the latter is more affected by cosmetics such as altering paydays or selling assets to meet the fixed deficit targets of the Gramm-Rudman-Hollings (GRH) legislation. The adjusted and consolidated deficit measure nets out intergovernment transactions and includes the receipts and expenditures of Canada and Quebec pension plans and public hospitals. (For details, see Conklin and Sayeed in Conklin and Courchene, 1983.) This measure is consistent with the macroeconomic definition of government spending. As Conklin and Sayeed state: "[A] meaningful measure of government activity must cover all levels of government" (in Conklin and Courchene, 1983, p. 14).

The Model

The open economy model developed, but not reported here, begins with a simple IS-LM framework and later introduces the aggregate supply function. The model allows us to investigate, in a broad sense, the impact of deficits on inflation. The model states that the domestic rate of inflation is, among other variables, a function of foreign income, domestic output, real deficits, and real money supply.

A linear econometrics model is used to empirically assess the inflationary effects of the Canadian deficits. The period of analysis begins in 1955 and ends in 1989. Sources of data, the model, and the empirical results of this analysis are available from the authors. We treated the United States (singly) and eight members of the European Economic Community (EEC) (jointly) as Canada's major trading partners. The EEC countries used include Belgium, Denmark, France, Germany, Italy, Ireland, United Kingdom, and the Netherlands. Given that the United Kingdom is Canada's second largest trading partner, this sample is not unreasonable.

Since the Canadian dollar began to float in the early 1970s, it was necessary to make adjustments for this policy change. Accordingly, a dummy variable was included in the model that increased the number of independent variables to fourteen. We encountered a high degree of multicollinearity among several pairs of independent variables when we estimated the model via the ordinary least squares (OLS) method. To correct for multicollinearity, we applied the principal components (PC) method to the entire set of independent variables. This method determines a set of highly correlated independent variables that could collectively form a component (factor) to be used as an independent variable in explaining the variation in the dependent variable. (For justification and statistical reasoning, see Basilevsky, 1981, particularly pp. 110–114. For econometric modeling, see Koutsoyiannis, 1977, pp. 251–252, 425.)

The application of the principal components results in less variance among the artificially created "independent" variables than that contained in the original independent variables. Additionally, it is difficult to give any specific economic meaning to these artificial independent variables (Koutsoyiannis, 1977, pp. 251–252). Adopting Kloek and Mennos' (1960) method to select correlated variables, we took the following steps. First, the Pearson correlation coefficient matrix was estimated using all thirteen independent variables, excluding the

dummy variable (D). Second, nine variables with a significant degree of multicollinearity were identified. Next, the principal components method was applied to these nine variables to determine the number of factor(s) required to
best explain the variation among them. (See Basilevsky [1981] and Koutsoyiannis [1977] for more details.)

Two factors cumulatively explain more than 98 percent of the variance of the
above nine variables. Given the nature of variables used in the principal components analysis and the high degree of multicollinearity among them, this outcome was to be expected.

The estimated inflation equation incorporates elements of money market,
product market, and foreign trade sector. In addition, it contains the crucial full
employment measure of deficit variable. This equation, essentially, is a reduced
form of the IS-LM model involving real variables. Two different versions of
regression results, versions (1) and (2), are obtained by either treating the United
States as Canada's major trading partner or treating the EEC as Canada's major
trading partner.

CONCLUSIONS

A close examination of the empirical results reveals that changes in the dependent variable (the rate of inflation) are explained, with a high degree of
reliability, by changes in the independent variables. The Canadian income measures exert a positive and significant effect on the rate of inflation; the Canadian
rate of inflation responds significantly and positively to variations in the GDP
of Canada's trading partners as well. Under a system of flexible exchange rate,
domestic prices and exchange rates move in opposite direction, whereas under
the fixed exchange rate, imports and exports respond to T, Dornbusch's terms
of trade. Since the latter term includes e (exchange rate), it is reflective of both
flexible and fixed exchange rate systems. The negative coefficient of the foreign
trade sector variable confirms the preceding statements.

The deficit variable carries a negative sign and its coefficient is highly significant in all cases. These negative coefficients are consistent with Eisner's
(1989, p. 88) results that "each percentage point of deficits as a ratio of GNP
subtracts 0.2 percentage point from the rate of inflation the next year, and 1.6
percentage point in the long-run." Bullard (1991, p. 53), using Marcet and Sargent's (1989a, 1989b, 1989c) model, has shown that in a perfect foresight dynamic world a permanent increase in government deficits with the low inflation
steady state raises the stationary inflation rate. However, at the high-inflation
steady state, a permanent increase in deficits lowers the stationary inflation rate.
This inference is consistent with Wilton and Prescott's (1987) observation that
"recent Canadian evidence clearly contradicts the hypothesis that large or growing government deficits causes inflation" (p. 424). Higher deficits might have
increased expenditures on infrastructural amenities, thus permitting private sector investment to flourish, leading to higher output and thus the "crowding-in"
phenomenon (Heilbroner and Bernstein, 1989).

The rate of inflation is positively and significantly affected by the foreign interest rate, as is expected in an open economy such as Canada where capital is perfectly mobile. In an open environment, capital flows are extremely sensitive to fluctuations in foreign interest rates, particularly those of the United States. Interest rates are also sensitive to price differentials and exchange rate variations in two different money centers.

The coefficient of money supply variable is negative and statistically significant in all the estimated models. At first glance, this seems to be contrary to the received theory. Darrat (1985), similarly, found a negative relationship between the rate of inflation and the rate of growth of nominal money supply. An explanation of this negative relationship may be found in the financial innovation hypothesis. Another explanation for negative relationship between the rate of inflation and money supply may be due to what Rasche (1987) calls a "shift in drift." This phenomenon attributes changes in M1 velocity to the decline of inflationary expectation and instability of the economy. This hypothesis holds that financial innovations of the late 1970s and early 1980s have rendered M1 less useful as a monetary policy target. Tatom (1990) and Rasche (1987), for instance, found an inverse relationship between the first difference of the rate of growth of M1 and nominal GNP and unanticipated inflation. Both of these authors, as well as Hoffman and Rasche (1991), however, found no empirical support for the financial innovation hypothesis. Hoffman and Rasche (1991, p. 673), for instance, found "a strong evidence for the existence of stationary linear combinations of both M1 and monetary base velocity and the Treasury Bill rate" in the United States.

The estimation results indicate that the Canadian inflation rate moves and is very sensitive to the U.S. inflation rate. This is consistent with Eisner's (1989) position that attributes inflation, particularly since the 1970s, to "escalating oil costs and rising prices of agricultural products in the world markets" (p. 89). Imported inflation in Canada is transmitted through a higher cost of imported goods and a higher price of imported inputs. These effects, in turn, place an upward pressure on internally generated inflation within Canada.

Finally, it is important to recall that the Canadian dollar was allowed to float in the early 1970s. A dummy variable included in the models estimated is designed to capture the influence of this policy change. The coefficient of the dummy variable carries a positive sign and is significant in three out of four models reported. An implication is that the structural shift in the exchange rate policy affects the rate of inflation.

REFERENCES

Abizadeh, Sohrab, and Mahmood Yousefi. 1986. "Political Parties, Deficits, and the Rate of Inflation: A Comparative Study." *Journal of Social, Political and Economic Studies*, Vol. 11, pp. 393–411.

———. 1988. "Government Deficits and Inflation." *Journal of Social, Political and Economic Studies*, Vol. 13, pp. 396–404.

Abizadeh, Sohrab, Mahmood Yousefi, and Michael Benarroch. 1996. "A Multilevel Government Model of Deficits and Inflation." *Atlantic Economic Journal*, Vol. 24, pp. 118–130.

Bahmani, Oskoee, and Mohsen Payesteh. 1993. "Budget Deficits and the Value of the Dollar: An Application of Cointegration and Errors—Correction Modeling." *Journal of Macroeconomics*, Vol. 15, pp. 661–677.

Barro, Robert J. 1974. "Are Government Bonds Net Wealth?" *Journal of Political Economy*, Vol. 82, pp. 1095–1117.

———. 1978. "Comment from Unreconstructed Ricardian." *Journal of Monetary Economics*, Vol. 4, pp. 569–581.

———. 1979. "On the Determination of the Public Debt." *Journal of Political Economy*, Vol. 87, pp. 940–971.

Barth, James R., George Iden, and Frank Russak, Jr. 1986. "The Economic Consequences of Federal Deficits: An Explanation of the Net Wealth and Instability Issues." *Southern Economic Journal*, Vol. 53, pp. 27–50.

Basilevsky, Alexander. 1981. "Factor Analysis Regression." *Canadian Journal of Statistics*, pp. 109–117.

Bernheim, B. Douglas. 1989. "A Neoclassical Perspective on Budget Deficits." *Journal of Economic Perspectives*, Vol. 3, pp. 55–72.

Boskin, Michael J. 1982. "Federal Government Deficits: Some Myths and Realities." *American Economic Review*, Vol. 72, pp. 296–303.

Buchanan, James, and Richard Wagner. 1978. *Democracy in Deficit*. New York: Academic Press.

Bullard, James B. 1991. "Learning Rational Expectations and Policy: A Summary of Recent Research." *Federal Reserve Bank of St. Louis Review*, Vol. 73, pp. 50–60.

Cebula, Richard J., and Rupoert G. Rhodd. 1993. "A Note on Budget Deficits, Debt Service Payments, and Interest Rates." *Quarterly Review of Economics and Finance*, Vol. 33, pp. 439–445.

Conklin, David W., and Thomas J. Courchene, eds. 1983. *Deficits: How Big and How Bad*. Special Research Report. Toronto: Ontario Economic Council.

Conklin, David W., and Adil Sayeed. 1983. "Overview of the Deficit Debate." In David W. Conklin and Thomas J. Courchene, eds., *Deficits: How Big and How Bad*. Special Research Report. Toronto: Ontario Economic Council, pp. 12–54.

Crozier, Robert B. 1976. *Deficit Financing and Inflation: Facts and Fiction*. Occasional Papers No. 3. Conference Board of Canada.

Darrat, Ali F. 1985. "Inflation and Federal Budget Deficits: Some Empirical Results." *Public Finance Quarterly*, Vol. 13, pp. 206–215.

Domar, Evsey D. 1993. "On Deficits and Debt." *American Journal of Economics and Sociology*, Vol. 52, pp. 475–478.

Dua, Pami. 1993. "Interest Rates, Government Purchases, and Budget Deficits: A Forward-Looking Model." *Public Finance Quarterly*, Vol. 21, pp. 470–478.

Dwyer, Gerald P., Jr. 1982. "Inflation and Government Deficits." *Economic Inquiry*, Vol. 20, pp. 315–329.

Eisner, Robert. 1986. *How Real Is the Federal Deficit?* New York: Free Press.

———. 1989. "Budget Deficits: Rhetoric and Reality." *Journal of Economic Perspectives*, Vol. 3, pp. 73–93.

Eisner, Robert, and Paul J. Pieper. 1984. "A New View of the Federal Debt and Budget Deficits." *American Economic Review*, Vol. 74, pp. 11–29.

Evans, Paul. March 1985. "Do Large Deficits Produce High Interest Rates?" *American Economic Review*, Vol. 75, No. 1, pp. 68–87.

Giffen, Phillip E., James H. McComber, and Robert E. Berry. 1981–1982. "An Empirical Examination of Current Inflation and Deficit Spending." *Journal of Post Keynesian Economics*, Vol. 4, pp. 63–67.

Gramlich, Edward M. 1989. "Budget Deficits and National Savings: Are the Politicians Exogenous?" *Journal of Economic Perspectives*, Vol. 3, pp. 22–35.

————. 1990. "U.S. Federal Deficits and Gramm-Rudman-Hollings." *American Economic Review*, Vol. 80, pp. 75–85.

Hafer, R. W., and Scott E. Hein. 1988. "Further Evidence on the Relationship between Federal Government Debt and Inflation." *Economic Inquiry*, Vol. 26, pp. 239–251.

Hamburger, Michael J., and Burton Zwick. 1981. "Deficits, Money and Inflation." *Journal of Monetary Economics*, Vol. 7, pp. 141–150.

Hamilton, James, and Marjorie A. Flavin. 1986. "On the Limitations of Government Borrowing: A Framework for Empirical Testing." *American Economic Review*, Vol. 76, pp. 808–819.

Heilbroner, Robert, and Peter Bernstein. 1989. *The Debt and the Deficit*. New York: W. W. Norton.

Hoffman, Dennis L., and Robert H. Rasche. 1991. "Long-Run Income and Interest Elasticities of Money Demand in the United States." *Review of Economics and Statistics*, Vol. 58, pp. 665–674.

Horrigan, Brian R., and A. A. Protopapadakis. 1982. "Federal Deficits: A Faulty Gauge of Government's Impact on Financial Markets." *Business Review* (Federal Reserve Bank of Philadelphia), pp. 3–16.

Inman, Robert P. 1990. "Public Debts and Fiscal Politics: How to Decide?" *American Economic Review*, Vol. 80, pp. 81–85.

Kawai, Masahiro, and Louis J. Maccini. 1995. "Twin Deficits versus Unpleasant Fiscal Arithmetic in a Small Open Economy." *Journal of Money, Credit and Banking*, Vol. 27, pp. 639–658.

Kloek, Teun, and L. B. M. Mennos. 1960. "Simultaneous Equation Estimation Based on Principal Components of Predetermined Variables." *Econometrica*, Vol. 28, pp. 45–61.

Kneebone, Ronald D. 1992. "Centralization and the Size of Government in Canada." *Applied Economics*, Vol. 24, pp. 1293–1300.

Kormendi, Roger C. December 1983. "Government Debt, Government Spending, and Private Sector Behavior." *American Economic Review*, Vol. 73, pp. 994–1010.

Koutsoyiannis, Anna. 1977. *Theory of Econometrics*, 2nd ed. London: Macmillan.

Macklem, Tiff R. 1993. "Terms-of-trade Disturbances and Fiscal Policy in a Small Open Economy." *Economic Journal*, Vol. 103, pp. 916–936.

Marcet, Albert, and Thomas J. Sargent. 1989a. "Convergence of Least-Squares Learning in Environments with Hidden State Variables and Private Information." *Journal of Political Economy*, Vol. 97, pp. 1306–1322.

————. 1989b. "Convergence of Least-Squares Learning Mechanisms in Self-Referential, Linear Stochastic Models." *Journal of Economic Theory*, Vol. 48, pp. 337–368.

————. 1989c. "Least-Squares Learning and the Dynamics of Hyperinflation." In William A. Barnett, John Geweke, and Karl Shell, eds., *Economic Complexity: Chaos, Sunspots, Bubbles, and Nonlinearity*. Cambridge: Cambridge University Press, pp. 119–140.

Mathis, Stephen, and Hamid Bastin. 1992. "Tax Discounting vs. Crowding Out." *Contemporary Policy Issues*, Vol. 10, pp. 54–62.

McCallum, Bennett T. 1984. "Are Bond-Financed Deficits Inflationary? A Ricardian Analysis." *Journal of Political Economy*, Vol. 92, pp. 123–135.

McMillan, W. Douglas, and T. Randolph Beard. 1982. "Deficits, Money and Inflation." *Journal of Monetary Economics*, Vol. 10, pp. 273–277.

Modigliani, Franco. 1983. "Government Deficits, Inflation, and Future Generations." In David W. Conklin and Thomas J. Courchene, eds., *Deficits: How Big and How Bad*. Special Research Report. Toronto: Ontario Economic Council, pp. 55–71.

Morely, Samuel A. 1984. *Macroeconomics*. Chicago: Dryden.

Nicoletti, Giuseppe. 1992. "Is Tax-Discounting Stable Over Time?" *Oxford Bulletin of Economics and Statistics*, Vol. 54, pp. 121–144.

Niskanen, W. A. 1983. "Responses." In W. C. Stubblebine and T. D. Willet, eds., *Reaganomics: A Mid-term Report*. San Francisco: ICS Press, pp. 79–107.

Ott, A. F. 1983. "Controlling Government Spending." In W. C. Stubblebine and T. D. Willet, eds., *Reaganomics: A Mid-term Report*. San Francisco: ICS Press, pp. 79–107.

Perri, Timothy J., and Gary L. Shelley. 1996. "Structural Change in Federal Spending and Deficits: Legislative and Cyclical Influences." *Atlantic Economic Journal*, Vol. 24, pp. 33–42.

Plosser, Charles I. 1982. "Government Financing Decisions and Asset Returns." *Journal of Monetary Economics*, Vol. 9, pp. 325–352.

Rasche, Robert H. 1987. "M1 Velocity and Money Demand Functions: Do Stable Relationships Exist?" In Karl Brunner and Allen H. Meltzer, eds., *Empirical Studies of Velocity, Real Exchange Rates, Unemployment and Productivity*. Amsterdam: North-Holland, pp. 9–88.

Rosensweig, Jeffrey A., and Ellis W. Tallman. 1993. "Fiscal Policy and Trade Adjustment: Are the Deficits Really Twins?" *Economic Inquiry*, Vol. 31, pp. 580–594.

Seater, John J. 1993. "Ricardian Equivalence." *Journal of Economic Literature*, Vol. 31, pp. 142–190.

Streeter, William, and Yves Lemay. 1993. "Provincial Fiscal Perspective." *Government Finance Review*, Vol. 9, pp. 39–41.

Tatom, John A. 1984. "A Perspective on the Federal Deficit Problem." *Review*, Vol. 66, pp. 5–17.

————. 1990. "The Link between Monetary Aggregates and Prices." St. Louis: Federal Reserve Bank of St. Louis, Working Paper No. 90-002.

Turnovsky, Stephen J. 1985. *Macroeconomic Analysis and Stabilization Policies*. Cambridge: Cambridge University Press.

Wilton, D.A., and D.M. Prescott. 1987. *Macroeconomic Theory and Policy in Canada*, 2nd ed. Toronto: Addison-Wesley.

Yellen, Janet L. 1989. "Symposium on the Budget Deficit." *Journal of Economic Perspectives*, Vol. 3, pp. 17–21.

Yousefi, Mahmood, and Sohrab Abizadeh. 1992. "Growth of State Government Expenditures: Empirical Evidence from the United States." *Public Finance*, Vol. 47, pp. 322–339.

Chapter 8

Budget Deficits and Financial Markets

BRUCE COLLINS

One consistent characteristic of the U.S. economy for the last 27 years is the annual budget deficit. However, over the same time period the total returns to the S&P 500 stock index were 2250 percent, or 12.22 percent per year compounded annually. The annual compound yield before 1969 was 9.75 percent. These two periods meet in 1969 when the last budget surplus occurred. While budget deficits are a post–World War II phenomenon, there has been a historic pattern of deficits associated with economic contractions. This pattern was fundamentally altered in the 1980s when a combination of large tax cuts and increases in government expenditures generated unprecedented peacetime budget deficits. Since the Reagan administration ushered in a period of high deficits, investors have become increasingly aware of the potential adverse effects of deficits on financial markets, on the economy, and on their economic future. The subject of this chapter is the impact of federal budget deficits on financial markets. We focus primarily on the domestic stock and bond markets but also reference the foreign exchange market. In the sections that follow, the economics of deficits and financial markets is discussed, followed by an empirical look at the relationship between budget deficits, the economy, and financial markets.

The importance of the financial market connection is that the economic mechanism of growth, behavior, and policy all operate through the purchase and sale of financial assets. For example, during a period of expansionary monetary policy, the impact on interest rates takes place through the portfolio allocation decisions of investors and businesses. Investors with excess cash buy financial assets, causing prices to rise and rates to fall ceteris paribus. Given the importance of interest rates, it is equally important to examine the role of financial markets within the context of federal budget deficits.

ECONOMICS OF DEFICITS AND FINANCIAL MARKETS

The argument over the impact of budget deficits on financial markets is essentially rooted in the economics of the budget deficits and the attitudes of investors. If budget deficits have little or no impact on interest rates and do not alter the dynamics of supply and demand for loanable funds, then the impact on financial markets and financial asset pricing is probably minimal. The second influence is the impact of budget deficits on investor attitudes. Although indirect, investor attitudes are in practice integrally related to interest rate determination. If the persistent existence of large budget deficits negatively influences public opinion and investor sentiment, then deficits clearly could affect financial asset prices. If we assume this is true, then we would expect stock returns to be negatively correlated with budget deficits in some way.

The key link between sectors of the economy and the general level of economic activity is through financial markets and interest rates. This relationship has been examined by economists through a discussion in the literature of the effectiveness of monetary and fiscal policy. The effectiveness of policy is dependent on how economic units are expected to respond to changes in relevant economic variables. Investors respond to events they believe will influence economic activity, interest rates, and financial asset prices. Thus, investors will anticipate outcomes based on forecasts by making portfolio adjustments that feed back into the economy. For example, an increase in the Commerce Department's Labor Cost Index will spark inflationary expectations, which is bad for interest-sensitive assets. This will lead to the sale of financial assets with a high risk to inflation and the purchase of those with a resistance to inflation. For a simple economy with two assets, cash and interest-bearing bonds, this would involve selling bonds and raising sufficient cash to sustain the current level of transactions. Cash is a lower duration asset than bonds, which means that interest rate changes affect bonds more. A 100 basis point increase in interest rates might cause bond values to fall by 10 percent, thus reducing the purchasing power of the sale value of bonds by that amount. If a 100 basis point increase in interest rates was the result of an increase in inflation by 1 percent per annum, then the purchasing power of cash would fall by only that amount. If, for example, investors could hold $100 in cash or in bonds, the purchasing power today is $100 for both. On the other hand, suppose our forecast suggests an increase in inflation for the next year that causes the bond value to fall to $90. Bondholders will be able to convert each bond to $90, while the cash holders still have $100. Thus, for bondholders acting on forecasts, the appropriate response is to sell bonds. The act of selling bonds in the face of higher inflation is what causes the bond price to fall and rates to rise. This is the process by which budget deficits could impact financial markets. Financial markets, however, offer a larger set of options for investors than two assets. There are, nonetheless, two major asset classes that still dominate the investment landscape: stocks and bonds.

The influence of budget deficits on financial markets is controversial. Two schools of thought have emerged. The first argues that persistent budget deficits lead to so-called crowding out among competing interests for limited loanable funds. The increased demand for loanable funds causes interest rates to rise, resulting in lower financial asset prices and lower rates of return on stocks and bonds. The longer the duration of the asset, the greater the impact on price. In addition, the value of the dollar rises as foreigners increase demand for the greenback due to higher returns expected from dollar-denominated assets. The interest rate effect filters through investment, consumption, and net export functions to cause the growth in the economy to subside. The alternative view has its roots in the thinking of David Ricardo and is aptly referred to as the Ricardian view. According to this view, a tax-induced budget deficit will produce greater savings to pay for the deficits, which avoids the problem of crowding out. Thus, the increase in demand for loanable funds is offset by an increase in supply, leaving rates unchanged.

The conventional point of view embraced by financial market professionals is that budget deficits do lead to crowding out, higher interest rates, lower economic growth, and lower corporate earnings. Consequently, a combination of higher interest rates and lower earnings lead to underperforming financial assets. In other words, budget deficits depress stocks and bonds or at least slow down their appreciation versus a deficit-free situation. Furthermore, to Wall Street it doesn't matter if deficits are bond financed or money financed. The former will produce government borrowing that will crowd out borrowings for business investment. The consequence is higher capital costs, reduced capital formation, reduced productivity, and slower economic growth. Bond-financed deficits increase the supply of bonds and the demand for loanable funds. This is what puts upward pressure on interest rates. Higher rates are required to induce investors to reallocate a portion of their portfolio holdings to bonds. Ultimately, deficits find their way into stock prices through lower corporate earnings and higher interest rates. In the latter case, money creation leads to inflation, which has a devastating effect on interest rate–sensitive financial assets. The government is exchanging printed fiat money for real assets, and there is a limit to how much exchange can take place.

The impact of deficits also depends on the current state of the economy. The behavior of economic variables may be different during periods of full or near full employment than when there is slack in the economy. During periods of economic slack, there is room for fiscal or monetary stimulus brought about by lower taxes and increases in banking reserves. This has a positive impact on real income, savings, and the availability of loanable funds. A tax-induced deficit under these circumstances will not lead to crowding out. At full employment, however, the demand for capital rises, and crowding out may occur. Thus, in order to assess the impact of budget deficits on financial markets, we must separate cyclical deficits arising from the current state of the economy and structural deficits.

The Economic Consequences of Budget Deficits

BUDGET DEFICITS AND FOREIGN EXCHANGE RATES

The influence of deficits can then be traced through the economics of i ment and savings. The budget deficit can be presented as the sum of dc savings surplus above investment and the trade deficit. Thus, deficits funded by an excess of savings or by foreign sources. Investment and s is important to our analysis because it takes place through financial mar the purchase of financial assets. The two sources of credit for deficit fin are priced in financial markets through domestic interest rates and the exc rate. In order to sustain current levels of investment, either increases in savings or foreign savings must emerge. The increased demand for lo funds and the dollar will be reflected in higher interest rates, lower fir asset prices, and a stronger dollar.

The conventional view of crowding out essentially ignores the trade by assuming it is small and slow to change. Under these conditions, defi financed out of domestic savings and subject to crowding out. At full e ment with fixed levels of real income and constant savings rates, budget are therefore likely to crowd out private investment and depress finan prices. Recall that the Ricardian belief is that private savings increa lower taxes because some of the tax savings is used to increase the loanable funds and the demand for financial assets. This process wil offset any increase in interest rates resulting from tax-induced budge Detractors supporting the conventional view, however, argue that in private savings are not sufficient to compensate for increased gover mand for funds. Consequently, higher interest rates and lower inve the result.

Increased foreign savings can throw a wrench into this analysis. M to consistently attract foreign capital, domestic interest rates must be attractive and combined with a strong dollar. An appreciating dollar increases the price of U.S. exports and lowers the price of imports. This situation exacerbates the trade deficit, which also must be financed. Thus, we have a scenario where trade deficits financed by foreigners also finance portions of the budget deficit and domestic investment. The impact of budget deficits is then related to the amount of foreign savings. The Japanese, for example, purchase large numbers of U.S. Treasury bonds. The foreign savings aspect of budget deficits explains the twin-deficit problem that emerged in the 1980s and the fall of the dollar in the late 1980s and early 1990s. Because competition for capital is global, crowding out can temporarily be avoided. It is unclear what the difference between interest rates is under conditions of crowding out with no support from the foreign sector and the interest rate required to attract foreign capital. Clearly, this differential is positive. The influx of capital in the 1980s supported not only U.S. budget deficits but also domestic financial markets as foreigners purchased U.S. stocks and bonds in record numbers. Operating through financial markets, foreigners have increased their holdings of U.S. financial and real assets tenfold since 1980.

The risk of this development from an investor's point of view is that the demand for dollar-denominated assets falls, causing the dollar to drop on foreign exchange markets. The depreciation of the dollar leads to capital outflows, reduced savings and loanable funds, and higher interest rates. Higher interest rates then are processed through the economy and financial markets. For this scenario to remain in check, the United States must continue to attract foreign capital by providing higher risk-adjusted investment opportunities vis-à-vis the rest of the world. The risk of a reversal grows as deficits persist.

The nature of budget deficits changed in the 1980s from cyclical to structural. The conventional outcome of crowding out did not unfold because deficits were financed in part by the expanding trade deficit. High real interest rates and a strong dollar ushered in the era of twin deficits facilitated by government policy. However, the higher rates did not eliminate domestic investment, economic growth, or a bull market in stocks. Gross domestic investment was up 70 percent in real terms, the economy was up 31 percent and the Dow Jones Industrial Average appreciated 228 percent. In the second half of the decade of the 1980s, deficits persisted while interest rates fell from double to single digits, triggering an economic expansion and an accelerating bull market in stocks. Meanwhile, the dollar began its long descent from 262 yen per dollar in 1985 to a low of 81 in 1995. In spite of improving trade conditions, trade deficits have persisted, possibly as a consequence of persistent budget deficits financed in part by foreign savings. In the 1990s, the United States has taken measures to reduce budget deficits. The last five years have produced a combination of low inflation and moderate economic growth that has supported the longest-running bull market in history. The markets have factored in an expectation of a balanced budget and a more disciplined approach to government spending programs. This, combined with a vigilant Federal Reserve with regard to inflation, has been positive for financial assets.

FINANCIAL MARKETS AND THE ECONOMY

Financial markets are a collection of individuals, institutions, and organizations that facilitate the flow of savings in the economy. The allocation of savings operates through the price mechanism within the infrastructure of financial markets. The flow of funds is regulated by interest rates and allocated to the economic unit willing to bid the highest. The ultimate use of savings after it passes through financial markets is investment in real assets, which drives the economy. None of this works, however, without efficient financial markets. It is important therefore to examine the impact budget deficits might have on this process and on financial assets. The circular flow of funds through the economy establishes the important link between what happens on Wall Street and what happens on Main Street. The decision to invest is made by financial managers within corporations and the decision to save by households. The capital budgeting decisions are made using methods such as net present value (NPV) or internal rate of return (IRR) criteria. In either case, the decision to invest is dependent on a positive differential between the returns on investment and the cost of funds. The process of crowding out refers to increases in the cost of funds that when filtered through investment criteria result in less investment in real assets. Higher interest rates simply make some capital investments unprofitable. The cost of funds is a hurdle rate that must be overcome for the investment to make sense. The level of interest rates is determined by the availability of loanable funds in the economy and the specific risk characteristics of an investment. The determinants of interest rates for capital budgeting purposes would include a global benchmark such as Libor or the rate on Treasury bills and a risk premium determined by the market. The benchmark incorporates the real rate of interest plus any forecast of inflation over the time of the loan. The factors that go into the risk premium include default risk (credit rating), liquidity risk (the risk of losing principal in transactions), maturity risk (longer-term loans are more volatile), and investor attitude toward risk.

The impact of budget deficits would occur in two ways. First, increased demand for funds may have direct consequences of crowding out. Second, a more subtle influence is distributed through the investment climate and impacts the risk premium. If higher and persistent budget deficits influence business confidence or investor sentiment, then expect interest rates to be higher due to a larger risk premium. For example, according to capital markets theory, the cost of capital can be estimated using the capital asset pricing model (CAPM), which states that the cost of capital is the sum of the risk-free rate and a market-risk premium. The market-risk premium widens when investors get nervous, and this impacts the cost of capital. Higher discount rates incorporated into equity valuation models would reduce the fair value of common stock prices. The rate on bonds will also rise, leading to an increase in funding costs for the two main sources of long-term capital for U.S. corporations: common stock and corporate bonds. This has rippling effects throughout the economy.

Economic units drive the economy through spending. The household sector is the major source of loanable funds, and the portfolio allocations of households are crucial to understanding the financial markets connection. In the process of engaging in economic activity, households build up a balance sheet that is a portfolio of assets and liabilities. One of the primary variables driving their allocation decisions is interest rates. Rising interest rates resulting from behavior in other sectors such as the government sector or the foreign sector will alter the portfolio choices of households and impact the availability of savings. In addition, the behavior of the household sector is driven by demographics. As the population ages, look for increases in savings and demand for financial assets. In 1996, a record amount of cash was invested in equity mutual funds. As of year's end, the value of mutual fund assets exceeded $2 trillion. This is, to a great extent, attributable to the demographic effect.

Business is the second major sector of the economy and is the primary supplier of financial assets and demander of loanable funds. Financial managers use financial markets as a means of financing capital investments. Unanticipated increases in demand will raise interest rates. Financial markets are also used for cash management and risk management purposes. Corporations will use derivative securities as part of cash management and risk management strategies in order to enhance short-term returns or manage financial risk. The impact of derivatives on the cost of capital is not known but expected to be downward. Derivative products have allowed corporations to reduce their exposure to financial risk and offset any increase in rates due to crowding-out effects. The proliferation of financing choices fostered by global competition and derivative products also serves to soften any crowding-out effects.

The three financial markets that are of interest include the stock market, the bond market, and the market for foreign exchange. The general financial asset pricing model is a discount function that simply states that the fair value of an asset is the present value of expected future cash flows. Stocks, bonds, and foreign exchange can be evaluated in terms of the time value of cash flows. The source of volatility in asset prices is twofold: uncertain cash flows and stochastic interest rates. The extent to which cash flows and discount rates are influenced by deficits will determine how financial assets and financial markets react to persistent deficits. The stock market is driven by a combination of four factors: expected earnings, expected interest rates, investor sentiment, and liquidity. The impact of budget deficits on financial markets can influence all of the above factors either directly or indirectly. Other factors that can influence stock prices will include investment opportunities in the economy, productivity improvements, technology, cost efficiency, global markets, demographics, and political events. The current bull market has been strongly supported by many of these factors in spite of persistent budget deficits. The fixed-income or bond market has a direct link to interest rates. The price of bonds is inversely related to interest rates. When payouts are fixed, the effects are well known. Any factor that can influence interest rates will impact the bond market in general and any single bond in particular. The value of the dollar is related to the U.S. economy through interest rates as well. An increase in domestic rates makes U.S. investments more attractive and the demand for dollar-denominated assets rise. Thus, budget deficits can also influence the value of the dollar through influencing interest rates. All three sectors of the economy can be influenced by budget deficits. However, the bond market and the dollar are influenced more directly than stocks.

The belief on Wall Street is that budget deficits are bad because they increase real interest rates through crowding out. This is a negative for financial assets. At a critical stage, the fear on Wall Street is that over time higher real interest rates will result in reduced investment and savings. This in turn will eventually spill over into stocks by adversely impacting price through lower corporate earnings and higher interest rates. A worst-case scenario would result in a spike in real interest rates, a falling bond market, a severe economic decline, and a stock market crash. The dollar's outcome is unpredictable, depending on the

Table 8.1
Deficits and Economic and Financial Asset Performance

Period	Deficit		GDP	Investment	Long Rates	S&P 500
1950-1954	-0.8%	down	27.6%	25.9%	3.22 rising	115.0%
1955-1959	-2.5	up	-13.1	27.2	2.97 rising	66.0
1960-1964	-1.0	steady	21.4	25.4	3.04 rising	48.5
1965-1969	-0.1	down	22.7	24.1	0.76 falling*	8.6
1970-1974	-0.6	steady	13.0	17.7	- 4.60 falling*	-25.6
1975-1979	-1.6	steady	16.9	23.3	- 3.19 rising**	19.7
1980-1984	-5.0	up	9.3	13.1	7.75 rising	23.2
1985-1989	-4.0	steady	16.6	3.5	3.52 falling	67.3
1990-1994	-3.9	steady	9.5	18.9	5.34 rising	28.8

Deficit is a percentage of GDP.
GDP, gross domestic investment, and S&P 500 cumulative growth over period.
*Falling real rates due to sharp increases in inflation.
**Rising rates as inflation rate falls.
Sources: Council of Economic Advisers, 1997; Federal Reserve Bank of St. Louis, various years;
   and Ibbotson and Associates, 1997.

reactions of the foreign sector to events in the United States. This outcome is more plausible with increased reliance on foreign savings (investment) and with an unwillingness of U.S. politicians to address the issue of budget deficits.

EMPIRICAL EVIDENCE

The Congressional Budget Office reported in 1984 that a set of 21 studies to date showed mixed evidence of a positive correlation between interest rates and budget deficits. The problem often cited with correlation statistics is that each variable is influenced by other factors. The difference between post-1980 deficits and historical deficits is in their magnitude and the conditions under which they emerged. Recent deficits are larger and have persisted longer, which makes statistical analysis more difficult. Historically, large deficits were short-lived and associated with economic cycles or political events such as war.

Table 8.1 reports the size of the U.S. deficit as a percentage of its gross domestic product (GDP), the cumulative growth in GDP and gross domestic investment, the level and direction of the interest rate on the 30-year government bond, and the cumulative price appreciation of stocks as measured by the S&P 500 stock index. The results were measured over five-year intervals. Conventional thinking would predict a positive relationship between deficits and the direction of interest rates and an inverse relation with GDP growth, investment, and stock performance. The data are not consistent with conventional thinking for the periods before the 1980s. There are times when the economy advances, investment expenditure is up, and stocks do well in spite of the deficit. Other

Table 8.2
Coefficient of Correlation between Deficits and Financial Assets

Period	Deficit/Stocks	Deficit/Bonds	Stocks/Bonds	Rates/Deficit
1944-1954	0.46	0.37	0.30	0.26
1949-1959	-0.27	-0.03	0.04	-0.30
1954-1964	0.30	-0.42	-0.64	-0.89
1959-1969	0.40	0.34	-0.31	-0.25
1964-1974	0.02	0.32	0.00	0.21
1969-1979	0.11	0.23	0.50	0.12
1974-1984	0.39	-0.16	0.19	-0.17
1979-1989	0.05	0.10	0.57	0.21
1984-1994	0.13	-0.10	0.70	0.58

Sources: Author's calculations based on Council of Economic Advisers, 1997; Federal Reserve Bank of St. Louis, various years; Ibbotson and Associates, 1997.

factors are influencing these variables. After 1980, the level of economic growth declines, as do investment expenditures. However, interest rates fell measurably after a period of 1970s inflation, triggering a bull market in stocks that some analysts would argue continues to this day. The relationship between stocks and the deficits is an inverse one over this period. This suggests that other factors can drive financial asset prices for an extended period. A closer examination of the 1980s reveals secular shifts in technology, a revolution in regulatory reform, and an explosion of financial product innovations combined with the opening of international flows of capital. It was at this time that the trade deficit began to finance budget deficits, thus reducing the impact of crowding out. In addition, financial investment sets expanded to provide investors with the potential for high returns here and abroad. The slowdown in investment expenditures was offset by increases in consumption encouraged by government policy. The movement in stocks over the time period is part of a secular movement up in stocks and unrelated to deficits. The stock market is driven by internal factors and the ability of the economy to generate earnings. The government's role is not significant enough to fundamentally impact this process. The size of government deficits is not enough to influence a market with daily trading volume that is 50 times larger in value than the annual budget deficits. The numbers simply are not there.

Table 8.2 reports the results of a statistical correlation between the deficit and financial variables using annual data. Since 1960, the correlation between stock and bond total returns has been strongly positive. This is expected because both are inversely related to interest rates. The performance between stocks and bonds can diverge significantly in the short run if earnings growth rates exceed increases in interest rates. The correlation between the deficit measured as a percentage of GDP and stock performance has almost always been positive but not significant. This is true whether measured over 10 or 15 years. The correlation between bond returns and the deficit is equally uncertain, with some positive correlation in the 1960s and 1970s. The correlation between the yield on the 30-year Treasury bond and the deficit was negative in the 1950s and 1960s and, until recently, insignificant. We report a snapshot of correlations in Table 8.2. We also produced rolling ten-period and fifteen-period correlations. The results show that stocks and bonds have been positively correlated since the mid-1970s, that stocks and the deficit have been positively correlated since 1970, but that the correlations are not always significant. Meanwhile, the correlation of bond returns and the budget deficit has been all over the board but also lacking in significance. Finally, interest rates have been positively correlated with the deficit, beginning with the late 1980s. The changes in interest rates in the 1990s have been more responsive to the prospect of reduced budget deficits than anytime in recent memory.

In order to further investigate the relationship between budget deficits and financial assets, we examined the last ten stock market crashes where the S&P 500 index reached a high, followed by a decline of at least 14 percent to a subsequent low before recovering. The data show that in the last seven cases beginning in 1969 interest rates were on the rise and in part responsible for declines in stock prices. For the seven cases, budget deficits were also expanding. Of the last ten stock market declines, four were market crashes without economic recession. These were periods of high speculation or market bubbles that burst without the accompanying economic decline. These periods tended to be of short duration (six months). Four of the stock market declines have occurred since 1980 and are of short duration and coincidental with large budget deficits. However, the recovery of stock prices was never associated with a reduction in deficits. The fact that deficits persisted during the sell-off in stocks appears coincidental rather than causal.

The results of our investigation are mixed. However, it appears that the impact of structural deficits of the 1980s have been hidden behind the globalization of capital markets and may have in some way contributed to hastening this process. Furthermore, the increases in trade deficits and a falling dollar have accompanied budge deficits. This is consistent with expectations and may account for the difficulty in finding a meaningful relationship between deficits and financial asset performance. The secular bull market of the 1980s and 1990s in stocks and the long-term decline in interest rates from their highs of the late 1970s and early 1980s are due to a combination of deregulation, technological advancements, and low inflation. Because of these powerful factors, the crowding-out expectation did not materialize. However, recent developments suggest that after a period of acclimation the attention of the investing public has moved to deficits. Politicians have made serious progress in creating an atmosphere of declining deficits, which has contributed to extending the bull market in stocks well into the 1990s.

CONCLUSION

Budget deficits have historically (before the 1980s) been relatively small and economically inconsequential. However, since 1981 and the creation of large peacetime deficits, there has been growing concern over persistent budget deficits. We find little evidence of budget deficits explicitly influencing financial markets and financial asset returns over most of the 1925–1980 period. However, since the 1980s, stock returns show a positive correlation with deficits in part because the rising awareness of deficits has forced the hand of politicians to pursue a balanced budget. This process has been positive for stocks and bonds as long-term interest rates remain under 7 percent. What we don't know is if the slower economic growth of the 1990s versus the 1980s can be attributable to persistent budget deficits and whether the cyclical nature of markets changed as a result. Nevertheless, the current bull market in stocks is the longest on record.

In summary, with a relatively fixed pool of private savings, budget deficits must necessarily be accompanied by trade deficits. This relationship suggests higher domestic interest rates and a stronger dollar are needed to maintain the flow of foreign capital required to finance the deficits. The extent of the increase in rates is reduced by the fact that the dollar is still the international currency and the United States is still regarded as a safe haven for investments versus the rest of the world. The decade of the 1980s produced high budget and trade deficits in the absence of war. The conventional expectation of high interest rates, slow economic growth, and falling financial asset prices did not materialize. Since 1982, despite high deficits, the U.S. economy has experienced almost uninterrupted economic growth and a bull market in stocks. By the time of the 1990s, when the awareness of budget deficits might show up as a recession and a bear market, government entities have taken strong measures at the state, local, and federal levels to reign in government spending and eliminate deficits. If this trend continues, the crowding-out effect may never be tested.

REFERENCES

Council of Economic Advisers. 1997. ''Statistical Tables Relating to Income, Employment, and Production.'' *The Economic Report of the President.* Washington, D.C.: U.S. Government Printing Office.

Federal Reserve Bank of St. Louis. Various years. ''Federal Reserve Economic Data (FRED).'' St. Louis: Federal Reserve Bank of St. Louis. Web site: http://www.stls.frb.org/

Ibottson Associates. 1997. *Stocks, Bonds, Bills, and Inflation 1996 Yearbook.* Chicago: Ibottson Associates.

Murthy Vasudeva, N. R. 1996. ''The Relationship between Budget Deficits and Capital Inflows: Further Econometric Evidence.'' *Quarterly Review of Economics and Finance*, Vol. 36, No. 4, pp. 485–494.

Rose, David C. 1995. ''Deficits and Interest Rates as Evidence of Ricardian Equiva-
    lence.'' *Eastern Economic Journal*, Vol. 21, No. 1, pp. 57–66.
Thorbecke, Willem. 1993. ''Why Deficit News Affects Interest Rates.'' *Journal of Policy
    Modeling*, Vol. 15, No. 1, pp. 1–11.

Chapter 9

The Twin Deficits: Fiscal Imbalances and Trade Deficits

HASSAN MOHAMMADI AND NEIL T. SKAGGS

During the 1980s, the United States experienced the unprecedented combination of large federal government budget deficits and large current account deficits. That the two deficits might be closely related ("twins") was a well-known theoretical possibility. The emergence of the first truly large peacetime budget deficits in U.S. history, shortly followed by huge trade deficits, led many observers to conclude that the theoretical possibility had become a reality.

The circumstantial evidence in favor of the twin-deficits hypothesis appears impressive. U.S. government budget deficits rose from 1.48 percent of gross domestic product (GDP) in 1979 to 6.11 percent of GDP in 1983 and remained above 3 percent of GDP through 1988. With a lag of about two years, current account deficits behaved similarly: They rose from a mere 0.4 percent of GDP in 1982 to a maximum of 3.7 percent in 1987. With the exception of 1991, when the United States received large payments from political allies to defray the costs of the Gulf War, the current account deficit remained in excess of 1 percent of GDP through 1996.

Nor was the United States the only economy to experience large budget and trade deficits during the 1980s and early 1990s. Other G-7 economies experienced much larger deficits, as a percentage of GDP, as did many smaller economies. In most cases, however, the seemingly clear pattern evident in the U.S. data does not appear; the data that led many American economists to consider seriously the twin-deficits hypothesis were less suggestive in most other cases. Nevertheless, the emergence of large government budget deficits and large trade deficits during the same time period triggered an outpouring of empirical studies intended to gauge the strength of the relationship, as well as a few new theoretical studies. Since trade deficits can be triggered by a number of factors besides the government's budget deficit, empirical work on the issue was needed.

In this chapter, we survey the theoretical literature on the relationship between budget and trade deficits, examine the empirical studies testing for the existence of such a relationship, and suggest some directions in which future research might prove fruitful.

THEORIES OF THE RELATIONSHIP BETWEEN THE DEFICITS

Studies of the twin-deficits relationship generally proceed from one of two theoretical bases. The hypothesis that increases in the government's budget deficit lead to increases in the economy's trade deficit follows directly from the Mundell-Fleming model (Fleming, 1962; Mundell, 1967). The Mundell-Fleming model is an open economy extension of the IS-LM model. As such, it is not fully "rational"; the assumptions made regarding expectations formation are asymmetric.

Current-period taxes are assumed to be fully perceived, but current-period government spending is implicitly assumed to be completely ignored by the private sector. In considering permanent disposable income, the private sector is assumed to be forward-looking in its assessment of income and taxation. The stock of government debt is nevertheless included as part of the stock of private wealth, the implicit assumption being that the private sector is too myopic to account for the effects of government debt on future taxes. (Kormendi 1983, pp. 994–995)

In the Mundell-Fleming framework, an increase in the government's budget deficit can generate an accompanying increase in the trade deficit through several channels. By increasing the disposable incomes and the financial wealth of consumers, the budget deficit encourages an increase in imports. To the extent that increased demand for foreign goods drives up the exchange rate, the effect on net exports is mitigated. However, the larger budget deficit also pushes up the interest rate (in large open economies), which encourages a net capital inflow and a larger decline in net exports. While the size of the effect is an empirical matter, the linkage between the deficits is clear.

In the 1970s, Robert J. Barro (1974) began applying the concept of rational expectations to questions of fiscal policy. Barro demonstrated that, under certain restrictive assumptions, debt financing produces the same responses by private economic actors as does tax financing—the Ricardian Equivalence proposition. If Ricardian Equivalence holds, the effects of deficit-financed fiscal policies on international trade should be minimal. For example, an increase in government purchases, financed by borrowing, has only a redistributive effect on aggregate demand. Government consumption or investment rises at the expense of private consumption. Any effect on net exports is minimal. Furthermore, since households save an amount equal to the government deficit, the interest rate is un-affected. Thus, the policy does not induce a net capital inflow and its accompanying decline in net exports. In the Ricardian case, the budget deficit and the trade deficit are unrelated to one another.

Trade imbalances can occur, of course, for reasons other than government budget imbalances. Three nonbudgetary causes of trade deficits are worth men-tioning. First, a decrease in an economy's saving rate coupled with unchanging investment (or an increase in investment accompanied by unchanged saving) produces a rise in the interest rate and a net capital inflow. Foreign economies earn the currency needed to supply capital by running trade surpluses against the economy with deficient saving. Given the relatively low U.S. saving rate, many economists argued that the trade deficits of the 1980s and early 1990s reflected deficient saving rather than government budget deficits. Note, however, that government budget deficits reduce national saving; if consumers/savers are not fully rational (in the Ricardian sense), government deficits can contribute to trade deficits through their effect on national saving.

Second, the early 1980s were years of political and economic instability in some parts of the world. Latin America, in particular, experienced great turmoil. Wealthy individuals in unstable countries often move their financial wealth to more stable capital markets. Massive movements of financial capital from Latin America to more stable economies could generate accompanying trade deficits in the stable economies.

Third, changes in foreign real incomes and resulting changes in foreign ag-gregate demands relative to domestic income and aggregate demand can gen-erate trade imbalances. For example, a recession in Europe reduces the demand for U.S. exports. If the U.S. economy continues to perform at a high level, net exports decline. Such a scenario might explain much of the increase in the U.S. trade deficit in the mid-1980s.

In addition to these macroeconomic factors, a number of microeconomic fac-tors might underlie the change in an economy's trade balance. Anything affecting the terms of trade can result in persistent trade deficits, providing other countries are willing to accumulate the debt of the deficit economy at a real exchange rate that does not equilibrate exports and imports. Given the significant number of potential causes of trade deficits, any relationship between the budget and trade deficits must be established empirically. A substantial number of econ-omists have accepted the challenge.

EMPIRICAL STUDIES OF THE RELATIONSHIP BETWEEN THE DEFICITS

Empirical examinations of the twin-deficits relationship have taken many forms, ranging from single-equation ordinary least squares (OLS) models to two-stage least squares models to small-scale structural models to unconstrained vector-autoregression (VAR) models to cointegration and vector-error-correction

(VEC) models. Each of these approaches has shortcomings, but some approaches are clearly superior to others. The results obtained are quite sensitive to the modeling technique chosen. As Tallman and Rosensweig (1991, p. 5) note, "Some studies using a Mundell-Fleming framework indicate that the twin deficit notion is consistent with the data. In contrast, other studies, finding no underlying relationship between government and trade deficits, are consistent with the predictions of Ricardian equivalence." Furthermore, results also depend upon the data chosen and the manner in which they are handled. The choice of variables to include in estimated equations is important, as is the form (levels, first differences, or percentage of gross national product [GNP]) in which variables enter the equations.

A survey of the empirical literature indicates that results depend importantly on the choice of variables. Ideally, the variables included in empirical models— and perhaps the estimated form of the models—should be dictated by economic theory. Omitting important variables can bias coefficient estimates. At the very least, including different sets of variables in purported tests of the same theoretical model makes it difficult to compare results across studies.

An important issue in choosing variables is the choice of appropriate measures of the budget and trade deficits. Theory implies that the relationship between deficits may be sensitive to the deficit measure used. Consider the basic macroeconomic saving-investment identity: $I + NFI = S_p + (T - G_c)$, where I is total (private plus public) domestic investment, NFI is net foreign investment, S_p is private domestic saving, T is total net tax revenue, and G_c is total government consumption expenditures. Suppose, for simplicity, that I and S_p remain constant, while G_c increases. In this case, NFI must decline. This implies a larger current account deficit, since $NFI = CA$. Also note the measure of the budget deficit: The deficit included in the aggregate investment-saving identity is the *total* government budget deficit, properly measured as net tax revenue minus government *consumption* expenditures.

No study of the U.S. twin-deficits relationship of which we are aware makes use of the appropriate measure of the budget deficit, since the U.S. government does not disaggregate purchases into consumption and investment components. (State and local governments do a much better job of accounting for investment spending.) If federal investment expenditures are positive (as they surely are), the standard definition of the federal deficit overstates the true amount of government dissaving. Changes in the measured deficit may or may not reflect changes in the theoretical deficit, depending on the components of revenues and expenditures that change.

Setting aside the issue of measurement error in the total budget deficit, most empirical studies use some other measure of the budget deficit. This is not necessarily inappropriate, since some components of the budget deficit might be more closely related to the current account deficit than are others. In particular, a number of investigators have used cyclically adjusted budget deficits in an effort to purge their estimates of cyclical influences, while better measuring the actual thrust of fiscal policy. Many others have used federal deficits, choosing to ignore the effects of state and local government budgets. Since state and local governments, in the aggregate, nearly always run surpluses, this leads to a persistent overestimate of the total deficit. It also runs the risk of overlooking intergovernmental symmetries, such as occur when the federal government shifts responsibilities for programs to the states without fully funding them. Such actions may simultaneously reduce the federal deficit, while also reducing state surpluses. Most studies make no mention of such issues when discussing their choice of variables.

The form in which variables are entered in equations also appears to be an important determinant of empirical results. Tallman and Rosensweig (1991, p. 7) note that the chances of finding a twin-deficits relationship appear to be greater if variables are entered as levels or as ratios to GNP, rather than as first differences. Yet the modern time series literature demonstrates that one should not arbitrarily choose variable forms. Regressing a variable that is nonstationary in levels on other nonstationary variables produces spurious coefficient estimates. What we know about the time series properties of many macroeconomic series should lead us to doubt the results of any study using data in levels. Less recognized are the problems that emerge from estimating VAR models that include cointegrated variables. Such VAR modeling can also lead to biased estimates, as we show below.

Early studies of the twin deficits (from the mid-1980s) typically relied on single-equation OLS or two-stage least squares models (e.g., Eisner, 1986, 1991; Summers, 1986). Such studies often found that changes in some measure of the budget deficit are correlated with changes in some measure of the trade deficit. For example, Eisner (1991) estimates an OLS equation using the ratio of net exports to GNP as the dependent variable and including the price-adjusted high-employment deficit as a percentage of GNP as an explanatory variable. He finds a positive effect of the budget deficit on the trade deficit, although the estimated coefficient is only marginally statistically significant. While Eisner's simple model avoids the nonstationarity problem inherent in using data in levels, its very simplicity—the only other explanatory variable is the change in the real interest rate—argues against taking the findings too seriously. The problems of simple single-equation models lead us to concentrate the remainder of our survey on representative multiequation specifications.

Zietz and Pemberton (1990) estimate a multiequation, structural, open economy model of the U.S. economy. Their model includes equations for short-term interest rates; the real trade-weighted exchange rate; domestic absorption; exports; imports; the domestic inflation rate; and trend absorption. They derive two-stage least squares estimates for each equation. Simulations of the model indicate a strong effect of budget policy on net exports, primarily through the effect of domestic absorption on imports. The effect through rising interest and exchange rates is minor. Despite the sizable effects of fiscal policy on net exports, Zietz and Pemberton conclude that less than half of the trade deficits of the 1980s can be explained by government policy.

A number of researchers have estimated VAR models in an attempt to account for the pervasive endogeneity among variables. Abell (1990b) estimated a seven-variable VAR model using monthly data for the period 1979.02–1985.02, which corresponds to the period of dollar appreciation in the early 1980s. The variables included in the system are the federal government budget deficit, the U.S. merchandise trade balance, the M1 money supply, Moody's AAA bond yield, the Dallas Federal Reserve Bank's 101-country trade-weighted dollar exchange rate, real disposable personal income, and the consumer price index (CPI). In a second paper, Abell (1990a) excluded disposable income and lengthened the sample period to 1977.01–1985.02 but used the same techniques.

Abell (1990b, p. 88) concluded that (1) ''budget deficits are not (directly) causally prior to trade deficits'' but (2) ''trade deficits are (directly) causally prior to budget deficits.'' He contended, however, that *indirect* causation running from the budget deficit through the interest rate and the exchange rate to the trade deficit exists. His reported impulse response functions showed a positive response of the trade deficit to a one-standard-deviation shock to the budget deficit. The size of the effect is, however, quite small. In variance decompositions, innovations in the budget deficit explain only 5.5 percent of the variation in the merchandise trade balance over a 24-month horizon, using an ordering that produces the most conservative estimated effect.

Abell's study is open to criticism because his choice of sample period invites spurious correlation. He intentionally examined a period of continuous dollar appreciation. His use of monthly data with an eight-month maximum lag length is also problematic, since it may not capture the true relationship among variables.

Bachman (1992) tested the twin-deficits hypothesis using quarterly data for the period 1974–1988. (He also tested the relationship between the trade deficit and three other ''causal variables'': gross domestic investment, relative productivity, and the exchange rate risk premium.) All of his analysis is bivariate. Finding no evidence of cointegration between the current account and the budget deficit, Bachman estimated bivariate VARs. His results suggested unidirectional Granger causation from the federal deficit to the current account. An impulse response function indicated that an innovation to the budget deficit of approximately 0.7 percent of GNP produces a current account response of about 0.4 percent of GNP after ten quarters.

The major problem with Bachman's study is the complete absence of any explanatory variables besides the federal budget deficit. Bivariate equations raise the possibility of misspecification. The unusually large response of the current account to an innovation in the budget deficit could simply be an artifact of the bivariate approach. Furthermore, the absence of bivariate cointegration does not preclude their cointegration in a larger system (as we shall demonstrate).

Kearney and Monadjemi (1990) estimated five variable VARs for eight countries (Australia, Britain, Canada, France, Germany, Ireland, Italy, and the United States). They did not include the government budget deficit as a separate variable, choosing instead to include government expenditures and tax revenues. Their VAR equations include "monetary creation" and the (real, effective) exchange rate but not income or an interest rate. The results vary widely across countries. For the United States, the authors found bidirectional causality between government spending and the current account but only unidirectional causality from the current account to tax revenues. The variance decomposition—based on a 40-quarter horizon—shows that government expenditures explain a significant percentage of the prediction error in the current account (36 percent). Innovations in tax revenues explain 21 percent of current account variation. On the other hand, innovations in the current account explain 17 percent of the prediction error in government expenditures and 14 percent in tax revenues. Simulation results show that the current account follows an oscillating pattern in response to a shock to government expenditures, *regardless* of how the expenditures are financed, a result that applies to all countries.

Kearney and Monadjemi summarized their findings as "indicating the existence of a temporary twin deficits relationship between the stance of fiscal policy and performance on the current account of the balance of payments, which does not persist over time" (p. 216). The absence of income as a variable in the VAR equations makes comparison of the results with other studies somewhat difficult.

Tallman and Rosensweig (1991) estimated a four-variable VAR system that includes measures of the real interest rate and the real exchange rate. They found that the government deficit (as a ratio to GNP) Granger causes the trade deficit (as a ratio to GNP) but not vice versa. They reported no variance decompositions or impulse response functions. Their findings reinforce those of Darrat (1988), who examined the existence of Granger causality between the real federal budget deficit and the "real trade deficit" using a system of unconstrained multivariate equations for both the budget deficit and the trade deficit. In addition to the two deficits, Darrat considered the effects of a trade-weighted exchange rate, the monetary base, the three-month T-bill rate, the inflation rate (GNP deflator), foreign real income (U.S. trade weighted), real GNP, a long-term government bond rate, and the hourly average industrial wage rate. He found bidirectional causality between the deficits (and between most other pairs of variables—an unusual result). Since Darrat did not estimate a complete VAR system, he presented no variance decompositions or impulse response functions.

Enders and Lee (1990) also estimated a VAR system, which they derived from a consumer optimization model of the economy consistent with the Ricardian Equivalence hypothesis (REH). They estimated a six-variable unconstrained VAR for the postwar period (1947.III–1987.I), covering both fixed and flexible exchange rate regimes. Their model contains government expenditures and changes in the federal debt as separate variables. Variance decompositions show a small but significant effect of both government spending shocks and debt shocks on net exports (15.9 percent and 12.9 percent, respectively). Plots of impulse response functions show a sustained decrease in net exports in response to both a government spending shock and a government debt shock. The latter result is, of course, contradictory to the REH. However, when Enders and Lee imposed theoretical restrictions drawn from the Ricardian theory on the model and tested their validity, they were unable to reject Ricardian Equivalence.

Miller and Russek (1989) estimated both VAR and cointegration models of the twin-deficits relationship, using quarterly data for the period 1946.I–1987.II. They transformed their data by both deterministic and stochastic methods and compared the VAR results for flexible and fixed exchange rate periods. Miller and Russek found evidence of causation from the federal deficit to net exports for the flexible exchange rate period using various transformations of the data. However, they found no evidence of cointegration for this period. The most obvious shortcoming of the Miller-Russek study is the bivariate nature of the analysis. As the authors noted, the absence of cointegration could be due to omitted variables—as could some of their VAR results.

In these studies (and in others not discussed), the estimated effect of budget deficits on the trade deficit range from the substantial (Kearney and Monadjemi, 1990) to the economically small and statistically insignificant (Enders and Lee, 1990). The presumed transmission mechanism changes from study to study. In some studies, the budget deficit appears to affect the trade deficit through the interest rate and the exchange rate (e.g., Abell, 1990a, 1990b). In others, the interest rate–exchange rate channel is insignificant; the budget deficit affects the trade deficit through domestic absorption (Zietz and Pemberton, 1990). Several studies do not even include domestic income or absorption, making comparisons across studies difficult.

In an attempt to surmount these difficulties and bring some order to the study of the twin deficits, we conducted a broad investigation that resulted in the estimation of a five-variable vector-error-correction model for the U.S. economy for the period 1973.I to 1991.IV (Mohammadi and Skaggs, 1996). For our baseline model we chose variables consistent with the Mundell-Fleming model: the real current account balance, the real total government budget surplus, the growth rate of the M2 money supply, the log of real GDP, and the real exchange rate (the trade-weighted average exchange value of the U.S. dollar against currencies of the industrial countries, adjusted by the ratio of export-to-import price indexes). We paid great attention to the univariate and multivariate time series properties of the variables and to the specification of our autoregressive models. This was necessary because models estimated in levels with nonstationary series can lead to spurious regression results, and models estimated in first differences are misspecified if the series are cointegrated and converge to stationary long-term equilibrium relationships.

Testing for nonstationarity in the individual data series using the augmented Dickey-Fuller procedure showed that the variables are nonstationary in levels but stationary in first differences. Next, we investigated the multivariate properties of the variables using the maximum likelihood procedure of Jøhansen (1988) and Jøhansen and Juselius (1990). We found evidence in favor of at least one cointegrating vector, which led us to estimate VEC models and compute the corresponding variance decompositions and impulse response functions. Significantly, we did not find bivariate cointegration between the deficits—a result consistent with that of Bachman and of Miller and Russek.

For purposes of comparison, we examined the effects of variable ordering on the estimated results. Because the extent of current period endogeneity of variables in a VEC or VAR system depends arbitrarily on the order in which the variables are entered, we were able to choose orderings that were most favorable to the twin-deficits hypothesis (the Mundell-Fleming ordering) and least favorable to the hypothesis. Estimating both orderings allowed us to set bounds on the estimates. We also estimated the system as an ordinary VAR, examined the effects of changing our measures of the budget and trade deficits, and investigated the effect of alternative lag lengths in the estimated equations. Our results enabled us to explain much of the variation of results across previous studies.

A substantial portion of the different results across studies can be explained by modeling choices. Longer lag lengths, more favorable variable orderings, and the use of broad measures of budget and trade deficits virtually guarantee relatively large estimated effects of budget deficits on trade deficits. Estimated effects also increase in size when a VEC model is used to estimate a cointegrated system; estimates are biased downward when VAR estimation is applied inappropriately. Yet even these "relatively large" effects are modest in economic terms. We found that a one-standard-deviation innovation in the budget deficit would, after eleven quarters, alter the current account to GDP ratio by less than 40 percent of the change in the total government budget deficit to GDP ratio. Translating our results into dollar levels measured at an annual rate, "a reduction of the total budget deficit of $86 billion in the first quarter of 1990 (from $131.7 billion to $45.7 billion) would have reduced the current account deficit in the fourth quarter of 1992 by less than $37 billion (from $99.7 billion to $63.0 billion)" (Mohammadi and Skaggs, 1996, p. 681).

The major twin-deficits relationship found in our broad study is the reverse of what might have been expected. We found that innovations in the trade deficit explain a larger percentage of the forecast-error variance in the budget deficit than vice versa. This holds for both orderings and for all measures of the deficits. The twin-deficits relationship tells us more about why the budget deficit behaves as it does than about why the trade deficit evolves as it does.

WHAT WE KNOW

All but one of the studies reviewed above focuses solely on the United States. Although most of the studies found some positive relationship running from the budget deficit to the trade deficit, the size of the estimated effect is nearly always small. The large changes in the U.S. budget deficit during the 1980s explain, at most, considerably less than half the changes in the current account balance. Factors other than the budget deficit are more important determinants of the current account balance.

The primary channel through which changes in the budget deficit are transmitted to the trade deficit appears to be real income. Several studies (Abell, 1990b; Enders and Lee, 1990; Zietz and Pemberton, 1990; also Karras, 1993) have found little influence through the interest rate or the exchange rate, while others have found larger effects of innovations in the budget deficit on real income or absorption (Zietz and Pemberton, 1990; Mohammadi and Skaggs, 1996). Since the majority of twin-deficits studies do not include income in the estimated systems, this result should be viewed as suggestive only.

WHAT WE NEED TO KNOW

Nearly everything we know about the twin-deficits relationship applies only to the U.S. economy. Thus, the first order of business would seem to be to apply the techniques developed for evaluating the U.S. economy to other economies, appropriately modifying the systems as necessary to conform to the theory of small open economies.

Beyond extending empirical work to other economies, a natural extension of the VEC methodology would be to estimate a structural VEC system to which testable restrictions based on economic theory can be applied. Such an approach would enable researchers to discriminate between theories, as well as to identify more precisely the channels through which the twin deficits interact.

REFERENCES

Abell, John D. July 1990a. "The Role of the Budget Deficit during the Rise of the Dollar Exchange Rate from 1979–1985." *Southern Economic Journal*, Vol. 57, pp. 66–74.

———. Winter 1990b. "Twin Deficits during the 1980s: An Empirical Investigation." *Journal of Macroeconomics*, pp. 81–96.

Bachman, Daniel David. October 1992. "Why Is the U.S. Current Account Deficit So Large? Evidence from Vector Autoregressions." *Southern Economic Journal*, Vol. 59, pp. 232–240.

Barro, Robert J. 1974. "Are Government Bonds Net Wealth?" *Journal of Political Economy*, Vol. 82, pp. 1095–1117.

Darrat, Ali F. October 1988. "Have Large Budget Deficits Caused Rising Trade Deficits?" *Southern Economic Journal*, Vol. 55, pp. 879–887.

Eisner, Robert. 1986. *How Real Is the Federal Deficit?* New York: Free Press.

———. 1991. "The Deficits and Us and Our Grandchildren." In James M. Rock, ed., *Debt and the Twin Deficits Debate*. Mountain View, Calif.: Mayfield Publishing Co., pp. 81–107.

Enders, Walter, and Bong-Soo Lee. August 1990. "Current Account and Budget Deficits: Twins or Distant Cousins?" *Review of Economics and Statistics*, pp. 373–381.

Fleming, Marcus. November 1962. "Domestic Financial Policies under Fixed and Floating Exchange Rates." *IMF Staff Papers*, pp. 369–379.

Jøhansen, Søren. 1988. "Statistical Analysis of Cointegration Vectors." *Journal of Economic Dynamics and Control*, Vol. 12, pp. 231–254.

Jøhansen, Søren, and Katarina Juselius. 1990. "Maximum Likelihood Estimation and Inference on Cointegration—with Applications to the Demand for Money." *Oxford Bulletin of Economics and Statistics*, Vol. 52, No. 2, pp. 169–210.

Karras, Georgio. Winter 1993. "Sources of U.S. Macroeconomic Fluctuations: 1973–1989." *Journal of Macroeconomics*, Vol. 15, pp. 47–68.

Kearney, Colm, and Mehdi Monadjemi. Spring 1990. "Fiscal Policy and Current Account Performance: International Evidence on the Twin Deficits." *Journal of Macroeconomics*, Vol. 12, pp. 197–220.

Kormendi, Roger C. December 1983. "Government Debt, Government Spending, and Private Sector Behavior." *American Economic Review*, Vol. 73, pp. 994–1010.

Miller, Stephen M., and Frank S. Russek. October 1989. "Are the Twin Deficits Really Related?" *Contemporary Policy Issues*, Vol. 7, pp. 91–115.

Mohammadi, Hassan, and Neil T. Skaggs. January 1996. "U.S. Fiscal Policy and Trade Deficits: A Broad Perspective." *Southern Economic Journal*, Vol. 62, pp. 675–689.

Mundell, Robert A. 1967. *International Economics*. New York: Macmillan.

Summers, Lawrence H. 1986. "Issues in National Savings Policy." In F. Gerard Adams and Susan M. Wachter, eds., *Savings and Capital Formation*. Lexington, Mass.: Lexington Books.

Tallman, Ellis W., and Jeffrey A. Rosensweig. 1991. "Investigating U.S. Government and Trade Deficits." *Economic Review* (Federal Reserve Bank of Atlanta), pp. 1–11.

Zietz, Joachim, and D. K. Pemberton. July 1990. "The U.S. Budget and Trade Deficits: A Simultaneous Equation Model." *Southern Economic Journal*, Vol. 57, pp. 23–34.

Chapter 10

Economic Growth and Fiscal Imbalances

SIAMACK SHOJAI

In August 1995 the U.S. Congressional Budget Office estimated that balancing the U.S. budget by the year 2002 could increase the growth in the United States by 0.1 percentage point every year. In August 1997 the Congress and the president of the United States agreed on a five-year accord that would balance the budget by 2002. In fact, the U.S. economy has shown a remarkable achievement in reducing its budget deficit from a high of more than $350 billion a few years ago to $22.6 billion in fiscal year 1996–1997 and an estimated budget surplus of $70 billion in 1998. Ball and Mankiw (1995) estimate that eliminating the budget deficit would increase the gross national product (GDP) by $30 or $40 billion a year. According to these estimates, a reduction in budget deficits enhances real economic growth. This chapter inquires into the link between fiscal imbalances and real economic growth. The theoretical and empirical foundations of this issue are discussed briefly.

According to the pioneering work of Harrod (1948) and Domar (1946), economic growth is achieved as a result of capital formation and labor force growth. Capital is accumulated and formed in the economy through savings. Nations with a high saving rate, generally, achieve a higher rate of economic growth. The economic model developed in Chapter 5 demonstrates that the national saving is identical to the excess of total output over households' consumption and government purchases. The national accounts identity reveals that the national saving equals the sum of net exports and investment. Thus, any fiscal activity that reduces national saving must cause a reduction in net exports or investment. The impact of budget deficits on trade balance was discussed in Chapter 9. Here we suffice it to say that budget deficits that reduce national saving would cause a reduction in investment, capital formation, and real economic growth.

Gokhale (1993) demonstrates that the net national saving rate in the United States averaged more than 9 percent in the 1960s, dropped to less than 4 percent in the 1980s, and in the early 1990s was less than 2 percent. Among many other factors, he attributes the decline in the net saving rate to the fiscal redistribution across generations caused by huge budget deficits.

According to traditional economic theory, an increase in budget deficits raises the cost of borrowing (real interest rates), which in return crowds out private spending on capital goods, leading to a lower rate of GDP growth. In Chapter 6 we discussed the Ricardian Equivalence hypothesis, which provides the opposing view on the impact of budget deficits on interest rates. We recall that, according to this hypothesis, the private sector, in anticipation of higher tax burdens in the future, increases its savings during deficit spending periods. Thus, deficits do not matter.

The empirical work in this area is ambiguous and does not resolve the theoretical controversies. Seater (1993) and Bernheim (1987) provide two opposing surveys of this debate. Researchers such as Hutchison and Pyle (1984), Ford and Laxton (1995), and Tanzi and Fanizza (1995) have provided empirical evidence in support of the traditional view. Their estimates indicate that higher deficits in industrial countries have caused real interest rates to be higher by 150 to 450 basis points. However, other authors' (Barro and Sali-I-Martin, 1990; Evans, 1987) empirical models provide support for the Ricardian Equivalence hypothesis. Barro (1991) concludes that it is the size and the composition of a government's budget that affect long-term economic growth.

GLOBAL DEBT REDUCTIONS

In the May 1996 issue of the *World Economic Outlook* prepared by the staff of the International Monetary Fund (IMF), the MULTIMOD simulation model of the IMF is utilized to investigate the effects of a deficit reduction in the United States on its economy and the spillover effects on the economy of industrial countries and developing nations under three different scenarios. In the first scenario, only the U.S. government debt is reduced by 1 percent of GDP through a permanent government spending reduction. The simulation assumes that there is no change in the debt of other countries, and there is no change in the monetary policy to offset government spending reduction. The simulation results indicate that in the long-run capital stock increases by 2.2 percent in the United States, leading to a 0.6 percent permanent rise in the United States real GDP. Other industrial and developing countries experience a real GDP increase of 0.4 and 0.3 percent, respectively.

The second scenario assumes no change in the U.S. debt while other industrial countries reduce their government spending. Since other industrial countries together are larger than the United States, the increase in the real GDP of all countries in the long run is larger than before. The U.S. real GDP rises by 0.7 percent, while other industrial countries' real GDP increases by 1.2 percent. The developing creditor countries' real GDP goes up by 0.7 percent, compared to a 0.8 percent rise in the real GDP of developing debtor countries.

In the last scenario, deficit reduction in the United States is achieved through tax increases. The simulation results indicate that deficit reductions through tax increases are less beneficial than those achieved through spending cuts. The real GDP rose across all nations by only 0.2 percent when debt was reduced through tax increases. This simulation exercise seems to reject the Ricardian Equivalence hypothesis. However, the MULTIMOD model cannot shed much light on this academic debate because it stipulates that a significant portion of consumers cannot borrow against their future labor income, wealth-constraint consumers don't care about the tax burden passed to future generations, aggregate consumption and saving are not very sensitive to interest rate changes, and monetary policy is neutral in the face of debt reduction policy.

DEFICIT REDUCTION IN DEVELOPING COUNTRIES

The size, nature, and causes of budget deficits in developing countries are discussed in Chapter 13. Government spending on education, health, and productive infrastructure in developing countries enhances economic growth. But expenditures on current consumption by government could lower the rate of economic growth. The *World Economic Outlook* (1996) concludes that during the mid-1980s a group of developing countries with high fiscal imbalances had significantly lower economic growth than countries with low to medium budget deficits. The real GDP growth was only 3 percent in the 1990–1995 period in high-deficit countries compared to 7 percent in low-deficit developing countries. The same study shows that in the developing countries with the highest reduction in fiscal imbalances, as a percentage of GDP, between 1980–1985 and 1990–1995 output was 40 percent higher during the latter period compared to the former.

Deficit spendings that are financed by the central bank can also lead to inefficiencies in the financial markets and cause high inflation in the developing countries. In addition, budget deficits distort the real exchange rates and interest rate, which in turn undermines the international competitiveness of the economy. Nevertheless, in the face of market failures, some studies have pointed to the beneficial effects of government spending on infrastructure, health, education, and productive development projects. The pioneering work of Rao (1953) demonstrates that government spending on productive development projects in developing countries is not as inflationary as it might be assumed because of the greater output growth. Eisner and Pieper (1987) report a positive impact of cyclically and inflation-adjusted budget deficits on economic growth in the United States and other Organization for Economic Cooperation and Development (OECD) countries.

In a recent study, Nelson and Singh (1994) utilize data on a cross section of 70 developing countries during two time periods, 1970–1979 and 1980–1989, to investigate the effect of budget deficits on GDP growth rates. Among the explanatory variables in this study are government budget deficits, government revenue, defense spending, domestic private and public investment, population growth rate, per capita income, education, and the inflation rate. The estimation results of the growth model suggest that defense spending and private investment have had a significant positive impact on economic growth both in the 1970s and the 1980s. Government revenue has a negative impact on the growth. The education variable provides no conclusive effects. Public investment has positively affected economic growth in the 1980s but has had no impact in the 1970s. The study concludes that budget deficits have had no significant effect on the economic growth of these nations in the 1970s and 1980s.

CONCLUSION

This chapter has provided the traditional view of the effect of government budget deficits on the economic growth in developed and developing countries. The traditional view suggests that deficits raise interest rates and crowd out private investments. Because private investments are more efficient and productive than public spending, economic growth is hampered by deficit spending. The Ricardian Equivalence hypothesis provides an alternative view, which holds that deficits are inconsequential because the public adjusts its savings in anticipation of future tax burdens caused by deficit spending.

The empirical work does not remedy the theoretical controversy. Differences in the measures of deficits, time periods, the properties of the economic models, and the estimation techniques have resulted in opposing empirical conclusions. Perhaps a better approach to resolve some of these controversies is to investigate the effects of different components of government spending on the level of aggregate demand and demand for private goods produced by the private sector. It would be interesting to inquire into the impact of government spending on the health and strength of major, high-technology industries in the industrial world. Perhaps the level of investments on research and development by many firms in the United States would be different in the absence of a strong demand by government. After all, technological improvements are a significant source of capital formation and real economic growth.

In the developing countries, more research must be done on the potential differential impact of government provision of social goods compared with production of those goods. Many developing countries may suffer not only from excessive government deficit spending but also from excessive ownership of the productive means of production. A real and honest privatization program accompanied by fiscal discipline may be much more effective in enhancing economic growth.

REFERENCES

Ball, Laurence, and Gregory N. Mankiw. 1995. "What Do Budget Deficits Do?" In *Budget Deficits and Debt: Issues and Options*. A symposium sponsored by the

Federal Reserve Bank of Kansas City, Jackson Hole, Wyo., August 31–September 2, pp. 95–119.

Barro, Robert J. May 1991. "Economic Growth in a Cross Section of Countries." *Quarterly Journal of Economics*, Vol. 106, No. 2, pp. 407–443.

Barro, Robert J., and Xavier Sali-I-Martin. April 1990. "World Real Interest Rates." National Bureau of Economic Research Working Paper No. 3317.

Bernheim, B. Douglas. 1987. "Ricardian Equivalence: An Evaluation of Theory and Evidence." *NBER Macroeconomics Annual*, pp. 263–304.

Domar, E. April 1946. "Capital Expansion, Rate of Growth and Employment." *Econometrica*, Vol. 14, No. 2, pp. 137–147.

Eisner, R., and P. J., Pieper. 1987. "Measurement and Effects of Government Debt and Deficits." In B. Jacquillat, A. W. Sametz, M. Sarnat, and G. P. Szego, eds., *Economic Policy and National Accounting in Inflationary Conditions.* Studies in Banking and Finance. Amsterdam: North-Holland.

Evans, Paul. September 1987. "Do Budget Deficits Raise Nominal Interest Rates? Evidence from Six Countries." *Journal of Monetary Economics*, Vol. 20, pp. 281–300.

Ford, Robert, and Douglas Laxton. March 1995. "World Public Debt and Real Interest Rates." IMF Working Papers WP/95/30. International Monetary Fund, Washington, D.C.

Gokhale, Jagadeesh. 1993. "The Decline in U.S. Saving Rates: A Case for Concern?" *Economic Commentary* (Federal Reserve Bank of Cleveland, Ohio), September 15, pp. 1–6.

Harrod, R. F. 1948. *Towards a Dynamic Economics.* New York: Macmillan.

Hutchison, Michael M., and David H. Pyle. Fall 1984. "The Real Interest/Budget Deficit Link: International Evidence, 1973–1982." *Economic Review* (Federal Reserve Bank of San Francisco), No. 4.

Nelson, Michael A., and Ram D. Singh. 1994. "The Deficit-Growth Connection: Some Recent Evidence from Developing Countries." *Economic Development and Cultural Change*, Vol. 13, pp. 167–91.

Rao, V. K. R. V. February 1953. "Deficit Financing, Capital Formation and Price Behavior in an Under-developed Economy." *Indian Economic Review*, Vol. 1, No. 3, pp. 55–91.

Seater, John J. 1993. "Ricardian Equivalence." *Journal of Economic Literature*, Vol. 31, pp. 142–190.

Tanzi, Vito, and Domenico Fanniza. May 1995. "Fiscal Deficits and Public Debt in Industrial Countries, 1970–1994." IMF Working Papers WP/95/49. International Monetary Fund, Washington, D.C.

World Economic Outlook. May 1996. Washington, D.C.: International Monetary Fund.

Part III

The Political Economy of Deficits

Chapter 11

The Welfare State and Entitlements: Resisting Retrenchment in the 1990s

ROBERT C. A. SORENSEN

The welfare state has been defined as "a state which takes a prime role in ensuring the provision of a minimum standard of life to all its citizens. The main aspects of 'welfare' are medical care, education, income maintenance (which includes old age insurance as well as unemployment insurance—RCAS), personal social services, and housing" (Hague, Harrop, and Breslin, 1992, p. 472). The level of benefits is not necessarily limited to a minimum, nor are benefits necessarily limited to persons of low income or limited wealth. Benefits may depend on need or may be offered in the same form to all without "means testing." In any case, the benefits are automatically available to all who fall into a designated category and in that respect constitute "entitlements," a fundamental component of the welfare state concept.

While varying paths were taken in the elaboration of different national systems, there are broad parallels in the entitlement programs developed in the United States and other advanced industrial societies, including the member states of what is now the European Union (Heidenheimer, Heclo, and Adams, 1983). Similar parallels may be seen in the critiques leveled at these systems and policy alternatives introduced in the late 1970s and 1980s in response to recession, budget pressures, and political sentiments (Organization for Economic Cooperation and Development, 1981). Adjustments to or even the "rolling back" of welfare state policies and entitlement programs seemed to have been at their height in the 1980s as championed and symbolized by the persons and governments of Margaret Thatcher and Ronald Reagan and endorsed by leaders and governments elsewhere (Krieger, 1986; Pierson, 1994). Yet despite economic, political, and policy pressures, welfare state entitlements appear to retain popular support in the mid- to late 1990s.

The main point of this chapter will be to show how recent electoral developments in the United States and in Europe support research showing widespread, continuing approval of the fundamentals of welfare state systems and popular resistance to cutbacks proposed by political elites (Shapiro and Young, 1989; Pierson, 1996). In this respect, the argument upholds the view of a consolidation of enduring support for welfare state policies with increasing parallels among advanced industrial societies despite national differences in the development of these policies and popular orientations to them.

One signal aspect of the current situation therefore is the manifestation of enduring favor for the welfare state in spite of evidence in the 1970s and 1980s to the contrary—hence, the need for responsive governments to continue to provide entitlement programs.[1] Another is the indication of increased saliency of economic policy making for the general population and hence the potentially increasing reality of democratically contested political economy. The broader theoretical context of these topics points to the relationship between public sentiment and public policy, the workings of this relationship in the context of democratic politics, and the conflicts generated under conditions in which public sentiment and macroeconomic policy and market forces may be at odds.

WELFARE STATE EXPANSION

Welfare state policies date back to social insurance programs introduced in Germany in the late nineteenth century. Social insurance systems to deal with industrial accidents, health, retirement pensions, unemployment, and family support were developed with varying degrees of similarity in advanced industrial societies after that time and throughout the first half of the twentieth century (Flora and Heidenheimer, 1981). Education and housing were additional areas of public funding innovation. In spite of differences between them, the advanced industrial countries came to provide even more substantial welfare programs in broadly comparable categories after World War II, accounting generally for between one fifth and one third of gross national product (GNP) (Furniss and Tilton, 1977; Siegel and Weinberg, 1977). The years after World War II brought such substantial expansion in these programs that "the period from 1960 to 1980 may indeed have been a golden age in the long history of welfare state spending and taxation" (Heidenheimer, Heclo, and Adams, 1983, p. 10).[2] As the portions of the population entitled to benefits expanded, they came to include middle- and even upper-class beneficiaries.

Still, variations in the levels of welfare state expenditure as percent of gross domestic product (GDP) or in terms of relative size of different programs do exist. Not surprisingly, a correlation exists between the wealth of a society and the percentage of its wealth that is devoted to welfare entitlements (Wilensky, 1975). The relevance of this point to the expansion of welfare systems during the growth years of the 1960s and 1970s is evident, but differences in economic development do not explain all the variations in the national programs.[3] Entitlement programs are more elaborate in some countries than in others along lines tied to history, culture, and political structures, as opposed to simple measures of national wealth. Such national differences might enhance rejection of or support for welfare state policies.

Heidenheimer, Heclo, and Adams, (1983) distinguish between welfare states on the basis of ''inherited (popular) attitudes towards government initiatives and intervention.'' In this context, they discuss elements of classical liberalism in the cultures of the United States and Great Britain, in contrast to carry-overs from feudalism in Sweden, France, and Germany. In the case of the former countries, a more limited role for the state and greater reliance on private efforts might be expected, while in the latter, the authoritative role of the state and maintenance of established status hierarchies would be more likely to be accepted (pp. 16–17).

Esping-Andersen (1996) further distinguishes between welfare states on the basis of commitment to equality, income redistribution, level of benefits, and inclusiveness of beneficiaries, along with the degree of political power exercised by labor unions and social democratic political parties. The ''universal'' welfare states of the Scandinavian countries, where social democratic parties dominated government in the first three decades after World War II, are examples of the most ambitious systems in this regard. Here egalitarian principles tended to support policies with more generous benefits available universally without necessarily requiring either means-testing or worker contributions. Germany, France, and Italy, where parties of the Left had less influence during this period, are seen as examples of a second ''conservative welfare state'' category in which the welfare provisions, while substantial, are tolerant of the persistence of class and status differences. The United States falls into a third category of ''liberal'' welfare states in which benefits are more limited both in substance and in scope of beneficiaries. Contemporary opinion polls have revealed patterns of public opinion, policy preferences, and ideologies supporting differences between national welfare state systems (Smith, 1987).

THE BACKLASH AGAINST THE WELFARE STATE

By different margins and with somewhat different timing, by the early 1980s, majorities of voters in the United States and many European countries, including the United Kingdom, Germany, France, and even Sweden, apparently supported efforts to control or reduce entitlements and public spending in general. Majority support appeared to shift from parties of the Left to conservative alternatives whose leaders were committed to cutbacks or reversals of welfare state programs. The Swedish Social Democrats lost control of the government in 1976, after dominating national politics since 1932. Margaret Thatcher led the Conservatives to victory in the United Kingdom in 1979 and government control until 1997. Ronald Reagan was elected president in the United States in 1980, reelected in 1984, and was succeeded by his vice president and fellow Republican George Bush in 1988. After thirteen years of liberal-social democratic government in Germany, Helmut Kohl became head of government in 1982 with a conservative-liberal coalition supported by voters in elections the next year and in three subsequent rounds of national elections. France would seem to provide an exception to this movement to the Right: Socialist François Mitterand ended the over two-decade-long neo-Gaullist era with his election as president in 1981 and the accompanying socialist victory in the National Assembly. But by 1986, the socialist majority in the National Assembly was lost to conservative forces, and Mitterand was forced into the first Fifth Republic experience of "cohabitation" with then Prime Minister Jacques Chirac and the new neo-Gaullist parliamentary majority.

Criticism of the welfare state systems was based in large part on financial considerations tied to steadily rising levels of expenditures. Two leading sectors of welfare state entitlements, those tied to old age insurance and medical coverage, were directly affected by patterns of increasing longevity throughout the advanced industrial societies and more advanced and more expensive medical treatment technologies. Higher expenditures led to greater revenue needs, largely met through higher levels of taxation, which tended not to be universally acclaimed, but also through deficit spending. Other entitlement programs were seen by some as contributing to unexpected and undesirable forms of dependency, workplace absenteeism, and diminished levels of labor productivity. In the late 1970s and early 1980s, the global economy experienced the recession that advanced industrial countries all shared in. Reduced tax revenues further burdened the welfare state systems. Additionally, welfare state policies and entitlement programs were seen by some not only as socially destructive and fiscally burdensome policies within the nation-state but as liabilities for societies in the competitive context of international economic interdependence.

Taxes and legally mandated nontax contributions from employers increased the cost of labor. Governments with high welfare state expenditures had less funds to offer in support of research and development and other subsidies to the private sector. Esping-Andersen (1996) summarizes these "diagnoses of welfare state crisis" as the critique tied to the long-term effect of population aging, the "market distortion" view, and the perspective based on "the consequences of the new global economy, which mercilessly punishes profligate governments and uncompetitive economies," and he grants a certain validity to all three perspectives.

Economic and political criticism generated policy attacks and calls for retrenchment via-à-vis the welfare state throughout advanced industrial societies. In European countries, the challenges to the welfare state arose at first largely on a national basis in the late 1970s and 1980s, then came prominently to be tied in the 1990s to the economic belt-tightening associated with consolidation and advancement of the European Union (Dinan, 1994). In the United States, the critique was articulated dramatically by the administration of Ronald Reagan and carried on, if less vocally, by his successor, George Bush. After the 1992 election of President Bill Clinton, a Democrat, plans to reform the existing welfare state and entitlement programs were under review by his administration, but the attack more broadly was continued by members of the "Republican Revolution" before and after their takeover of the U.S. Congress in 1994.

Differences between national welfare systems manifested themselves to some degree in the timing and severity of the anti–welfare state backlash. Nevertheless, given the literature on differences among countries and welfare state programs, it is the parallels in the problems associated with the programs and, at the same time, the relatively limited effects of the instances of backlash that are striking.

Notably, electoral challenges to the welfare state came earliest in countries with the most substantial programs. Sweden, where the Social Democrats had effectively dominated the government since 1932, provided a signal contribution to the pattern when the parliamentary elections led to a moderate-conservative government coalition under Prime Minister Thorbjörn Fälldin in 1976. The Social Democrats made up the opposition for the next six years, until their return to effective power in 1982, losing their place again in 1991 and regaining it in 1994. The Swedish approach to the welfare state is distinctive because of "comprehensive, universalistic, and generous" programs but also because of its commitment to maximizing employment through public sector hiring (Esping-Andersen, 1996; Stephens, 1996). The system, funded by relatively high levels of taxation, was strained under conditions of reduced economic growth. Popular support wavered, as evidenced in part by the electoral history, but reforms introduced by parties of both the Right and the Left have been characterized more as adjustments than as fundamental changes or reversals in policy (Pierson, 1996; Stephens, 1996).

Prime Minister Margaret Thatcher's attack on the United Kingdom's welfare state, initiated in 1979 and carried on through the 1980s, stands out for its extreme form and in the substantial powers available to implement her policies in the context of the British constitutional system. Thatcher, in particular, pursued privatization of publicly owned properties. Her policy was actually quite well received by those directly affected in one area, especially, the sale of public housing to tenant residents. On the other hand, her consideration of privatizing part or all of the very popular National Health System was enormously unpopular and did not go anywhere. Polls showed revival of support for welfare state policies in general within the first years of her government, and Thatcher's efforts to undermine the welfare state at the local level by changing the local tax system contributed in particular to her downfall (Shapiro and Young, 1989; Pierson, 1996). While Thatcher's successor, John Major, softened the tone of Conservative positions, the orientation of his government was very much in the Thatcher style, including a continued unwillingness to commit the United Kingdom to the "Social Charter" provisions of the European Union's Maastricht Treaty. Nonetheless, Pierson (1996) argues that toward the end of the Major administration, the changes in the British welfare state were still not substantial.

While François Mitterand's election as president of France in 1981 and the related Socialist majority in the National Assembly pointed in a different direction, the legislative majority was lost to a conservative coalition five short years later while Mitterand was still in office. Mitterand was reelected president three years later, and a Socialist minority government was formed after new legislative elections, but conservatives gained a 465-seat majority after National Assembly elections in 1993. Support for enhancing the French welfare state during this period might well be called mixed, as conservatives showed strength in the two parliamentary victories of 1986 and 1991 and, more recently, in Jacques Chirac's election as president in 1995. The Socialists struggled against trends of an increasingly competitive and constrictive global economic environment, which worked against increased public spending, and a contentious electorate divided between demanding supporters and anxious critics. The Socialists functioned under a particularly heavy burden of high expectations, coming to power in 1981 after 23 years of conservative government in France's Fifth Republic. The ambitious scope of programs for change in the early years of Mitterand's first term may have contributed to support for the opposition.

The 1995 election of neo-Gaullist Jacques Chirac as president of France might have been taken as a definitive reorientation of French politics to the Right. Promising jobs to voters troubled by high unemployment through solutions tied to the private sector, he was not the candidate of the welfare state; but it is not at all clear that his electoral success came from this. In fact, Chirac's attacks on the welfare state, implemented by his prime minister, Alain Juppe, readily engulfed the new conservative regime and the country in strikes and popular discord. The justification of these policies by the president and prime minister on the basis of the French commitment to achieving standards set for a common European Union currency and ''Economic and Monetary Union'' was not adequate to quiet widespread and debilitating opposition.

In Germany the challenges to the welfare state came later and somewhat more gently than in many other states.[4] Helmut Kohl had been the chancellor of a moderate-conservative coalition of conservatives and liberals since 1982. Although there were initiatives to benefit the private sector and some departures from programs and levels of spending of the previous Social Democratic administrations under Helmut Schmidt and, before him, Willy Brandt, until recently Kohl's coalition government essentially maintained the ''social market economy'' perspective set out by its partisan forefathers for the Federal Republic in the early post–World War II years. The German economy had been the strongest in Europe, and despite an increasingly lively partisan scene in national politics, the underlying impulses and institutions of consultation and consensualism all helped to maintain the viability of the substantial German welfare state system (Wilensky, 1981). Nevertheless, the costs of the country's entitlement programs rose particularly rapidly in recent years to impose difficult levels of economic strain and budget deficits in the 1990s.

Germany had not escaped the problems of human longevity and high-cost labor and recession-related unemployment that challenged the welfare state systems of other advanced industrial societies. But the country's welfare system was additionally burdened by high numbers of political asylum-seekers and immigrants, particularly families of "guest workers," initially recruited from abroad in the 1960s, and ethnic Germans from Eastern Europe and the former Soviet Union. Even more significantly, the unification of East Germany with the Federal Republic in October 1990 meant that a new population group making limited revenue contributions to public and private welfare programs brought very substantial new demands on the welfare system, spurred by high levels of unemployment. At the same time, Germany, like France, had been falling short of meeting the standards set for the Economic and Monetary Union processes of the European Union, which generally called for cuts in public spending, not increases. Entitlement programs were adjusted to gain savings through measures supported by characteristic consultation between the government and representatives of all affected interests; however, the welfare system in the mid-1990s remained basically unchanged in Germany (Pierson, 1996).

In the "liberal" welfare state of the United States, policy in opposition to existing programs came about more through the Reagan and Bush administrations' support for the private sector and neglect of public programs than through actual changes in the latter. On the one hand, the favor of those governments for the private sector and market forces contributed to substantial growth in the 1980s of income and wealth discrepancies. Through government inaction, the "relative value" of benefits through the two major public programs for the nonelderly—Aid to Families with Dependent Children (AFDC) and Unemployment Insurance—declined (Esping-Andersen, 1996; Myles, 1996). While reducing the costs of the major welfare programs of Social Security and Medicare was increasingly at issue, the fate of other entitlement programs appeared more directly threatened by the Republican Party resurgence in the early years of the Clinton presidency. Myles (1996) argues that the low level of electoral participation of low-wage workers and minorities in the United States, the particularly diminished influence of labor unions, and the relative lack of power of inner-city mayors all contributed to a "democracy deficit" tied to these issues. This, along with the persistence of race as a political issue with a strong association for some with welfare programs, as well as the continuing fiscal constraints on the state, all suggested a further decline in welfare state programs in the United States.

PERSISTENCE OF POPULAR SUPPORT FOR THE WELFARE STATE

While there appeared to be a backlash against the welfare state in the United States and European countries in the late 1970s and 1980s, the picture, as described above, is not clear, and exactly what was happening has been debated. A fundamental point, as frequently noted, is that relatively little actually changed in entitlement policies and funding levels (Esping-Andersen, 1996; Pierson,

1996). Another point is that while government elites announced the prospect of policy change, to what extent the policy initiatives were broadly favored by voters is uncertain. It has been argued that while votes were cast for leadership favoring rolling back welfare policies, public support for the broad idea of the welfare state and component policies was maintained in a relatively stable fashion (Wilensky, 1981; Shapiro and Young, 1989; Papadakis, 1992; Papadakis and Bean, 1993; Pierson, 1996).

As alternatives to objections to welfare state policies, popular discontent might have been based on particular methods or forms of taxation, high levels of government spending in general as opposed to government spending on welfare policies per se, or perceived inefficiencies or even oppressiveness of government operations (Shapiro and Young, 1989). Shapiro and Young, along with Pierson, argue that renewed support for maintaining welfare state commitments to entitlements was in fact stimulated precisely by efforts on the part of political leadership to remove entitlements increasingly relevant to growing segments of national electorates.[5] Pierson argues that the "negativity bias" of welfare state beneficiaries increased readiness to oppose cutbacks, especially given these groups' concentrated interests in contrast to the more diffuse and uncertain societal gains tied to proposed reductions. He also emphasizes the enormous expansion in the number of individuals and groups in advanced industrial societies affected by the various welfare programs: large new constituencies, sensitive to the prospect of loss, vocal, and electorally active (Pierson, 1996; also see Kosonen, 1992). Electoral contests and policy debates in the mid-1990s show shifts in public choice away from leadership committed to reducing the welfare state.

In Europe, confrontation over the welfare state took on new intensity in the context of the European Union evolution, which gained renewed momentum with the implementation in the early 1990s of the European Single Market and the Maastricht Treaty. These developments included efforts to generate systems of welfare state standards and institutions for Europe as a whole, but the undertaking was still in process and not without controversy, as illustrated by the unwillingness of the government of John Major to sign the Social Charter of the Maastricht Treaty (Leibfried and Pierson, 1995). More readily apparent were the potential constraints that the European Union presented to the independence of welfare state arrangements in any given member state.

Standardization of taxation and entitlements to avoid market distortions and the prospect of moving toward the lowest common denominator represented a difficult scenario for societies with more elaborate programs (Kosonen, 1992). More specifically, it was in movement toward Economic and Monetary Union and the creation of a common European currency, the *Euro*, to be implemented in January 1999, that tensions over reducing or maintaining welfare state systems came to a newly pronounced pitch. While there had been progress toward realizing these ambitious goals of "ever closer union," development in the mid-1990s revealed previously unimagined obstacles of various sorts tied to the economies of the member states and the moods of public opinion. Challenges were most pronounced in three larger members of the European Union, the United Kingdom, France, and Germany, although developments in Sweden—as of January 1996 one of the three newest members of the European Union— were also related to this phenomenon.

In Sweden, one of the Nordic European countries in which the anti–welfare state backlash came earliest, the holding power of welfare state programs was also revealed relatively promptly. There was little departure from the status quo during the three moderate conservative governments between 1976 and 1982. At the height of the backlash elsewhere, the Social Democrats once again guided the Swedish government for nine years from 1982 to 1991. While they were out for four years, the welfare state was not dismantled, and the Social Democrats regained power in 1994. Sweden's economic problems and those of its entitlement programs were exacerbated in the early 1990s as the country began being reoriented for changes in the global economy and membership in the European Union. Part of the formula contributing to Sweden's past successes had been the consensually oriented relations between different interest groups, including business and labor, and government actors in what has been referred to as a corporatist or neocorporatist system (Wilensky, 1981). While still present, this system had been weakened over the past two decades by both public and private efforts to deal with repercussions of the domestic welfare state and a changing international economic environment (Stephens, 1996). Changed government policies allowed for new capital movement, and companies gave new attention to trimming costs and pursuing competitive stature. Government revenues were increasingly strained to meet obligations growing rapidly from an already very expansive base of welfare state expenditures. Yet even during the latest period of conservative government, welfare state programs were left essentially intact. Pierson (1996) notes that public opinion polls showed "overwhelming" support for maintaining existing levels of social spending in 1992, and in 1994, the Social Democratic Party was returned to power with "one of its highest vote totals ever."

In the United Kingdom, eighteen years of Conservative Party government came to an end on May 1, 1997, when the British voters gave the Labor Party, led by Anthony Blair, an overwhelming majority in the House of Commons. Defeated Prime Minister John Major was not particularly popular but was forced by the constitution to call the election no more than five full years since the last. Many measures of the economy lent themselves to his party's electoral prospects: GNP was up, and unemployment was down. The Conservatives carried the burden of being the familiar, long-term incumbents; they suffered from a series of embarrassing scandals and division within the party over relations with the European Union. Nonetheless, ultimately John Major also remained the standard-bearer of a welfare state cutback policy, privatization, and the rearrangement of British society with a growing discrepancy between rich and poor and greater austerity for those in between. Tony Blair, the new prime minister, was not an advocate of the traditional welfare state. Blair's campaign was for a "new Labor" party that he promised would leave behind much of the party's past ideological commitments and that he asserted in many ways would proceed without departure from policies of the Conservative Party. Nevertheless, he *was* the leader of the Labor Party, "new" or not, and Labor's victory brought Conservative rule to an end and passed control of the government to the party more closely identified with welfare state policies and entitlements.

While the European Union became an issue toward the end of the brief campaign period, it was not a substantial one and did not figure directly in the political debate of the elections. The positions of the two major parties hardly differed on Europe, broadly speaking, except that the Labor Party favored Britain's acceptance of the Social Charter agreement, which the Conservative government had refused to endorse. Despite the wariness of the government of John Major concerning the European Union and the outright rejection of the Union by many of his Conservative Party associates, the issue was more one of nationalism than one of economic policy. The economic policies of the Thatcher and Major governments, which had aimed for reduced public spending and support for the free market, happened to have been quite consistent with the standards targeted for Economic and Monetary Union and had brought the British economy, with a predicted 1997 budget deficit below 3 percent of GDP, to a relatively good position for future cooperation with its fellow European Union member states. The campaign of Tony Blair and the Labor Party tried to minimize its criticism of Conservative Party economic policies, yet indirectly, these policies, with their inherent fit for Economic and Monetary Union advancement, provided some of the basis for the Labor Party's victory, given the burdens imposed on Labor's traditional working-class constituency, as well as elements of the middle class.

While the Conservative defeat in the United Kingdom was anticipated, the outcome of the British elections was still startling in its scope and, inevitably, in its basic element of change. Elections in France were not expected at all in 1997, and yet they came about, with completely unexpected, disastrous results for the conservative government under President Jacques Chirac. When Chirac became president in 1995, he inherited a substantial conservative majority in the National Assembly, which had been elected in 1993. Passage of any proposals initiated by the government of Chirac's appointed prime minister, Alain Juppe, was essentially assured. Principal policy goals were reduced government expenditures, in general, and reductions in the cost of France's extensive welfare state programs, in particular.

As the government of one of the major member states of the European Union, the Chirac-Juppe administration saw meeting the standards for the common currency project to be a goal of primary importance. Out of several requirements, however, a 1997 budget deficit no greater than 3 percent of GDP turned out to be particularly unlikely to be achieved for France (as for most of the other European Union states). The path Chirac and Juppe wished to follow, by cutting government outlays for the public sector and entitlement programs, while at the same time reducing access to benefits by tightening requirements or postponing eligibility, generated protests, strikes, and intense public hostility in the fall of 1995, within the first months of the new president's accession to power. In spite of the institutional evidence of conservative dominance in French politics and government, the popular political mood revealed itself to be quite difficult. The government backed down in the confrontation. The scenario repeated itself in 1996, while the deadline for meeting the European Union standards came nearer. High unemployment, reaching 12.8 percent in early 1997, turned more people toward public programs just as the government attempted to reduce costs. New legislative elections would normally not have taken place until 1998, but Chirac decided a fresh popular mandate for the conservative agenda was needed to allow his government to implement the reforms and cutbacks that were being so actively resisted. It was within his constitutional powers to call new elections, and he did. The opposition parties attacked the government precisely for the austerity measures and the priority given to European monetary union. After the second round of voting for the National Assembly on June 1, 1997, the Socialists came close to a majority and were able to achieve one through a coalition with the Communists and the environmentalist Green Party. President Chirac, far from having achieved a new mandate, appointed Socialist Lionel Jospin as his new prime minister.

In the case of Germany, there were no recent national election returns at the time of this writing to provide a clear measure of the popular mood on welfare state cutbacks, but the situation of the ruling coalition under Chancellor Helmut Kohl was not happy. Unemployment in early 1997 was 12.2 percent nationwide. The federal government had allocated and spent very substantial funds for eastern Germany, but unemployment in that region was still over 20 percent. In a familiar pattern in the context of this chapter, demands on government programs increased at precisely the same time efforts were being redoubled to reduce public expenditures, and deficit spending increased. Employees in the country's large public sector protested throughout the summer of 1996 against proposed changes in working conditions, rates of wage increases, and benefits. Germany, the economic powerhouse of the European Union, would probably not meet the 3 percent requirement for 1997 budget deficit compared to GDP, and the majority of the German public was apparently pleased with neither Chancellor Kohl nor the European monetary union project. In early 1997, more than half of all Germans were opposed to the introduction of the new European currency, and opinion polls showed leaders of the Social Democratic Party, the principal opposition party, more popular than the chancellor.

The Social Democrats, in opposition since 1982, noted the success of the British Labor Party and France's Socialists and hoped to emulate it. The previous parliamentary elections in Germany were held in 1994. An electorate increasingly concerned over the financial burdens of unification and the early signals from the Kohl government of welfare state cutbacks once again gave a majority to the conservative-liberal coalition, but with a margin of only ten seats in the Bundestag, the lower house of Parliament that elects the chancellor. The next elections were held in the fall of 1998. Chancellor Kohl announced he would lead his party for the fifth time in the contest for seats in the Bundestag and control of government. He remained committed to current goals of the European Union, including the Euro, and the austerity measures required to implement them. The Social Democrats had to choose between a traditional left strategy, like that of France's Socialists, and a more centrist one, like that of Britain's "new Labor" Party. As it turned out they argued for the maintenance, if not the elaboration, of the welfare state and entitlement programs. Receiving the plurality of the vote, the Social Democrats won the right to form the new government, headed by Gerhard Schröder.

In the United States, the tensions generated by welfare state cutbacks, proposed or implemented, were not as substantial as in the European countries. In large part this was because the more vocal debate was over the relatively small income maintenance programs, like AFDC, while political elites tried to avoid significant reforms of the far more ample Social Security and Medicare entitlement systems (Myles, 1996). Yet while Americans were seen to be critical of the tax burden and government intervention associated with the welfare state, they also showed support for maintaining certain entitlement programs (Shapiro and Young, 1989; Pierson, 1996; Uchitelle, 1997). Clinton's first election in 1992 could hardly be taken as a clear mandate for the welfare state, but it did take the presidency from incumbent George Bush, Ronald Reagan's Republican successor, and gave it to Clinton and the political party more closely associated with welfare state policies. Clinton was dealt heavy blows during his first term in office, inter alia, by the defeat of his initiative on health insurance reform and by the Republican congressional victories in 1994, which intensified the condition of confrontation in the muted ideological context of American politics. The maintenance and even improvement of the Republican congressional majorities and Clinton's reelection in 1996 conveyed a mixed message for the popularity of a "liberal" agenda in the United States. Just before the election and with wide criticism from spokespeople for program beneficiaries and many of his own supporters, Clinton signed into law major changes in federal government welfare policies.

Nevertheless, in a clear-cut commitment to the most popular entitlement programs, candidate Clinton emphasized in his reelection campaign that while government expenditures had to be controlled, commitments to Social Security, Medicare and Medicaid, education, and the environment had to be protected. These positions were hallmarks for his candidacy, however little he distinguished himself in other ways from Republican challenger Senator Bob Dole.

Clinton's reelection might have been taken as a popularly imposed limitation on the proposals of the Republican leadership and perceived threats to entitlements. On the one hand, he received the endorsement of the voters. On the other, the Republicans were unable to capitalize on the popular support that gave them, once again, control of both houses of Congress. While Clinton's agreement to further modifications in the American welfare state is not unimaginable, his election and reelection, at a time of Republican resurgence, evidenced popular favor for the stand that he and his party were perceived to have taken in favor of protecting entitlement programs.

CONCLUSION

In their discussion of comparative public opinion and the welfare state, Shapiro and Young (1989) cite the lack of research on "the degree or frequency of the influence of public preferences on policies, a matter central to theories about democracy" (p. 85). Heidenheimer, Heclo, and Adams (1983) emphasize that the welfare state is a context in which to study "the politics of social choice." Public opinion, democracy, and choice are prominent variables in the latest developments discussed above, shown to deserve continued and increased research. In spite of differences in national approaches to the welfare state, popular majorities have recently opted along roughly similar lines for maintaining entitlements rather than closing them off.

While the "choices" are not totally clear-cut and might well be debated, all differing welfare state system variants display movement along this pattern: the European Nordic "universal" systems, as in the instance of Sweden, the "conservative" systems, as in France and Germany, and even the "liberal" systems, as in Great Britain and the United States. The case of the welfare state suggests evidence for the autonomy of popular sentiment vis-à-vis elite policy making, the vitality of electoral systems, and the potential for policy tension between elite and popular preferences in advanced industrial societies at the end of the twentieth century.

What appears to be the case for now is that the 1990s may be a period of maintenance and moderate readjustment of the policies of welfare state systems and entitlement programs rather than a time for their substantial reduction, as intended by some conservative political leaders. Governments that do otherwise will risk the censure of disappointed voters. The challenge remains for governments to function effectively, responding to constituent demands and preserving popular entitlement programs while dealing with economic problems associated with welfare state policies.

NOTES

1. The idea of voters having become committed to entitlements and reluctant to see these eroded, in spite of popular and elite criticism of the related tax burden, offers a straightforward political basis for maintaining and possibly even enhancing the welfare state. This point is fundamental for Pierson's treatment of the new difficulties in the politics of welfare state retrenchment (Pierson, 1996). Pierson contrasts understanding the retrenchment process with various explanations for welfare state development. For an earlier review and consolidation of explanatory theories, see Uusitalo (1984).

2. The period corresponds to the one Esping-Andersen refers to as "capitalism's postwar 'Golden Age' " (Esping-Andersen, 1996).

3. For a current look at the three most broadly accepted explanations for the development of welfare state systems, see Pierson (1996); and for a brief overview of the welfare programs in the United States and Canada, specifically, see Myles (1996).

4. Wilensky attributes the successes of certain societies in managing ostensible "crises" of the welfare state to the presence of neocorporatist institutions. He includes Sweden and Germany in this category of "corporatist democracies," while he considers the United States and the United Kingdom to fall into a contrasting category of "fragmented and decentralized political economies" (Wilensky, 1981). Esping-Andersen also emphasizes the corporatist nature of his "conservative" welfare state category, which includes France and Germany but not Sweden (Esping-Andersen, 1990).

5. This finding, which is noted frequently (e.g., Shapiro and Young, 1989; Esping-Andersen, 1996; Pierson, 1996), points to a major obstacle to one approach suggested to reducing entitlement expenditures: cutting benefits to middle-class and better-off recipients in order to target increasingly scarce resources on the poor and sick (see Snower, 1993).

REFERENCES

Dinan, Desmond. 1994. *Ever Closer Union? An Introduction to the European Community*. Boulder, Colo.: Lynne Rienner Publishers.

Esping-Andersen, Gøsta. 1990. *The Three Worlds of Welfare Capitalism*. Princeton, N.J.: Princeton University Press.

———. 1996. "After the Golden Age? Welfare State Dilemmas in a Global Economy." In Gøsta Esping-Andersen, ed., *Welfare States in Transition: National Adaptations in Global Economies*. London: Sage Publications, pp. 1–31.

Flora, Peter, and Arnold J. Heidenheimer, eds. 1981. *The Development of Welfare States in Europe and America*. New Brunswick, N.J.: Transaction Books.

Furniss, Norman, and Timothy Tilton. 1977. *The Case for the Welfare State: From Social Security to Social Equality*. Bloomington: Indiana University Press.

Hague, Rod, Martin Harrop, and Shaun Breslin. 1992. *Political Science: A Comparative Introduction*. New York: St. Martin's Press.

Heidenheimer, Arnold J., Hugh Heclo, and Carolyn Teich Adams. 1983. *Comparative Public Policy: The Politics of Social Choice in Europe and America*, 2nd ed. New York: St. Martin's Press.

"Insecure or Jobless, Europeans Renew Protests." 1997. *New York Times*, March 25, p. D4.

Kosonen, Pekka. 1992. "National Welfare State Models in the Face of European Integration." *History of European Ideas*, Vol., 15, pp. 47–54.

Krieger, Joel. 1986. *Reagan, Thatcher, and the Politics of Decline*. New York: Oxford University Press.

Leibfried, Stephan, and Paul Pierson, eds. 1995. *European Social Policy: Between Fragmentation and Integration*. Washington, D.C.: Brookings Institution.

Myles, John. 1996. "When Markets Fail: Social Welfare in Canada and the United States." In Gøsta Esping-Andersen, ed., *Welfare States in Transition: National Adaptations in Global Economies*. London: Sage Publications, pp. 116–140.

Organization for Economic Cooperation and Development (OECD). 1981. *The Welfare State in Crisis.* Paris: OECD.

Papadakis, Elim. March 1992. "Public Opinion, Public Policy, and the Welfare State." *Political Studies*, Vol. 40, pp. 21–37.

Papadakis, Elim, and Clive Bean. 1993. "Public Support for the Welfare State: A Comparison between Institutional Regimes." *Journal of Public Policy*, Vol. 13, No. 3, pp. 227–254.

Pierson, Paul. 1994. *Dismantling the Welfare State: Reagan, Thatcher, and the Politics of Retrenchment.* Cambridge: Cambridge University Press.

———. January 1996. "The New Politics of the Welfare State." *World Politics*, Vol. 48, pp. 143–179.

Shapiro, Robert Y., and John T. Young. 1989. "Public Opinion and the Welfare State: The United States in Comparative Perspective." *Political Science Quarterly*, Vol. 104, pp. 59–89.

Siegel, Richard L., and Leonard B. Weinberg. 1977. *Comparing Public Policies: United States, Soviet Union, and Europe.* Homewood, Ill.: Dorsey Press.

Smith, Tom W. 1987. "The Welfare State in Cross-National Perspective." *Public Opinion Quarterly*, Vol. 51, pp. 404–421.

Snower, Dennis J. May 1993. "The Future of the Welfare State." *Economic Journal*, Vol. 103, pp. 700–717.

Stephens, John D. 1996. "The Scandinavian Welfare States: Achievements, Crisis, and Prospects." In Gøsta Esping-Andersen, ed., *Welfare States in Transition: National Adaptations in Global Economies.* London: Sage Publications, pp. 66–87.

Uchitelle, Louis. 1997. "The Shift toward Self-reliance in the Welfare System." *New York Times*, January 13, p. A15.

Uusitalo, Hannu. 1984. "Comparative Research on the Determinants of the Welfare State: The State of the Art." *European Journal of Political Research*, Vol. 12, No. 4, pp. 403–422.

Wilensky, Harold L. 1975. *The Welfare State and Equality: Structural and Ideological Roots of Public Expenditures.* Berkeley: University of California Press.

———. 1981. "Democratic Corporatism, Consensus and Social Policy: Reflections on Changing Values and the 'Crisis' of the Welfare State." In OECD, *The Welfare State in Crisis.* Paris: OECD, pp. 185–195.

Chapter 12

Wherefore a Prudent Fiscal Policy?

HERSCHEL I. GROSSMAN

Both professional and popular commentators in the United States express obsessive concern about the growth of the public debt. This hand-wringing about budget deficits might be appropriate if the United States were at the brink of a fiscal disaster. The reality, however, is that the United States has pursued, and continues to pursue, a prudent fiscal policy. Most important, the public credit remains sound. The government continues to roll over its existing debt and continues to be able to issue new debt with no difficulty. The markets still regard U.S. government securities to be the benchmark risk-free asset. The markets have never thought that the budget deficit has been out of control or that the burden of debt servicing has threatened to become so large that the U.S. government would succumb to the temptation to repudiate its debts.

To what can we attribute the continued prudence of American fiscal policy? This question probably has a different answer in the present than it had in the past. In recent years the traditional rationale for limiting the size of the public debt, based on cycles of war and peace and of depression and prosperity, probably has lost much of its relevance. Nevertheless, fiscal policy in the United States has remained under control mainly because the American public harbors warranted fear of the potential consequences of an imprudent fiscal policy. The alarmist tone of the ongoing discussion about budget deficits and the public debt reflects, and also reinforces, the public's perceptions about the dangers of fiscal imprudence.

THE TRADITIONAL NORMATIVE THEORY OF PUBLIC DEBT

The traditional normative theory of public debt offers the following prescription for a prudent fiscal policy: A government should borrow whenever either its spending is temporarily high or its tax revenues are temporarily low.[1] Temporarily high government spending is most often associated with times of war but also can occur in times of economic depression, when the government is called on to relieve hardship. Temporarily low tax revenues can occur in times of either war or economic depression when the government's tax base is temporarily reduced.

The traditional theory also prescribes that in times of peace and prosperity the government should run budget surpluses and reduce the public debt. This prescription is an essential part of a prudent fiscal policy because all borrowers, even governments, face a potential ceiling on the amount of debt that they can incur. Lenders do not allow borrowers to incur unlimited amounts of debt because lenders know that no borrower would be able to resist the temptation to repudiate its debts, were its debt burden to become large enough. Reducing the public debt in times of peace and prosperity maximizes a government's ability to incur new debts during the next war or depression. For a growing economy the traditional theory generalizes to the prescription that the government should allow the public debt to grow relative to national income during wars or depressions but should reduce the public debt relative to national income in times of peace and prosperity.

In the traditional theory the possibility of incurring public debt is most important in a major war in which the government wants to spend on the war effort an amount that exceeds the maximum current revenue that it can obtain from taxation. In such a case, borrowing enables war spending to avoid the constraint on tax revenue implied by the Laffer curve. In some historical wars, a government's ability to borrow has been critical not only for avoiding defeat but also for securing the very survival of the state. For example, in his discussion of the Napoleonic Wars, French historian Fernand Braudel concludes, "The national debt was the major reason for the British victory. It had placed huge sums of money at England's disposal at the very moment when she required them" (Braudel, 1984, p. 384) Similarly, Keynes wrote in 1916, "If we go on giving the army what they want longer than the Germans can do this for theirs, we may *appear* to win by military prowess. But we really shall have won by financial prowess" (Johnson, 1971, Vol. 16, p. 187). Or as Alexander Hamilton wrote in 1795 in his famous "Second Report on Public Credit," "There can be no time, no state of things, in which credit is not essential to a nation, especially as nations in general continue to use it as a resource of war" (Syrett, 1961, Vol. 18, p. 125).

The traditional theory also allows a government to incur public debt in small wars and depressions even if by increasing tax rates it could raise sufficient tax revenue to pay for its desired spending. In these cases the purpose of borrowing is to mitigate the need to increase taxes to pay for a temporary increase in spending. The traditional theory would even permit incurring debt to allow a reduction in tax rates during a depression. The rationale for minimizing increases in taxes during wars and perhaps even reducing taxes in depressions is that such a policy would help to smooth the disposable incomes of taxpayers over time. Smoothing of disposable income is desirable because taxpayers typically prefer a constant stream of income and consumption to a fluctuating stream with the same average value. This preference reflects diminishing marginal utility of consumption.[2]

Under the traditional theory, paying off debts that were incurred during a war or depression requires a government to keep taxes higher than would otherwise be necessary when peace and prosperity return. The traditional theory prescribes that taxes should be kept permanently high enough to pay for the government's spending over the cycle of war and peace and over the cycle of depression and prosperity.

THE HISTORY OF THE AMERICAN PUBLIC DEBT

The traditional normative theory of public debt not only provides a prescription for fiscal policy, but it also describes the fiscal policy that the United States actually has followed for most of its history. Until recent years the U.S. federal government borrowed large amounts only during major wars and during the Great Depression. During all other times the American public debt decreased, at least relative to national income.[3]

It is also noteworthy that despite the importance of Keynesian ideas in academic and political discussions of fiscal policy from the 1930s until the 1970s the history of the public debt in the United States, as well as in Great Britain, during this period is explicable without any reference to Keynesian economics. In his classic study *The Fiscal Revolution in America* (1969), Herbert Stein claims that "by the time that tax cut of 1964 was enacted, budget balancing had ceased to have an important influence on fiscal decisions and compensatory finance had taken its place as standard doctrine and major, though by no means exclusive, determinant of action" (p. 454). But the Keynesian "fiscal revolution" to which Stein refers is not apparent in the historical data.

At first glance it might appear that American fiscal policy violated the prescriptions of the traditional theory when the government continued to allow the public debt to increase relative to national income after the major recession of 1981–1982 had ended. But this impression is superficial. Most of the decade of the 1980s, although a time of prosperity, also was a period of intense cold war, with higher military spending than in the years either immediately before or after. Military spending steadily increased from 4.7 percent of gross national product (GNP) in 1979 to 6.3 percent of GNP in 1986 but then began decreasing. By 1996, military spending was only 3.6 percent of GNP. At the same time, the budget deficit remained above 5 percent of GNP through 1986, but by the end of the decade of the 1980s, when the Cold War abated, the budget deficit had decreased to less than 3 percent of GNP, and the outstanding public debt leveled off at about 40 percent of annual GNP. Thus, the increases in the public debt during the 1980s seem to be in large part consistent with the traditional prescription for borrowing to finance a temporarily high level of war spending, albeit in this case spending to fight a cold war rather than a hot war.

The experience of the first half of the 1990s is more difficult to reconcile with the traditional theory. During these years, a period of unambiguous prosperity and peace, the budget deficit reached almost 5 percent of GNP, and the outstanding public debt jumped to 50 percent of annual GNP. An increasing public debt relative to national income during a time in which national income has been growing and military spending has been decreasing is surely inconsistent with the prescriptions of the traditional normative theory of public debt.

From the perspective of the traditional theory, American fiscal policy during the first half of the 1990s seems to have been imprudent. By not reducing the public debt and the cost of debt servicing relative to national income in a period of peace and prosperity, the government seemed to be acting as if it was unconcerned about its ability to borrow during the next war or depression.

To rationalize this behavior, one might plausibly argue that the prescriptions of the traditional theory are no longer relevant. Given the current economic and political situation, what is the probability that the United States will experience a major war or depression anytime in the future? Although historical experience warns against the view that we need no longer worry about major wars or depressions, it is arguable that advances in knowledge and technology have brought us to an unprecedented age of permanent peace and prosperity. If a future major war or a future depression is indeed highly unlikely, then it may be appropriate for fiscal policy to pay little attention to the prescriptions of the traditional theory.

Another possibility is that the large budget deficits of the first half of the 1990s were only a temporary aberration. The stance of fiscal policy changed radically in the second half of the 1990s. The budget deficit began decreasing in 1993, and by 1997 was less than 2 percent of GNP. Also, by 1997 the outstanding public debt was decreasing relative to national income. By 1998, the budget deficit had disappeared, and the budget was in surplus.

It is true that economists are warning us that demographic developments could result in a fiscal crisis sometime in the twenty-first century. Indeed, it is easy to concoct doomsday scenarios in which the aging of the population and currently legislated entitlements, together with current tax rates, imply an infeasible explosion of public debt. But what is more noteworthy is that politicians and other policy makers are paying serious attention to these warnings. The fact that the political process is worrying about a potential problem a decade or more in advance and is considering actions to avert the problem before the problem materializes is a truly remarkable exhibition of fiscal prudence.

THE PUBLIC DEBT AND ECONOMIC GROWTH

Interestingly, in the intense discussion about fiscal policy in the United States, the prescriptions of the traditional normative theory of public debt are rarely, if ever, mentioned. Instead, "responsible" commentators, especially economists, have focused on a different concern about fiscal policy, which is that budget deficits gobble up national saving and crowd out investment and, as a result, stunt productivity and depress economic growth.

From an individualistic perspective this concern with national savings and investment seems unwarranted. Any household that thinks that its current consumption is too high relative to its expected future consumption opportunities can increase its own private saving and investing. For example, suppose that the government were to reduce current taxes and increase its current borrowing, and that this policy implies higher taxes in the future. Any taxpaying household that objects to this policy and that would prefer not to consume more now and not to consume less in the future can completely offset the effects of this policy simply by increasing its current saving by the amount by which its current taxes are reduced. In the simplest case, it can use this increase in saving to buy public debt, and then it can use the interest that it receives to pay the higher future taxes.

For many economists these observations about individual options are not decisive. They argue, either explicitly or implicitly, that economic growth generates positive externalities and, consequently, that savings, investment, and economic growth should not be left to the outcome of individual choices. As examples of such positive externalities one might plausibly cite national strength and influence as well as social harmony.[4]

But even if we accept this externalities argument, it alone does not seem to provide an operational criterion for fiscal policy. If economic growth is good, then how far should the fiscal policy go in promoting economic growth? Should the government attempt not only to reduce its current budget deficit but even to achieve large budget surpluses that it could use to finance increases in investment? If so, how large should these surpluses be?

ALWAYS POSTPONE TAXATION?

By appropriately adjusting its savings behavior over time an individual taxpaying household could insulate its time path of consumption from the time path of government borrowing and taxation. However, this possibility is not available to a household that must pay taxes now but that has either temporarily low income or temporarily high expenses and that is credit constrained—that is, that cannot borrow against the security of its future income. For such households, low taxes now are desirable, even though government borrowing implies higher taxes in the future, because low current taxes enable them, if they so choose, to increase current consumption at the expense of future consumption. Moreover, low taxes do not constrain anybody. Any taxpaying household that does not prefer higher consumption now and lower consumption in the future can get exactly the time path of consumption that it wants by increasing its own current savings.

These observations suggest that a policy of government borrowing to pay for current spending is desirable, because this policy postpones taxation and allows those that desire it the option of higher current consumption than if current spending were financed by current taxation. But like concern about economic growth, this argument also does not provide a sensible operational criterion for fiscal policy. If government borrowing, which allows people to put off paying taxes, is good, then why collect taxes at all as long as the government can borrow to finance its spending? Why should not the government just borrow as much as it can until its credit runs out?

In recent decades, some governments actually seem to have followed this strategy. Italy is an example, and the Italian experience reveals the negative consequences of such a fiscal policy. The Italian government seems to have come close to exhausting its credit. Once a government is close to exhausting its credit, it must make whatever drastic fiscal adjustments are necessary to balance its budget, regardless of the pain that these drastic adjustments inflict. In addition, it is difficult to predict and, hence, to plan for the time at which the government's credit will be exhausted. In practice, lenders will cut off the government's credit whenever they sense that further increases in the public debt might cause the government to succumb to the temptation to repudiate its debts. The strategy of borrowing until the government's credit runs out leaves national welfare at the mercy of capricious lenders.

UNDERSTANDING FISCAL POLICY

Although the ongoing discussion about fiscal policy in the United States pays little or no attention to the prescriptions of the traditional normative theory of public debt, this discussion also has not provided a clear substitute for the traditional normative theory as a prescription for fiscal policy. How, then, can we explain the prudence of fiscal policy in the United States? The preceding discussion suggests, as a plausible hypothesis, that American fiscal policy reflects a balancing in the popular consciousness of several considerations. Despite understandable popular preference for postponing taxation, it appears that the American public supports a fiscal policy that limits the growth of the public debt, probably for a combination of several reasons.

What are these reasons? First, the concerns implicit in the traditional theory probably still carry weight. In its current incarnation the traditional theory prescribes that the government should limit the growth of the public debt in times of peace and prosperity so that it will be able to increase its borrowing in the event, however unlikely, of a future war or depression. Second, the preaching of economists that the social benefits of investment exceed the private benefits and that government borrowing crowds out investment possibly has had some influence. Third, and probably most important, the American public apparently understands that unless fiscal policy limits the growth of the public debt, the government's credit will run out at some unpredictable future time. The public also apparently understands that were the government to exhaust its credit, the consequent fiscal adjustments would be both drastic and painful. Fiscal policy in the United States is under control mainly because the public is sufficiently forward looking to recognize the importance of a prudent fiscal policy.

NOTES

1. The traditional theory also allows the government to borrow to finance capital expenditures, with the presumption that depreciation of the public capital is fully included in current spending. The problem of constructing a capital account for the public sector makes it difficult to make this prescription operational. The present discussion abstracts from this part of the traditional theory.

2. Some theories of consumption behavior assume that, regardless of the time path of taxation, each taxpaying household can use private saving and borrowing to smooth its own consumption. If this assumption were true, then the government would have no reason to be concerned about smoothing disposable income. Theorists who take this assumption seriously have invented another reason for avoiding tax increases during wars and depressions. This reason is the desirability of smoothing the distortions to the economy, such as disincentives to work, that result from taxation. These theorists assume that a constant tax rate causes less distortion than a fluctuating tax rate with the same average level. See, for example, Barro (1979).

Although this argument for avoiding tax increases is clever, the need to invoke it is questionable, because the assumption that taxpaying households can smooth their own consumption does not seem to be true for many, or even most, households. In practice, people can borrow only limited amounts against the security of future income. Accordingly, the traditional concern with smoothing disposable income seems to provide a sufficient rationale for a fiscal policy that avoids tax increases during wars and depressions.

3. The total American public debt, which includes debts incurred by state and local governments, has a similar historical pattern. The present discussion focuses on the public debt incurred by the federal government.

The traditional theory also seems to describe actual British fiscal policy from the beginning of the eighteenth century up until the present. The United States and Great Britain are the only major sovereign states whose accumulated public debts were not wiped out either by explicit repudiation or by inflation at some point in the twentieth century. See Grossman (1990) for an analysis and interpretation of the history of the American and British public debts. Even in the American and British cases, inflation was responsible for much of the decrease in the real value of the public debt during the second half of the twentieth century.

4. Professor Benjamin Friedman has been one of the more articulate proponents of the argument that the U.S. government should borrow less in order to leave a larger part of national savings available to finance private investment. See, for example, Friedman (1988, 1993).

REFERENCES

Barro, Robert. October 1979. "On the Determination of Public Debt." *Journal of Political Economy*, Vol. 87, pp. 940–971.

Braudel, Fernand. 1984. *The Perspective of the World*, Vol. 3. Librairie Armand Colin, 1979; English translation, New York: Harper & Row.

Friedman, Benjamin M. 1988. *Day of Reckoning: The Consequences of American Economic Policy under Reagan and After*. New York: Random House.

————. 1993. "The Clinton Budget: Will It Do?" *New York Review*, July 15, pp. 37–41.

Grossman, Herschel. 1990. "The Political Economy of War Debt and Inflation." In W. S. Haraf and P. Cagan, eds., *Monetary Policy for a Changing Financial Environment*. Washington, D.C.: American Enterprise Institute.

Johnson, Elizabeth, ed. 1971. *The Collected Writings of John Maynard Keynes, Activities 1914–1919*, Vol. 16. London: Macmillan.

Stein, Herbert. 1969. *The Fiscal Revolution in America*. Chicago: University of Chicago Press.

Syrett, Harold C., ed. 1961. *The Papers of Alexander Hamilton*, Vol. 18. New York: Columbia University Press.

Chapter 13

The Size, Nature, and Causes of Budget Deficits in Developing Countries

JAMES ALM AND RAUL A. BARRETO

INTRODUCTION

In the last several decades, many countries around the world have experienced large and persistent budget deficits. The existence of these deficits has been particularly pronounced in developing countries.

In this chapter, we examine several dimensions of the deficit experience of developing countries over the last several decades: the size of the deficit, its nature, and its causes. Our central themes are threefold. First, there is enormous variation in the size of the deficit (relative to national income), both across countries and across time. Second, the economic effects of large and persistent deficits are surprisingly controversial and unresolved. And third, the causes of deficits seem to depend largely upon the political and other institutional arrangements in each specific country, rather than upon any farsighted optimizing behavior on the part of the government; a particularly important factor in the determination of fiscal deficits is the amount of corruption in the economy, with more corrupt economies associated with greater deficits.

THE SIZE OF BUDGET DEFICITS

There are several ways to measure the size of budget deficits (Buiter, 1983). Perhaps the simplest and most useful is the public sector borrowing requirement, or the excess of expenditure over revenue for all levels of government. Other measures correct for the inflation component of interest payments (the "operational deficit") or exclude all interest payments (the "primary deficit").

This section presents some evidence on the size of the budget deficit for a representative sample of developing countries from Africa, Asia, and Latin

America for the period 1971 to 1985. The budget deficit is measured as the excess of central government expenditure over its revenues and is expressed relative to gross domestic product (GDP). The countries examined include:

Africa: Algeria, Cameroon, Egypt, Ghana, Kenya, Liberia, Morocco, Nigeria, Zaire, Zimbabwe

Asia: India, Indonesia, Iran, Korea, Malaysia, Pakistan, Philippines, Singapore, Sri Lanka, Thailand, Turkey

Latin America: Argentina, Brazil, Chile, Dominican Republic, Colombia, Ecuador, Jamaica, Mexico, Nicaragua, Panama, Peru, Trinidad and Tobago, Uruguay, Venezuela

These countries are chosen in part because of the availability of information on variables that are included in the empirical analysis of the causes of deficits. Data are from various issues of the International Monetary Fund's *Government Finance Statistics Yearbook*.

The budget deficit as a fraction of GDP for most of these countries indicates enormous variation in their deficit experiences this period. For example, Cameroon experienced a large and growing budget deficit, reaching over 10 percent of GDP by 1985 and averaging nearly 5 percent over the entire period. In contrast, Zaire had on average a near balance between expenditures and revenues over the entire period, with some fluctuation between deficits and surpluses over time, and Zimbabwe showed a consistent budget surplus over much of the period. Other African countries have markedly different patterns of deficits over time.

Similarly, there is no unique deficit pattern in Asian or Latin American countries. Indonesia and Singapore both had consistent and large central government budget deficits, averaging roughly 8 percent of GDP over the entire period; in Latin America, Trinidad and Tobago and Venezuela also show a significant deficit over this period, in both cases reaching roughly one quarter of GDP in some years and averaging nearly 10 percent of GDP over all years. Iran has had an average deficit of 5 percent of GDP over time, with variation from a deficit of 14 percent in one year to a surplus of 6 percent in another year. Nicaragua experienced on average a surplus of roughly 2 percent of GDP. Several other countries in both regions—India, Pakistan, Thailand, Argentina, Ecuador, Jamaica, Mexico, Panama, Peru, and Uruguay—had on average a rough balance between expenditures and revenues, with an average deficit/surplus of less than 1 percent of GDP. Table 13.1 summarizes these results.

In short, the experiences of most developing countries differ substantially across country and time.

THE NATURE OF BUDGET DEFICITS

An important issue to consider is the benefits and costs of a balanced budget. More precisely, why is it desirable to achieve a budget in which government

Table 13.1
Average Deficit as a Percentage of GDP, Various Countries of Africa, Asia, and Latin America, 1971–1985

Region	Country	Deficit	Region	Country	Deficit
Africa:	Algeria	0.1	Latin America:	Argentina	-0.8
	Cameroon	4.9		Brazil	4.1
	Egypt	0.8		Chile	2.4
	Ghana	-2.1		Colombia	2.2
	Kenya	1.2		Dominican Republic	4.0
	Liberia	2.9			
	Morocco	1.7		Ecuador	-0.1
	Nigeria	3.5		Jamaica	-0.5
	Zaire	0.2		Mexico	-0.1
	Zimbabwe	-2.5		Nicaragua	-1.9
Asia:	India	0.6		Panama	-0.8
	Indonesia	7.4		Peru	0.6
	Iran	5.2		Trinidad & Tobago	9.1
	Korea	2.9		Uruguay	-0.6
	Malaysia	2.2		Venezuela	9.5
	Pakistan	0.5			
	Philippines	2.4			
	Singapore	8.5			
	Sri Lanka	1.7			
	Thailand	0.5			
	Turkey	2.7			

Source: International Monetary Fund, various years.

expenditures equal tax revenues? In this section, we consider the different views on deficits. It turns out that there is a surprising amount of disagreement among economists about the economic impact of large budget deficits.[1]

The Keynesian View

Most economists agree that there are at least some circumstances under which deficits are actually desirable. This perspective on deficits (sometimes called the "Keynesian view") is based on the fact that the size of the deficit depends on two basic elements: discretionary tax and expenditure decisions, and the performance of the economy. When the economy moves into a recession, government expenditures automatically increase and revenues automatically decrease, due to the presence of automatic stabilizers in the government budget. Consequently, the deficit increases in such periods, even if the government takes no direct action on spending or taxes. Similarly, the deficit declines as the economy expands, again with no discretionary decisions by government. These automatic changes in the "cyclical deficit" are viewed favorably by most economists because the economy is stimulated when there is need for stimulus and restrained when there is need for restraint. However, if the deficit remains even when the economy is at full employment, then such a deficit is called a "structural deficit." Here the evaluation of deficits is considerably more controversial.

The Neoclassical View

In the "neoclassical view" of deficits, structural deficits are seen as the source of a variety of economic ills. The most frequently mentioned negative effect of deficits emphasizes its impact on interest rates and, through that channel, on private investment. Remember that a deficit occurs when the government borrows from the public to finance its expenditures. This borrowing necessarily competes with other borrowers for the available loanable funds, so that increased government demand for credit puts upward pressure on interest rates and crowds out private investors competing for the same funds. In the long run these deficits therefore reduce the private capital stock, which lowers economic growth and future standards of living. Put differently, the presence of government deficits means that public saving is negative, so that total national saving (or public plus private saving) is reduced.

Of course, the crucial—and often neglected—question here is how the government uses the funds that it has attracted at the expense of private borrowing. If the government invests the funds in productive capital, then the deficit leads to a substitution of public sector capital for private sector capital, and the burden on future generations is accordingly reduced; in fact, if public sector capital is more productive than the displaced private sector capital, then the deficit actually makes future generations better off. There is some limited evidence on the productivity of public infrastructure investments. However, deficits in most developing countries do not appear to have contributed in a consistent and significant way to such investments.

Another adverse effect of deficits stems from their impact on export sectors. To the extent that government borrowing increases domestic interest rates, domestic investment appears more attractive to foreign investors, and capital flows from abroad to the domestic economy. These capital inflows in turn increase the demand for the domestic currency, which then appreciates relative to other currencies. A more valuable domestic currency enables domestic consumers to buy foreign goods more cheaply; however, it also makes it more difficult for domestic businesses to sell their products overseas. Deficits therefore crowd out domestic exporters, which leads to a loss of employment and income in export sectors of the economy. Unlike the case of investment, there is substantial empirical evidence to support this argument, although its relevance for small, open economies is somewhat suspect.

When the debt issued to finance the deficit is held overseas, an additional burden emerges. The servicing of debt requires that interest on the debt be paid and that the principal ultimately be retired. When these payments are made abroad, they constitute a transfer from domestic citizens to individuals living overseas, thereby reducing the living standards of those citizens that must make the payments. Current and future generations are now burdened because current consumption increases at the expense of future consumption.

One last adverse consequence of deficits stems not so much from the deficit per se but from pressure that the existence of the deficit is thought to bring to bear on the government. One pressure is imposed on the monetary authority. There is some fear that large, persistent budget deficits may eventually force the monetary authority to monetize the debt; that is, the monetary authority may pay for the debt that it purchases by printing money. The result of this monetization is a growth in the money supply and so an increase in inflation. Such monetization has been a fairly common experience in many developing countries, especially those that have tried to repudiate large debts by inflation.

Another pressure is on the agency that issues the debt. The presence of a large deficit may lead to government default on the debt, if limitations on the ability of the government to issue new debt imply that the deficit cannot be serviced.

In sum, many economists believe that deficits are harmful primarily because some individuals and sectors are burdened now by increased government borrowing and because future generations are burdened both by the involuntary taxes that they must pay to service the principal and the interest on the debt and also by the smaller capital stock that they receive from the current generation.

The Ricardian View

However, there are other economists who believe that these adverse consequences are both unsubstantiated and unjustified or who believe that deficits are primarily a symptom rather than a cause of the economic ills that are mistakenly attributed to deficits. These economists make several arguments.

The first argument is that tax and deficit finance are equivalent, in that the burden of each is on current, not future, generations. This argument was first made by David Ricardo over 150 years ago (hence, the name the "Ricardian view" of deficits) and more recently has been argued by Barro (1974). It rests on the notion that individuals should recognize when the deficit increases, by, say, $1, that their future taxes must also eventually increase by $1 in present value terms, since the $1 of additional debt requires debt service of $1 over its lifetime. If individuals recognize that deficits now require taxes later, then tax and debt finance are equivalent ways of financing government expenditures and so have the same effects. In both cases, the burden is felt by generations at the time the expenditure is made.

However, the assumptions upon which the Ricardian view is based are quite restrictive. These assumptions include: Individuals are infinitely lived (or are linked to all future generations by altruistically motivated transfers); there are perfect capital markets; there is no uncertainty; individuals are rational and far-sighted; and all taxes are nondistortionary, or lump-sum, taxes. There is little doubt that these assumptions do not hold in the "real" world, especially in developing countries.

A second argument is that the empirical evidence on the harmful effects of deficits is largely inconclusive, even for the United States where most research has been directed. In particular, empirical evidence only weakly supports the link between greater deficits and higher interest rates (Seater, 1993). It appears that many other factors (e.g., the overall state of the economy, the rate of inflation, monetary policy, international trade and financial developments, and so on) interact to determine the level of interest rates. Neither the amount of the deficit nor the amount of the outstanding accumulated debt appears to be a major factor in the determination of interest rates.

A third argument sees deficits as a symptom rather than a cause of economic problems. The notion here is that the government can finance any given level of its expenditures by taxing, by borrowing money from the public, or by expanding the money supply. Although the composition of finance is of some importance, the more crucial issue is the level of spending that must be financed. According to this argument, all the adverse consequences that are attributed to deficits are in fact due to excessive levels of government expenditures, not to the deficit itself.

This debate is not resolved. Most countries have only a limited experience with large peacetime deficits, and research especially in developing countries has only begun to address some of the issues raised in the above discussion. However, the consensus view of a clear majority of economists is that deficits create major problems for any economy, problems that may not appear in their most severe form until several years have passed.

THE CAUSES OF BUDGET DEFICITS

In this section, we examine the causes of budget deficits. We first begin with a discussion of the theoretical literature on the origin of deficit finance. We then use this literature to specify and to estimate a number of models of the determinants of deficits.

Theories of Deficits

Explanations for government use of budget deficits fall into two main categories, which can be roughly classified as normative and positive approaches. We consider each briefly.

One theory of deficit finance is based on a normative approach, in which deficits emerge as the result of optimal intertemporal choices by a rational government (Barro, 1979). This approach is sometimes called the "equilibrium approach" or the "tax smoothing approach." Here government must choose the time path of taxes in order to finance a known and given path of government expenditures. In choosing the taxes, the government is assumed to minimize the present value of the excess burden of taxation. If the excess burden of taxation is a convex function of the tax rate, then it is straightforward to show that the tax rate should be set at a constant level across all time periods needed to achieve budget balance. Deficits therefore emerge as the result of unexpected shocks to government spending: When spending is above (below) its permanent level, the government responds by running a temporary deficit (surplus), not by adjusting the level of taxes. This approach has received some empirical support for the United States (Barro, 1986) and other Organization for Economic Cooperation and Development (OECD) countries (Roubini and Sachs, 1989) but not for developing countries (Roubini, 1991).

A second approach is more explicitly positive and invokes various political economy, or public choice, theories of deficit finance.[2] In one theory (Buchanan and Wagner, 1977), for example, it is assumed that voters suffer from "fiscal illusion"; that is, voters are not fully aware of the intertemporal budget constraint of the government and systematically underestimate the true burden of future taxes needed to service the public debt. Self-interested politicians can then substitute deficit for tax finance and thereby gain electoral advantage. In another theory (Cukierman and Meltzer, 1989), deficits are viewed as a way of redistributing income from future generations (who obviously do not vote in the current period) to current generations. Other theories are based on the fact that the existence of government debt links past policies to future policies, and this linkage enables a current government to impose constraints on future governments (Persson and Svenson, 1989; Alesina and Tabellini, 1990). Some theories emphasize the role of distributional conflicts among different social groups (Weingast, Shepsle, and Johnsen, 1981; Alesina and Drazen, 1991). Finally, there are numerous studies that emphasize the impact of different budget institutions and laws (e.g., Which institution has the authority to draft/approve/implement government budgets? Which individuals play a role in the process? Are there constitutional limits on the deficit? Can the budget be amended easily? What is the time sequence of the budget process? Can specific items be deleted from the budget?). Empirical work seems particularly promising in this area (Roubini and Sachs, 1989; Roubini, 1991; Alesina et al., 1996).

In their entirety, these approaches suggest a number of variables that can be used to estimate the determinants of budget deficits. We present our empirical results based on these theories.

Empirical Evidence

We estimate the determinants of budget deficits using our sample of developing countries. Our dependent variable is the average budget deficit in the country as a proportion of GDP over the period 1971–1985.

We use a number of explanatory variables in different specifications. We include several economic variables: per capita real GDP in 1970, to control for the level of economic development; the share of the labor force employed in agriculture in 1970, also to control for the level of economic development; the average annual growth rate in per capita real GDP over the period, to control for cyclical effects on the budget deficit; the ratio of debt to GDP in 1970, to examine the impact of previous deficits on the further accumulation of debt; and the ratio of central government spending to GDP, to examine the effects of government size on deficit finance.

We also include several political/institutional variables. One is an index of political instability, measured from 1 to 10, with a higher number indicating greater political stability), to test the effect of political stability on the magnitude of budget deficits.[3] Another institutional variable is an index of the degree of "hierarchical" versus "collegial" approaches in budget institutions.[4] "Hierarchical" denotes a top-down approach to the budget process, in which the main decisions are made by a few individuals at the top of the process, while "collegial" implies a bottom-up approach that emphasizes the use of democratic rules at each decision stage. The index ranges from 0 to 100, with a greater number indicating a more hierarchical budget institution. The hypothesis here is that a more hierarchical process leads to greater fiscal discipline and so smaller deficits. The last institutional variable is an index of corruption, measured from 1 to 10, with a higher number indicating more corruption.[5] This variable is included to test the hypothesis that the ability of government to finance expenditures with taxes rather than deficits is weakened by a more corrupt institutional environment. It is important to note that the role of corruption in the determination of deficits has not been previously examined in empirical studies, despite the suggestion in some theoretical analyses that the extent of corruption (and other economic crimes like tax evasion) can have a significant impact on the optimal tax structure (Alm, 1996). The various specifications are estimated using ordinary least squares (OLS) methods.

The estimation results are somewhat sensitive to the precise specification. Nevertheless, there are several consistent findings. Countries with higher per capita GDP tend to experience larger deficits; similarly, more agrarian countries also run larger deficits. Perhaps surprisingly, countries in which the ratio of government spending to GDP is larger tend to have smaller deficits, while countries with a higher ratio of debt to GDP tend to have larger deficits. Most important, the political and institutional variables are found to have a consistent impact on the magnitude of deficits. Deficits tend to be larger in countries that experience greater political stability, that have more hierarchical budget institutions, and that have greater amounts of corruption.[6]

CONCLUSIONS

The deficit experience of developing countries suggests several major conclusions: that there are substantial differences in the magnitude of budget deficits across countries and across time, that the economic effects of these deficits are still uncertain, and that the causes of these deficits are capable of productive analyses, both from a theoretical and, especially, from an empirical approach. The last conclusion is perhaps the most intriguing. It should be apparent that the political and institutional arrangements within a country are critical factors in the determination of budget deficits and that these arrangements can overwhelm most tendencies toward farsighted and intertemporal optimizing behavior. Indeed, an implication of these empirical results is that government budget actors are for the most part shortsighted and self-interested in their management of the public finances, who act within the constraints imposed by various societal institutions. Put differently, individuals seem largely reactive in their decisions, rather than proactive, since the latter strategy would imply behavior more consistent with a farsighted actor. Individuals also seem interested mainly in maximizing their own wealth, by responding to opportunities for corruption. In all their choices, they are limited by the institutions of the society in which they operate. If it is deemed desirable to limit budget deficits, then appropriate policies cannot ignore these institutions.

NOTES

1. This literature is now quite large. For a detailed discussion of many of these issues, see Barro (1974), Bernheim (1989), and Eisner (1989). Seater (1993) provides a comprehensive survey of the theoretical and empirical literatures.

2. See Alesina and Perotti (1995) for a survey of theories that take a political economy perspective.

3. The political instability index is discussed in more detail in Barreto (1996).

4. This index is discussed and calculated by Alesina et al. (1996). Note that this index exists at present only for Latin American countries, so regressions that include this variable are limited to these countries.

5. The corruption index is discussed in more detail in Barreto (1996).

6. These estimation results are available upon request.

REFERENCES

Alesina, Alberto, and Allan Drazen. 1991. "Why Are Stabilizations Delayed?" *American Economic Review*, Vol. 82, No. 4, pp. 1170–1188.

Alesina, Alberto, Ricardo Hausman, Rudolf Hommes, and Ernesto Stein. 1996. "Budget

Institutions and Fiscal Performance in Latin America.'' NBER Working Paper 5586.

Alesina, Alberto, and Roberto Perotti. 1995. ''The Political Economy of Budget Deficits.'' *IMF Staff Papers*, Vol. 42, No. 1, pp. 1–31.

Alesina, Alberto, and Guido Tabellini. 1990. ''A Positive Theory of Fiscal Deficits and Government Debt.'' *Review of Economic Studies*, Vol. 57, No. 3, pp. 403–414.

Alm, James. 1996. ''What Is an 'Optimal' Tax System?'' *National Tax Journal*, Vol. 49, No. 2, pp. 216–233.

Barreto, Raul A. 1996. ''Corruption, the Public Sector and Economic Development.'' Ph.D. dissertation, University of Colorado at Boulder.

Barro, Robert J. 1974. ''Are Government Bonds Net Wealth?'' *Journal of Political Economy*, Vol. 82, pp. 1095–1117.

———. 1979. ''On the Determination of Public Debt.'' *Journal of Political Economy*, Vol. 87, pp. 940–971.

———. 1986. ''U.S. Deficits since World War I.'' *Scandinavian Journal of Economics*, Vol. 88, pp. 195–222.

Bernheim, B. Douglas. 1989. ''A Neoclassical Perspective on Budget Deficits.'' *Journal of Economic Perspectives*, Vol. 3, pp. 55–72.

Buchanan, James M., and Richard E. Wagner. 1977. *Democracy in Deficit: The Political Legacy of Lord Keynes*. New York: Academic Press.

Buiter, Willem H. 1983. ''Measurement of the Public Sector Deficit and Its Implications for Policy Evaluation and Design.'' *IMF Staff Papers*, Vol. 30, No. 2, pp. 307–349.

Cukierman, Alex, and Allan Meltzer. 1989. ''A Political Theory of Government Debt and Deficits in a Neo-Ricardian Framework.'' *American Economic Review*, Vol. 79, No. 3, pp. 713–732.

Eisner, Robert. 1989. ''Budget Deficits: Rhetoric and Reality.'' *Journal of Economic Perspectives*, Vol. 3, pp. 73–93.

International Monetary Fund. Various years. *Government Finance Statistics Yearbook*. Washington, D.C.: IMF.

Persson, Torsten, and Lars E. O. Svenson. 1989. ''Why a Stubborn Conservative Would Run a Deficit: Policy with Time-Inconsistent Preferences.'' *Quarterly Journal of Economics*, Vol. 104, No. 2, pp. 325–345.

Roubini, Nouriel. 1991. ''Economic and Political Determinants of Budget Deficits in Developing Countries.'' *Journal of International Money and Finance*, Vol. 10, pp. S49–S72.

Roubini, Nouriel, and Jeffrey D. Sachs. 1989. ''Political and Economic Determinants of Budget Deficits in the Industrial Democracies.'' *European Economic Review*, Vol. 33, pp. 903–938.

Seater, John J. 1993. ''Ricardian Equivalence.'' *Journal of Economic Literature*, Vol. 31, pp. 142–190.

Weingast, Barry R., Kenneth A. Shepsle, and Christopher Johnsen. 1981. ''The Political Economy of Benefits and Costs: A Neoclassical Approach to Distributive Politics.'' *Journal of Political Economy*, Vol. 89, No. 3, pp. 642–664.

Chapter 14

The Budget Process and Fiscal Imbalances in the New South Africa

ISMAIL ADAMS

This chapter focuses on the political economy of the budget reform process in the new South Africa, with particular reference to new intergovernmental fiscal relations. Following the first democratic national elections in early 1994, the incoming government inherited an administration with an apartheid mind-set, embodied in public institutions, an administration inappropriate and ill equipped to deal with and handle the demands expressed by the electorate. It is important to realize that the apparent smooth and easy speed of the South African transition is a consequence not only of the "political miracle" of 1994 but also of the negotiations conducted under the old apartheid regime. The negotiated settlement laid the foundation for the present government to pursue a neoliberal economic policy agenda, which was further influenced by the post–Cold War capitalist hegemony (Adams, 1997).

This chapter addresses the respective roles of the different tiers of government—national, provincial, and local—affecting resource allocation in reconstruction and development since early 1994. The democratic political system emerging in the new South Africa is not a sufficient condition to secure a stable society. It has to be underpinned by a growing and vibrant economy to sustain a successful transition and move the country toward full-fledged democracy. Although the African National Congress–led government has already promulgated acts of Parliament into a number of feasible socioeconomic policy initiatives in addressing the legacies of apartheid, the time has come for government to focus on the most crucial aspects of the policy process, namely, implementation within the policy environment. It is a fact that any strategy requires a budget that has to be financed from sources either locally or internationally. The method or source of finance adopted brings with it different sets of problems and concerns. For example, what will be the financial strategy both in the short to medium and long term for provincial and local governments in the delivery of social goods and services? In essence, the form, structure, and composition of intergovernmental fiscal relations will become a crucial element toward public sector reform in South Africa.

The structure of government in South Africa is highly centralized. The central government has access to more than 80 percent of the revenue collected by all tiers of government and is responsible for about 70 percent of total government expenditures. Local governments account for 10 percent of revenues and 7 percent of total government expenditures. Although the political changes in the country are directed toward creating a democratic and nonracial form of government, there are strong advocates for a decentralized form of government. Features of this are apparent and are reflected by the demarcation of regional/municipal boundaries and the creation of the nine provincial regions with greater fiscal responsibilities. In effect, 1994 will record the beginning of the devolution, and sharing, of important responsibilities to subnational governments—the implementation and planning of new decentralized arrangements with the added objective of restructuring and developing the economy in terms of the Reconstruction and Development Programme (RDP).[1]

The aim of this chapter is to differentiate several key drivers that will ultimately determine the extent of successfully implementing a system of intergovernmental fiscal relations in South Africa. The chapter covers four interrelated parts. The second section, which follows, deals with some matters of the new South African Constitution and how they will affect intergovernmental fiscal relations and economic performance. The constitutional dimensions will allow the creation of mechanisms through which the distribution of resources between the regions can be effected. The third section provides an overview of the budgetary reform process as required by the new Constitution, highlighting the principles underlying the approach pursued by government to accommodate a decentralized system of resource allocation. The fourth section reviews recent fiscal developments with an emphasis on reducing the budget deficit from 4 percent of gross domestic product (GDP) in 1997–1998 to an anticipated 3 percent of GDP by 1999–2000. This is in line with the government's macroeconomic strategy presented to Parliament on June 1996, the Growth Employment and Redistribution (GEAR) strategy. We also indicate some weaknesses of GEAR by arguing that this is an inappropriate macroeconomic strategy given the level of economic development in the country. The fifth section provides the new structure of intergovernmental fiscal relations in South Africa, highlighting the profound socioeconomic disparities between and within provinces and the efforts of central government to equalize fiscal inequities. The sixth section reviews the current output of the constitutionally established Financial and Fiscal Commission (FFC), which serves as an advisory body to Parliament to ensure greater transparency, efficiency, consistency, and predictability of fiscal policy. We also provide the variables of the base formula of the FFC and its consequential allocations to provinces. This is followed by a presentation of a new revenue sharing formula agreed to by the Budget Council that serves as a new basis for revenue resource allocations between the center and provinces and between provinces among themselves. In fact, the 1998–1999 national budget will be developed according to the Medium-Term Expenditure Framework (MTEF) and will also provide estimates for the following three years. Which of these drivers will predominate future intergovernmental provincial fiscal relations in South Africa will ultimately influence the extent of vertical and horizontal imbalances in the economy. Finally, we conclude with some challenges ahead.

CONSTITUTIONAL ISSUES

Constitutional principles provide the political framework within which different levels of government operate among themselves. However, the relationship between constitutions and economic performance is not clear and often misunderstood. In an illuminating article by Jon Elster (1994), he emphasizes, inter alia, that constitutions can be useful by serving as precommitment devices especially in the domain of two polar positions of economic performance: The first pertains to economic efficiency, and the second to well-being or security. He concludes that constitutions matter for economic performance to the extent that they promote the values of stability, accountability, and credibility. These issues are very important to the new South African democracy, for change has come about through a process of political accountability, and a new Constitution became effective on February 3, 1997, that establishes a unitary state with three levels of government: national, provincial, and local. Each of these is assigned certain powers and functions, be they exclusive, concurrent, or shared, and financial resources. A major concern is that of redistribution, given that the Gini-coefficient of 0.65 for the country is one of the worst in the world. The key question is, Will the process of political accountability be sufficient without a redistribution of assets to maintain the same level of political participation? In this regard the particular design of intergovernmental fiscal relations should ultimately reduce the profound economic disparities in the country. There is no doubt that constitutions and thereby institutions do have a profound impact on economic outcomes and performance reflected through the policy-making environment and process (Buchanan and Tullock, 1962). Moreover, the success or failure of the policy implementation process is heavily dependent on the cultural and political institutions in place (see Grindle and Thomas, 1991). This is very important in the South African context since the public sector is in the process of transforming itself away from the apartheid mentality syndrome toward a new democracy.

Schedule 5 of the Constitution allows for exclusive responsibility for a range of public services to the nine provincial governments. In turn, Schedule 4 of the Constitution specifies a number of shared central-provincial responsibilities that include, among others, agriculture; casinos, racing, gambling, and wagering;

airports other than international and national; education at all levels, excluding tertiary education; health services; housing; language policy; nature conservation; public transport; regional planning and development welfare services; and trade and tourism. The concurrent functions comprise about 58 percent of total government expenditure—and about 68 percent if expenditure on public debt is excluded. It is clear that the assignment of these functions to the provinces will have significant implications for the financial needs of provincial governments.

A very important issue in public policy implementation is the extent to which the national government should be responsible for financing the minimum standards of sector-specific services like education, health, and housing. There are various ways in which this could potentially be dealt with, each with different implications for fiscal equalization and the autonomy of provincial governments. On the one hand, the national government could be responsible for making conditional/earmarked grants to provincial governments for financing a minimum level of service. The provinces could also augment these services with their own funds to provide a better service if they so desire. On the other hand, national transfers to finance minimum standards of services could be limited to those provinces whose own revenues are insufficient to provide minimum standard services. In this case, transfers could play a major role in reducing fiscal inequalities. This option, however, requires extensive devolution of transfer of revenue sources to the provincial level.

Section 214 of the Constitution stipulates that each sphere of government shall have a constitutional right to an equitable division of revenue collected nationally. In general, Sections 227 through 230 defines fiscal powers to provinces and local governments as follows:

(i) Local government and each province is entitled to an equitable share of nationally collected revenue to enable it to provide basic services and exercise the functions allocated to it on recommendations by the FFC.

(ii) A province may impose taxes, levies, or duties (surcharges) other than the income tax, value-added tax, general sales tax, rates on property, or customs duties on recommendation of the FFC.

(iii) Municipalities are subject to the same limitations of tax assignment as provinces except that it can impose rates on property taxes and excise taxes.

(iv) A province or municipality may raise loans subject to recommendations of the FFC.

(v) Taxes levied and loans raised by provincial and local governments shall not be detrimental to national policies.

These constitutional provisions basically allow provinces and local governments their own taxing powers under certain conditions as well as the sharing on both an origin and a formula basis. However, the allocations to provinces shall be determined by an act of Parliament according to the following criteria: the national interest; after taking into account the national debt; fiscal capacity and performance of provinces and municipalities; development needs; economic disparities within and among provinces; the need for flexibility; and so on. It is therefore evident that the fiscal powers conferred to provinces are extremely limited if provinces are likely to exercise any autonomy. Moreover, the borrowing powers of provinces are likely to undermine the political autonomy provided by the Constitution. But revenue dominance by the central government is essential to underscore its responsibility for macroeconomic management and stability and income redistribution. The present constitutional arrangement brings forth a number of important fiscal implications.

First, revenue sharing implies that provinces can allocate the funds according to the priorities and preferences of their own residents, which guarantees a large degree of autonomy in the allocation of these funds. However, their autonomy will be less in the case of their own taxes where they can also determine their own tax rates. Second, the percentages of how each of these taxes (the income tax and the value-added tax) will be shared between provinces will be a high priority of the FFC (discussed later). Third, with regard to assigning expenditures, the crucial element is the allocation of the respective roles of central and subnational governments. Traditional public finance theory suggests that an "efficient" expenditure assignment between levels of government is based on the geographic dimension of benefits. That is, each jurisdiction should provide and fund services whose benefits accrue within its boundaries. Responsibilities for stabilization policies are typically assigned to central government, as is that of income redistribution. A transition economy like South Africa provides a special challenge to these basic principles of intergovernmental finance, because the responsibilities and nature of institutions and government are changing dramatically. Experiences of other more developed federal systems dictate that as fiscal decentralization develops, the expenditures of subnational governments increase relative to the center. Finally, we have a combination of revenue and expenditure mismatch resulting in subnational governments being left with inadequate resources to provide needed services. This will lead to a fiscal squeeze on the local provincial economy and will in effect force them to revert to "coping mechanisms" to deliver services, where otherwise they could not. These might include shifting budgetary outlays; resisting the privatization of enterprises; and the establishment of extra budgetary funds that make the budget less transparent. Because South Africa is plagued with a considerable diversity among regions, resource endowments, and ethnic groups, coping mechanisms may undermine national cohesion and nation building. Notwithstanding the constitutional political economy framework, the crucial challenge to provinces is whether they have the institutional capacity to implement national directives as well as the capacity to administer revenue from taxes under their competency. As this development process unfolds, one would expect that the central government would release more devolution. The impact of these fiscal dimensions on provinces is more clearly illustrated and discussed in a later section that deals with the provincial and local pattern of public sector activities.

BUDGETARY REFORM

The South African budget process has historically been based on the West-minster system used in the United Kingdom, which rests fundamentally on an annual planning cycle and expenditure controls managed by national and provincial treasuries. The incremental budget approach (adding a percentage to the previous year's allocation) is to be replaced by zero-based budgeting to take into account the fiscal implications emanating from the new Constitution, as mentioned above. The new Constitution requires significant reforms to the budgetary process with particular reference to legislation governing financial relations between the three tiers of government.

The current budget process contains several weaknesses that limit the ability of government to reprioritize public expenditure toward the objectives of the RDP. According to the Institute for Democracy in South Africa (IDASA, 1997), these include, among others, the absence of systematically monitoring the performance of spending agencies against agreed criteria; the lack of reporting on the incidence of expenditure; a weak chain of accountability between heads of agencies and officials within spending agencies responsible for implementing programs; and inadequate forward planning. These weaknesses as well as the incapacity of government at both the provincial and local level to carry out expenditure plans under the RDP manifested themselves in substantial ''rollovers'' of funds.[2] A recent International Monetary Fund (IMF) Staff Country Report (1997) indicates that rollovers increased from R1.5 billion in March 1993 (0.4 percent of GDP) to R8.9 billion by March 1996 (1.8 percent of GDP).

However, given the shortcomings of the past institutional budget framework, government has embarked on a comprehensive program of budget reform. Important changes are to be recommended by the end of 1998 in a White Paper on Budget Reform. The principles that underlie the government's approach in this regard include improved accountability, with devolved accountability for performance; clear setting of objectives, both in the medium term and on an annual basis, with transparent links between national and departmental objectives; a planning process that ensures that the budget contributes to those objectives, and with a role for the legislature in budgetary planning; transparent reporting based on generally accepted accounting practice; and the adoption of a revised format for the Estimates of Expenditure. In line with these principles, government has already implemented two very important initiatives deviating from the past. First is the adoption of an MTEF as part of a multiyear approach to fiscal planning (see below). Second, as indicated before, is the shift from incremental to zero-based budgeting.

Although the budget process has already undergone substantial changes, it is a long-term process and will in the future change to accommodate the unfolding decentralized fiscal resource allocation system of the FFC. Some of the key reforms that have been proposed to improve public sector performance entails, first, the expenditure evaluation of inputs, outputs, and outcomes. In the past the budget process was shrouded with secrecy and was regarded as a control mechanism for recording expenditure conforming to separate development (apartheid). Moreover, budgetary decisions were of an ad hoc nature without consulting the broader civil society, which inevitably led to poor public sector performance. Several countries have embarked upon budget reform to improve government strategic planning, priority setting, accountability, control, and legislative oversight. The new dispensation in South Africa gives impetus to these reforms since the old centralized methods are no longer tenable. Second, the government also indicated a change from the cash accounting system to the more acceptable *accrual based system* of accounting. This will facilitate true costing of outputs and performance measurement. Third is the introduction of performance agreements between heads of line departments, as is, for example, the practice in New Zealand. The philosophy behind this approach is the intention of creating incentives for either promotion or nonobstruction of efficient resource management in order to achieve outputs at lowest possible cost. A fourth proposed reform is integrating planning and budgeting through the MTEF. And a fifth reform is the reprioritization of expenditure to meet RDP objectives, since with limited resources and the massive demand for public goods and services government cannot hope to meet all the aspirations of the electorate. Thus, it is clear that government has to make appropriate trade-offs in the prioritization process, especially in regard to social sectors like education, health, and welfare. In addition to the FFC, a Budget Council has also been established as a cooperative decision-making body consisting of the minister and deputy minister of finance, the nine provincial ministers of finance, and officials of the Department of Finance, State Expenditure, and Provincial Treasuries. The Budget Council is charged with recommending the revenue-sharing arrangements to the national government, taking into account the FFC recommendations.

RECENT FISCAL DEVELOPMENTS AND GEAR

Before going into a discussion about the fiscal imbalances between the central and provincial governments, we briefly present an overview of the economic environment prior to the election of April 1994. Table 14.1 presents the structural indicators of the South African economy prior to the transition. South Africa's real GDP growth had been declining since 1965. In the first half of the 1960s it was almost 6 percent per year; by the 1970s it dropped below the population growth rates; and by the mid-1980s it had fallen to around 1 percent. It should be noted that in the past 20 years South Africa managed to achieve an annual economic growth rate of more than 5 percent—in 1980, in 1981, and in 1984. With a present population of approximately 40 million, growing at about 2.6 percent per year, per capita GDP growth has been negative since 1982 but recovered slightly after the elections of 1994. During the succeeding 2 years, growth exceeded the population growth rate, increasing real GDP per capita

Table 14.1
Structural Indicators for South Africa

	1980	1990	1993	1994	1995	1996	1997
GDP (real ,% change)	6.6	-0.3	1.3	2.7	3.4	3.1	1.5
Inflation % p.a.	15.0	14.4	9.7	9.0	8.6	7.4	8.0
GDFI (% GDP)	26.2	19.6	15.5	16.0	16.9	17.0	17.4
Domestic Savings (% GDP)	34.5	19.5	17.2	17.1	16.8	16.5	15.2
Budget Deficit (% GDP) [FY]	0.9	3.2	10.1	5.7	5.7	5.4	5.2
Public Debt (% GDP) [FY]	31.6	38.6	48.4	48.6	54.8	56.0	55.8

Notes: The fiscal year begins April 1. Data prior to 1994–1995 are not comparable with those thereafter because the 1994–1995 budget incorporated figures from the former homelands: Transkei, Bophusthatswana, Venda, and Ciskei.
Sources: *World Development Report*, 1995, 1996; *South African Reserve Bank Bulletin*, 1995, 1996; *Budget Review*, 1997.

marginally for the first time after many years. However, this growth momentum is far too low, and there are indications that the expected growth rate for 1997 would again be less than the population growth rate (see Table 14.1).

It is suggested that a real growth rate of between 7 and 8 percent would be needed to absorb new entrants into the labor market and to really make a dent in the unemployment rate of around 38 percent. Since mid-1985, there has been a massive decline in investment, especially by parastatals contributing to the decline in growth. Table 14.1 indirectly alludes to this in that the ratio of gross domestic product to savings has declined twofold since the 1980s, from 34.5 percent in 1980 to a low of 16.5 percent in 1996.[3] Prior to the elections, a major concern by policy makers was whether South Africa was heading for a "debt trap," as the public debt as a percentage of GDP increased by about 25.4 percent from 1990 to 1993. Since then the new government has adopted austerity measures to reduce the budget deficit at all costs, despite the apparent disagreement to this fiscal approach by the South African labor movement. In addition, civil society is also starting to put pressure on government to restructure its public debt,[4] the bulk of which was incurred under the apartheid era. It is appropriate in this context to reiterate a key point raised earlier: Will the process of political accountability be sufficient without a redistribution of assets to maintain the same level of political participation?

Against this background, apartheid intensified inequality in South Africa beyond that expected in a country at its level of development. As indicated earlier, the income distribution in the country is one of the worst in the world, with a Gini-coefficient of 0.65.[5] According to McGrath and Whiteford (1994), there was some redistribution of income from whites to blacks in the 1970s and 1980s, but "almost all the increased incomes accruing to the black population has flowed to the richest 20% of black households. Simultaneously the economic position of the remaining 80% of black households has worsened and in real terms they were poorer in 1991 than in 1975" (1994, p. 8). The social fabric and living conditions for the majority of people at the time of the transition were some of enormous disparities and inequities across and within the nine provinces. It is for these fundamental reasons that the macroeconomic policy initiatives underpinned by the RDP base document and the MERG (1993) report recommended as a first priority a "rapid improvement in the quality of life of the poorest, most oppressed and disadvantaged people."

However, the initial conditions of the economy in 1994 were those of extreme instability of the kind that had characterized some developing countries at the point of their economic and political transition. Haggard and Kaufman (1995) pointed out that (on the basis of twelve Latin American and Asian countries) in those countries that had achieved a "modicum of macroeconomic stability" at the beginning of their economic and political reform, policy options other than orthodox, neoliberal ones "ought to command greater attention" (pp. 310–316, as reported by Michie and Padayachee, 1997). The message here is clear: South Africa's first democratic government ought not to have embarked on a neoliberal economic policy stance by focusing on inflation and reducing budget deficits (which was not unreasonable) but should rather have opted for an aggregate demand management approach driven primarily by increased public investment. This approach would have directly targeted the improvement of social and physical infrastructure for the most disadvantaged, a notion underpinned by the publication of the RDP.

It advanced a number of key initiatives in support of economic and social transformation, with the state playing a major initiating and interventionist role in the economy. In fact, the RDP was construed by many as the first "development strategy" of the government. As indicated in Table 14.1, the two years following the elections, the economy was manifested by slow economic growth and rising unemployment. In an effort to rebuild confidence, the government announced GEAR in June 1996.

Although the objectives of GEAR are desirable and agreeable to almost everybody, the choice of policy instruments in achieving the objectives is where the difference lies. This is so because the choice of each policy instrument within a particular paradigm generates its own outcome, which in turn brings forth different implications for economic growth and development. The GEAR strategy acknowledges that the major constraint on economic growth remains the country's low savings and hence poor investment (see Table 14.1). There is therefore a twofold strategy: first, to reduce government dissaving by cutting the budget deficit to 3 percent of GDP by fiscal year 1999–2000; and second, to encourage foreign investment inflows. Under GEAR the budget deficit is required to fall to 4 percent in 1997–1998, to 3.5 percent in the following year, and toward a sustained 3 percent from 1999–2000—a target apparently made respectable and to be adhered to under the Maastricht requirements for the European Monetary Union. However, the current performance of the economy does indicate that South Africa has no chance of achieving the economic growth projections as projected under the GEAR strategy.[7] It has been indicated before that the GEAR document and the budgetary proposals represent a marked shift of policy by the government away from the RDP proposals. Adelzadeh (1996) provides a systematic and devastating critique of GEAR: the flawed modeling exercise, its questionable methodology, its contradictions, and the contrived analysis on which the GEAR proposals are based. Not only is the GEAR strategy "out of gear," but the government's philosophy of development approximates that which free market liberals advocated in the 1970s and the 1980s—maintaining an orthodox economic stabilization package as described in the previous section.

Michie and Padayachee (1997) argue that the rationale for government's predilection with its macroeconomic strategy "appears to be that growth would best be promoted by freeing the private sector from the fetters of the distorted, racist logic and constraints of the country's past" (p. 225). Moreover, they maintain that "[t]he government's position . . . appears to extend beyond the removal of all vestiges of racially based economic interventions (which all progressives would . . . support) to all other state interventionist measures such as tariff protection, financial regulation, state ownership and the like" (p. 225). For example, with its trade liberalization stance, the government announced proposals in June 1995 where the motor and textile industries were subjected to major tariff cuts by the year 2003, giving them just eight years to adjust instead of the twelve years agreed to by the World Trade Organization (WTO) and the General Agreement on Tariffs and Trade (GATT). Earlier it was indicated that the projected growth rate is largely dependent on the rapid success of government stimulating the private sector. This is to be done through cutting the budget deficit to 3 percent by 1999. This will reduce interest rates and in turn is expected to stimulate private investment. The economic logic behind this kind of reasoning is the "crowding-out" argument: When the state borrows to finance a deficit, it competes with the private sector for funds, thus pushing up interest rates. However, there is no consensus among economists about the importance of crowding out, and no empirical evidence exists to suggest that it has ever occurred in South Africa.

Furthermore, the strategy document is unclear as to where the sources of output growth and employment growth are to come from. This aspect generates another major weakness of GEAR in that it is not integrated or coordinated into a development strategy or a five-year development plan. For instance, there is no clear linkage between it and the RDP, except to say that GEAR agrees with the objectives of the RDP. Issues of developing human resources, health and welfare, meeting basic needs, and all facets of the RDP seeking to address the most disadvantaged sections of the South African society are barely treated in GEAR. In fact, the absence of a development strategy does not imply that government is not addressing the social sectors. On the contrary, a number of acts of Parliament have already been approved pertaining to the transformation and reconstruction of education, health, and welfare. Most of the legislature addresses procedural issues of responsibility at the different levels of government in striving toward equity and efficiency. However, no development strategy and not making available to the general public the econometric model upon which the GEAR strategy is based dampen or reduce the ability of the public to criticize government, despite its claim to transparency. Amartya Sen (1997) puts it this way: "The point of having a *conscious* development strategy is to subject the implicit choices [of government] to explicit scrutiny" (p. 26). To reiterate, a much larger and a more fundamental problem of the government's strategy is that it is almost entirely based on the formalistic, theoretical and empirically based forecasting model to derive its policy recommendations.

PROVINCIAL AND LOCAL PATTERNS OF PUBLIC SECTOR ACTIVITY

Earlier we said that the Constitution of South Africa integrated the previous apartheid-based jurisdictions into nine provinces. Across and within these provinces there are considerable differences in economic and social well-being. Table 14.2 provides indicators of revenue, expenditure, and social diversity among the nine provinces. The economic and development indicators reveal that disparities between the provinces are significant. However, the existing patterns of taxes and revenues and other social indicators across the provinces form the starting point for considering the implications of regional government.

A key issue in assessing the consequences of moving to a system of regional government that would take over the responsibility for certain areas of taxation and public spending involves both the sustainability of current standards of public spending and public services in the new system and the problem of fiscal equalization. Table 14.2 shows that the population distribution across provinces is very uneven. While four provinces have populations, expressed as a percentage of total population, between 6 and 9 percent, KwaZulu-Natal takes up 21.1 percent of the country's population. In sharp contrast, the Northern Cape has the lowest population in the country, representing only 1.8 percent of the total, although it is the largest region in terms of land space. There is also considerable variation between the provinces in economic performance and living standards. Government statistics indicate that Gauteng accounts for close to 37 percent of the country's GDP, while the Northern Province accounts for just 3.1 percent. Unemployment in the Western Cape is less than one in seven, compared to KwaZulu-Natal's one in four.

In addition, the magnitude of the differences in spending needs between provinces is depicted by the variances in social and development indicators. Table 14.2 also indicates that per capita personal income tax per province relative to the national average in the 1995–1996 fiscal year differs considerably between

Table 14.2

Indicators of Revenue, Expenditure, and Social Diversity among Provinces

	Northern Cape	Mpum-alanga	Free State	North West	Western Cape	Northern Province	Gauteng	Eastern Cape	KwaZulu-Natal
1997/98 provincial revenue(%):									
Revenue/GDP	0.3	0.8	1.0	1.1	1.5	1.7	2.2	2.3	2.6
National transfers/total prov. revenue.	96.6	96.0	92.2	95.5	94.4	95.4	94.1	97.8	95.3
Share of transfer/total national trnf.	2.5	6.0	6.9	8.4	10.9	12.9	16.1	17.1	19.3
1997/98 share of provincial expenditure for:									
Education	34.5	42.2	35.6	38.6	34.7	36.8	36.7	34.4	37.7
Health	15.9	21.1	23.3	16.7	26.0	15.5	34.3	18.8	22.8
Welfare1/	27.0	....	14.9	15.4	23.8	14.4	17.1	20.2	20.6
Other functional categories	22.7	25.7	26.3	29.2	15.5	33.3	12.0	26.6	18.8
Wages and salaries	46.3	....	53.3	....	....	59.9	50.7	55.2	....

Social indicators (%):

Prov. Population/total population	1.8	7.3	6.7	8.1	9.0	13.1	17.1	15.7	21.1
Adult illiteracy rate (1991)	20.0	25.0	16.0	31.0	5.0	26.0	8.0	28.0	16.0
Rural pop./provincial popln (1995)	27.0	68.0	4.07	72.0	14.0	91.0	6.0	65.0	63.0
Poverty rate in province (1993)	57.0	52.0	66.0	57.0	23.0	57.0	19.0	78.0	53.0
Prov. Poverty/natnl. Poverty (1993)	1.0	9.0	9.0	9.0	4.0	18.0	6.0	24.0	21.0
Children aged 5-17 (1995)	26.0	29.0	26.0	28.0	26.0	36.0	23.0	31.0	31.0
Pensionable aged group (1995)	6.0	5.0	5.0	5.0	6.0	5.0	6.0	6.0	5.0
Personal income tax/national ave.2/	110.0	99.0	88.0	57.0	163.0	28.0	221.0	44.0	75.0

1. Health and welfare combined for Mpumalanga, and shares refer to 1996–1997 budget.
2. Per capita collections per province relative to national average in 1995–1996 fiscal year.
Sources: Financial and Fiscal Commission, May 1996; International Monetary Fund, 1997, table 1, p. 55.

the regions. Gauteng and the Western Cape had a per capita personal income tax of 221 and 163, respectively. This is followed by the Northern Cape (110) and Mpumalanga (99). The Eastern Cape is the poorest region, with a per capita personal income tax of 44.

These pronounced variations in economic and social conditions and performance mean that the existing patterns of spending per head, and of tax revenue per head, vary considerably between the provinces. Spending on social security benefits (once introduced) will tend to be higher in the poorer areas, while income tax revenues will tend to be higher in the more prosperous provinces. Moreover, during the 1997–1998 fiscal year, almost two thirds of provincial expenditure is expected to go to education and health, of which over three quarters is for the payment of wages and salaries (Table 14.2). These disparities will in turn have to be considered in deciding on the form of equalization to be adopted by the FFC.

These figures will obviously change once the FFC's formula is in place. However, the longer the delay in implementing a formula that is more objective than annual ad hoc subjective decisions, the more provinces will use the previous year's allocation as a basis for projecting future allocations. This is contrary to the government's commitment to zero-based budgeting. The method and approach of financing provincial government constitute a major objective of the FFC. However, the appropriate basis for financing regional government will depend in part on the prior question of its role and functions.

Where regional government is principally concerned with the efficient implementation and administration of policies determined by central government, it may be appropriate for regional government to be financed largely or entirely through financial transfers from centrally collected tax revenues (currently in practice in South Africa). There would be little need for regional government to be assigned its own sources of tax revenue and to have the power to vary the rates of tax that are levied on its local population. In contrast, where regional government is intended to function as a more independent level of democratic decision making, giving regional voters the power to make choices that differ from those in other regions or that differ from the choices that would be made by central government, there is a much greater case for assigning some tax powers to regional government. In this case, some independent power over revenue is essential if the opportunity for regional government to make independent choices is not to be a meaningless fiction. Moreover, to ensure "accountability" when regional decision makers choose to set higher levels of spending, it is essential that the additional revenues required to finance any extra spending chosen by independent regional governments be raised from the regional population, through regional taxes; as little as possible of the tax burden should fall outside the region.

These requirements do leave open a considerable range of possibilities. The final choice that will be made will have to coincide with the appropriate provisions of the Constitution. Table 14.3 is perhaps the core of analyzing the

Table 14.3
Total Provincial Revenues (R million, real)*

Province	1996/97 Budget (base yr)	1997/98	1998/99	1999/00	2000/01	2001/02	2002/03
Western Cape	8729	8722	8719	8721	8729	8773	8838
Eastern Cape	14123	14386	14657	14956	15225	15455	15696
Northern Cape	1834	1810	1786	1761	1737	1712	1691
KwaZulu-Natal	15260	16030	16825	17645	18490	19327	20182
Free State	5471	5634	5804	5981	6165	6353	6550
North West	6801	7041	7288	7544	7809	8059	8318
Gauteng	11926	12958	14036	15162	16337	17722	19163
Mpumalanga	4715	4960	5212	5474	744	6023	6311
Northern	9818	10244	10681	11129	11587	11992	12397
Total	78678	81786	85010	88353	91821	98418	99147

*Grants plus own revenue.
Source: Financial and Fiscal Commission, May 1996.

effects of provincial allocations, for it indicates the extent of horizontal fiscal disparities across provinces. Equalizing per capita incomes across provinces will be a long-term objective. As is generally known, the rationale for central grants is (1) to adjust for different revenue capacities and for the costs of providing the same level of public service and (2) to encourage lower-level governments to pursue services and programs that spill over to adjacent jurisdictions.

The new Constitution provides a framework for local government, including a schedule of assigned functions. Section 214(1) of the new Constitution stipulates that an act of Parliament must provide for an assignment of revenue to local government as part of the equitable division between the national, provincial, and local spheres of government. Provision is also made for other conditional allocations to municipalities. Compared to a province, the local government has a larger tax base. Own-generated revenue accounts for almost 90 percent of its budget, thus requiring a smaller proportion of local government revenue than that at the provincial level.

Section 215(2) of the new Constitution indicates that legislation must prescribe the form and structure of municipal budgets. The Constitution also provides for the regulation of taxes, rates on property, surcharge on fees, and other levies or duties through national legislation. The 1997–1998 intergovernmental grants to local government have been allocated through the various provincial budgets as required by the interim Constitution.

Government grants to municipalities include a program for the elimination of infrastructural backlogs, based on an affordable level of service standards. The program also aims to promote local economic development through investment in municipal services. The municipal infrastructure program is coordinated by the Department of Constitutional Development, as are local government service grants for agency and delegated functions from national and provincial departments (such as ambulance and primary health care) and for subsidization of municipal services like libraries, bus transport, and firefighting. Although the national government will assist municipalities in financing their infrastructural needs for rendering basic services, recurrent expenditure is the responsibility of local government and must be covered from its own revenue sources.

Unlike the provincial level, the distribution of revenues to local governments is not addressed explicitly in the FFC formula. The existing transfers that go to local government via the transfer to provinces are captured in the Basic Grant. The FFC believes that the current intergovernmental transfers from national government to local authorities that are included in the global amounts going to the provinces are unsatisfactory because the criteria on which such grants are made are subject to doubt. The FFC is of the view that equity between the second and third spheres of government can be promoted only in a dispensation where no finance is made available on an arbitrary basis, as currently appears. The FFC favors a mechanism for transfers to local government that is based on considerations similar to those used in the provincial grants formula. On designing a system of local government grants, the focus of the FFC will be on a number of key issues: vertical fiscal balance; horizontal fiscal balance; types of grants; local government "basic services"; equity considerations; own revenue; and data needs.

FINANCIAL AND FISCAL COMMISSION

Institutional Structure and Base Formula

As can be observed from the previous sections, the present framework for fiscal relations in South Africa has three main features. First are the revenue-sharing arrangements between the provinces and the national government that are constitutionally guaranteed. Second is the assignment of taxation powers to the provinces and the national government. Lastly, the constitutionally established Financial and Fiscal Commission has a strong role to play in regard to administering the informational requirements needed to facilitate the smooth functioning of finances within a fiscal decentralized system. Such information will form the basis for their recommendations regarding the fiscal needs of the various tiers of government. Its role will be similar to the Australian Grants Commission. The FFC should ensure that the operation of financial flows within government will be more transparent, rendering the public service more accountable and more efficient.

As alluded to before, the central task of the FFC is to achieve interprovincial equity with respect to central government transfers. This is to be done through implementing two processes. First is the division of resources between national government and provincial governments to address the problem of a vertical fiscal imbalance. The second is the division of resources among provincial governments to address a horizontal fiscal imbalance. In terms of the first category, the FFC estimates that nationally collected revenue plus provincial revenues from a surcharge on personal income tax phased in from 1 percent to 7 percent will increase from 51.85 percent in 1996–1997 (base year) to 54.85 percent by fiscal year 2002–2003. This implies that the national share will decrease from 48.15 percent to 45.15 percent for the same period, assuming greater decentralization of functions to subnational levels of government. With regard to the second category, a grant formula of five elements is used to alleviate a horizontal imbalance. The recommended formula comprises the following elements:

$$P = S + m + T + I + B$$

where P is the total provincial allocation; S is a minimum national standards grant to provide for primary and secondary education and primary and district health care; m represents a spillover grant to provide for the financing of those services that have interprovincial spillover effects; T is a fiscal capacity equalization grant; I is an institutional grant to provide funds for each province to finance the core of the legislature as required by the Constitution; and B is a basic grant to enable provinces to establish and maintain the institutions necessary for the fulfillment of their constitutional obligations according to their own priorities.

Table 14.3 indicates the amounts in real terms to provinces by applying the formula over a period of five years. It shows that all the provinces receive an increase in allocation with the exception of the Northern Cape. The table also indicates that funds are directed away from the relatively well-endowed provinces to those with fewer facilities, in line with the Constitution. If these figures are expressed in per capita terms, then a very even pattern emerges between the provinces by the target date of 2002–2003, varying between R1,872 and R2,010 per capita. However, if revenue-raising powers and the formula are not implemented simultaneously, then provinces that are highly funded will face dwindling transfers and no other resources. This will exacerbate provincial deficits.

However, these were recommendations from the FFC which, as stated earlier, is a statutory advisory body accountable to Parliament. The national cabinet decides on the final allocations between the three spheres of government and presents these in the form of the budget for parliamentary approval. Moreover, the Intergovernmental Fiscal Relations Act, which took effect on 1 January 1998, establishes a formal process for considering intergovernmental budget issues. The Act is designed to facilitate and regulate a process of consultation to promote a budget-making process that is fair. The 1999 budget will be the first budget guided fully by the requirements of the Intergovernmental Fiscal Relations Act.

Other than these problems, the FFC's recommendations also raise several other issues. First, the recommendations imply the creation of a uniform financial management system across provinces so that accurate national data can be compiled for planning, implementing the formula, and monitoring the results. In fact, the government held a national census in October 1996 to improve the efficacy of the country's database, which will no doubt entail an adjustment to initial allocations since the formula is population biased. Second, the proposals also assume that the provinces possess the high levels of financial accountability and managerial efficiency to determine and control their own budgets. This is of major concern to national government as indicated earlier where approximately R1.6 billion represents carry-through costs of the RDP from two previous fiscal years.

A New Financial Framework

As indicated earlier, national policy on the allocation of funding to provinces and their degree of financial autonomy has evolved considerably over the last few years. On the revenue side, recommendations on how provinces should be funded were made by the FFC in May 1996. Subsequently, the Budget Council made a set of amended recommendations in line with the principles agreed at the Finance Lekgotla in April 1997. These form the basis for the current mechanism for determining the allocation from national to provincial government.

Currently, provinces' ability to raise their own revenue is small. Although the FFC recommended that provinces should be given the power to levy a personal income tax surcharge, this proposal has not become policy so far. Provinces do have the legal power to borrow, but this power is not likely to be exercised in the immediate future. These limitations have an important impact upon provincial expenditure since, in effect, the provincial budget becomes a cash budget with little ability to cover deficits.

On the expenditure side, the areas of budgetary authority for the provinces largely correspond to the areas of legislative competence as listed in Schedules 4 and 5 of the Constitution. The year 1997–1998 was the first year provinces were given full responsibility for budget allocation between their departments. The current budget formulation process is therefore a significant transfer of fiscal responsibility to provinces from national government. For the 1998–1999 budget, a new MTEF is being introduced by national government to provide a mechanism for budgetary planning over a rolling three-year period (see "The Medium-Term Expenditure Network" below).

A new revenue-sharing formula devised by the national Budget Council is in operation from 1997–1998 onward. This formula attempts to provide an equitable mechanism for dividing up resources both between national and provincial governments as well as between provincial governments. Given the importance of national revenue to the provincial government, the basis of the formula is described below.

The formula is based on two "splits": The *vertical split* determines the proportion of the available funds that is allocated to national departments and the proportion to be allocated to provinces; the *horizontal split* determines the distribution of the provincial funds between all of the nine provinces. The Budget Council formula takes total national budget expenditure and subtracts standing appropriations, debt service costs, and a new policy reserve. This gives the total expenditure to be shared between national and provincial. The vertical split between national and provincial is then based on the actual split in 1996–1997—that is, 42.1 percent for national; 57.9 percent for the provinces. The Budget Council proposes that these shares of spending, excluding debt interest and policy reserve, should remain the same for the next five years. Viewed from a total budget spending perspective, Table 14.4 illustrates the percentage shares of the total budget attributable to the four major components.

The horizontal split between provinces is allocated by splitting the total to be shared into four categories: conditional grants; unconditional grants for social security; tax share grants; and an "equitable share." Table 14.5 shows the distribution of the different grants between all the provinces for 1997–1998.

Conditional Grants

Conditional grants are for the following services: tertiary and academic health services; vocational education and teacher training colleges; RDP expenditure; and intergovernmental grants to local government. The exact services in each province that qualify are still to be determined.

Table 14.4
Percentage Shares of Total Budget Spending

Category	1997/98	1998/99	1999/00	2000/01	2001/02	2002/03
National	32.7	31.9	31.8	31.9	32.0	32.1
Provincial	44.9	43.9	43.7	43.9	44.0	44.1
Policy Reserve	1.0	2.5	2.7	2.8	2.9	3.0
Debt interest	21.4	21.7	21.8	21.4	21.1	20.8
Total	100.0	100.0	100.0	100.0	100.0	100.0

Source: Budget Council, 1997.

Unconditional Grants for Social Security

The intention of this grant is to provide provinces with the ability to meet their social security obligations. There is some discussion about transferring responsibility for social grants back to the national government, but in the meantime, social grants remain a provincial responsibility. In addition, social grants budgets will change significantly with the phasing in of the envisaged new child support program.

The Budget Council proposes a formula that incorporates weights based on the Age 0–4 and Age 60+ populations and on the size of the urban and non-urban populations. The intention is to phase in this approach over five years, allowing a real increase of 2 percent a year. However, although provinces retain the responsibility to meet social security obligations, the grant for social security is discretionary and can therefore be spent in whatever way the province deems appropriate. This component of the formula will be of great importance to those provinces where a high proportion of people are receiving welfare.

Tax Share Grants

The intention of this grant is to allocate part of the financing on the basis of an estimate of the tax contributed by each province. The Budget Council recommends that 10 percent of the funds remaining after subtraction of the conditional and social grants should be allocated for distribution in tax share grants. This will be around R6 billion, rising to R7.5 billion. The Budget Council proposes the use of the gross geographic product as a proxy for the tax base of each province.

"Equitable Share"

The remainder of the total to be shared between the provinces—the "equitable share"—is allocated to each province based on a demographic formula with four components:

Table 14.5
Distribution of Grants between Provinces, 1997–1998

1997/98	Conditional grants	Social Grants	Tax shares	Equitable share	Total
Western Cape	1,340	1,700	843	5,295	9,178
Eastern Cape	1,048	3,200	455	9,516	14,219
Northern Cape	65	500	125	1,348	2,038
KwaZulu-Natal	1,643	3,100	892	10,651	16,286
Free State	700	900	371	3,799	5,770
North West	359	1,000	333	5,313	7,005
Gauteng	3,190	1,700	2,258	6,306	13,454
Mpumalanga	326	800	488	3,355	4,969
Northern Province	655	1,800	221	8,292	10,968
Total	9,326	14,700	5,986	53,875	83,887

Source: Budget Council, 1997.

- A *basic share*, which is allocated according to the size of the population of each province; 20 percent of the equitable distribution is allocated in this way.
- An *education component*, which is calculated based on the percentage of the population aged five to nineteen and the percentage of full-time educational enrollment; 45 percent of the equitable distribution is allocated in this way.
- A *health component*, which is split equally between all the provinces to provide for the institutional foundation of provincial governments; 30 percent of the equitable distribution is allocated in this way.
- An *institutional component*, which is split equally between all the provinces to provide for the institutional foundation of provincial governments; the remaining 5 percent of the equitable distribution is allocated in this way.

The Medium-Term Expenditure Framework

A Macroeconomic Policy Working Group has been established to formulate long-term expenditure guidelines and quantify national economic objectives. The framework has been designed to encourage the alignment of departmental programs and budgets within the overall budget constraint. The Unit for Fiscal

Analysis in the Department of Finance, the Department of State Expenditure (DSE), and the Central Statistical Service have been collaborating in designing the MTEF. The problem with long-term planning is that over time the needs of communities change, the global economy changes, and projects that looked good need to be updated regularly, as economic circumstances and priorities change.

It is envisaged that the MTEF currently being defined will:

spell out the future financial implications of departmental policies and programs

help to evaluate policy trade-offs by highlighting policy and program trade-offs

enable spending agencies to plan ahead with greater certainty

assist the cabinet in evaluating policy options and setting expenditure priorities

reduce the need for rollovers and promote reprioritization

The Medium Term Expenditure Framework (MTEF) sets out three-year spending plans of the national and provincial governments. It aims to ensure that budgets reflect government's social and economic priorities and give substance to government's reconstruction and development commitments. The MTEF is one of the most important reforms of the budgetary process the government has introduced. The Minister of Finance released the *Medium Term Budget Policy Statement 1997* on 2 December 1997. The Statement sets out the policy framework for the 1998–1999 budget. It describes the government's goals and objectives and explains the economic environment within which these objectives are addressed. Broadly speaking, it reflects the macroeconomic and fiscal policy targets of the GEAR strategy and the RDP objectives.

The methods used in the MTEF are those of identifying unit costs, projecting the target client population (e.g., children under five, clinic patients, etc.), and combining these with quantified policy aims (e.g., pupil-teacher ratios) to give an estimate of costs of policy options. These are set against projected resources availability to test the feasibility of policies and to allow the prioritization of options within probable budget constraints. The MTEF is linked to the budget in that it will be an annual exercise rolling forward to form the basis of the budget.

Moreover, the MTEF is intended to allow effective policy making through taking a longer-term view and balancing options against resources to be made available. In the published version, a three-year forward view is taken, although often decisions will have implications for longer periods, and the Budget Council has made projections for future resources over a five-year period. For the present, allocations (two and three years) are said to be indicative of future plans only. A working MTEF system would have an annual cycle like that for the budget, and it is usual that the indicative allocations shown for year two will roll forward at the end of a planning year to form the basis for the next year's budget figures. As the system rolls forward, accumulated data on spending patterns and target achievements will form the basis of analysis and policy performance review.

For 1998–1999 to 2000–2001, the Department of State Expenditure has requested that provincial governments supply their expenditure figures in the form of the MTEF. The MTEF has two key innovations:

Multiyear expenditure planning. Provinces are requested to provide both their forthcoming budget as well as estimates for the following three years.

Cost-drivers. This is a mechanism determining the factors that are likely to drive costs in the large spending departments (Education, Health, Welfare, and Transport). The cost-drivers approach allows departments to see the impact of demographic changes on the cost of meeting national norms and targets.

Both of these innovations are welcome. Multiyear budgeting allows for better planning of projects and programs; the use of cost-drivers provides provinces with a tool with which to assess the implications of different levels of service delivery.

CONCLUSION

The establishment of appropriate intergovernmental fiscal relations in South Africa constitutes one of the major challenges for government. As indicated at the beginning, the Constitution provides the broad policy for a system of intergovernmental finance. There is an urgent need to translate the appropriate constitutional provisions into practice and to ensure that the monitoring process is in place. In this regard, the theoretical foundations of intergovernmental fiscal relations as well as the experience of other countries provide some useful directions, although these issues were not formally discussed here. The FFC's input into this process is of major significance, as it links the operation of the constitutional structure and the fiscal relations between the three spheres of government.

In this regard the budget reform process as discussed in this chapter serves to steer the economy into a system of decentralized resource allocation, of which two institutions are paramount. One is the Budget Council, followed by the recommendations of the FFC. The recent fiscal developments in the country are focused primarily on reducing the budget deficit and bringing the public debt in line with the government's macroeconomic strategy GEAR. Although the objectives of GEAR are realistic and reasonable, the approach adopted in achieving them in the short term are deflationary in the sense of exacerbating present inequities and social delivery expectations. We have indicated a number of weaknesses of GEAR and predicted that its projections will not be achieved in the short term.

The following are some of the most important broad challenges regarding the fiscal relations between the different levels of government (MERG, 1993): First, the need to prioritize development is imperative, for priority must be placed on developmental aims as outlined in the RDP whereby each level of government will act as a developmental agency reinforcing the broader macroeconomic policies of government. The fiscal relations between the various layers of government must complement the objectives of the RDP in order to "promote the goals of poverty reduction, greater equality through human development, and economic growth and employment." In this connection, as stated before, the present macroeconomic strategy of government may dampen or diminish RDP objectives. Second concerns the maintenance of macroeconomic stability. A third issue is that taxes should be levied by the jurisdiction that can do it most efficiently. This was referred to earlier as the tax assignment issue where the government has awarded the most important tax bases to the central government. This is appropriate considering the level of inequality in the country. A fourth principle deals with the efficient delivery of services, where the responsibility for the various functions of government should be given to the level of government that can most effectively be held accountable for its efficient delivery. In this case the impact of transfers and grants could perhaps be an issue that deserves constant monitoring and research, for the outcome of such research would assist in the refining of transfers and grants so that they can have the desired impact.

NOTES

1. The RDP is a coherent, interrelated program that seeks to address the legacy of apartheid but points to the action necessary to take us to the future. The central pillars behind the RDP are meeting basic needs, developing human resources, rebuilding the economy, democratizing the society, and financing the RDP.

2. Rollovers result from underspending, mainly from capital projects, relative to the original budget allocations. The minister of finance approves the amounts that may be rolled over on a case-by-case basis. Generally, rollovers must be spent by the end of the following fiscal year.

3. See Fallon and de Silva (1994) for a review of South Africa's past economic performance.

4. South African's public debt at fiscal year 1997–1998 is R305.8 billion, of which 96.2 percent (R294.3 billion) represents domestic debt and a foreign component of only R11.5 (3.7 percent). The interest on total government debt is R38.5 billion (19.8 percent) of total expenditure. This is the second largest expenditure item in the budget after education (20.8 percent). Presently, there is a campaign under way for the cancellation of apartheid's foreign debt upon an established precedent within international jurisprudence, the Doctrine of the Odious Debt (see Rudin, 1997). There is also a campaign in place driven by nongovernmental organizations for the restructuring of the domestic debt (see Dyffy, 1997).

5. Whites have personal incomes per capita of about 9.5 times those of Africans, 4.5 times those of blacks, and 3.0 times those of Asians. Social indicators such as infant mortality and life expectancy at birth for whites are comparable to those of developed

countries, while for the African majority, they are broadly in line with poorer developing countries. These extremes tend to confirm the view that there are really two South Africas—a First World society for whites and a Third World society for blacks.

6. The GEAR document details an economic reform program directed toward a competitive, fast-growing economy that creates sufficient jobs for all work seekers; a redistribution of income and opportunities in favor of the poor; a society in which sound health, education, and other services are available to all; and an environment in which homes are secure and places of work are productive. Five sets of new policy proposals were offered to achieve these goals: faster fiscal consolidation; a ''regulated, flexible'' labor market; accelerated tariff reductions; and additional exchange control liberalization.

7. This is the view of a sample poll of some 30 leading South African and international forecasting units. GEAR looks for growth of 2.9 percent in 1997, 3.8 percent in 1998, and 4.9 percent in 1999. The average prediction of the poll, carried out by Reuter, instead offers only 2.1 percent in 1997, 3.1 percent in 1998, and 3.8 percent in 1999 (*F&T Weekly*, July 11, 1997).

REFERENCES

Adams, I. 1997. ''The State and Development in Post-Apartheid South Africa.'' Occasional Paper Series No. 3. Department of Economics, University of the Western Cape, Bellville, South Africa.

Adelzadeh, A. 1996. ''From the RDP to GEAR: The Gradual Embracing of Neo-Liberalism in Economic Policy.'' *Transformation*, No. 31, pp. 66–95.

Buchanan, J., and G. Tullock. 1962. *The Calculus of Consent*. Ann Arbor: University of Michigan Press.

Budget Review. March 1997. Pretoria, South Africa: Department of Finance.

Constitution of the Republic of South Africa. 1996. Government Printer, RSA.

Development Bank of Southern Africa. 1994. *South Africa's Nine Provinces: A Human Development Profile*. Pretoria, South Africa: DBSA.

Dyffy, G. 1997. ''The Political Economy of South Africa's Public Debt.'' Glassbox Consulting Co. Rondebosch, Cape Town, South Africa.

Elster, Jon. 1994. ''The Impact of Constitutions on Economics Performance.'' Proceedings of the World Bank Annual Conference on Development Economics 1994, World Bank.

Fallon, P., and L. A. P. de Silva. 1994. ''South Africa: Economic Performance and Policies.'' Discussion Paper 7. World Bank, Southern Africa Department, Washington, D.C.

Financial and Fiscal Commission (FFC). 1995. *Framework Document for Intergovernmental Fiscal Relations in South Africa*. Pretoria, South Africa: FFC.

———. May 1996. *Recommendations for the Allocation of Financial Resources to the National and Provincial Governments for the 1997/98 Financial Year*. Pretoria, South Africa: FFC.

Grindle, M. S., and J. W. Thomas. 1991. *Public Choices and Policy Change: The Political Economy of Reform in Developing Countries*. Baltimore, Md.: Johns Hopkins University Press.

Growth, Employment and Redistribution, a Macroeconomic Strategy. 1996. Pretoria, South Africa.

Haggard, S., and R. R. Kaufman. 1995. *The Political Economy of Democratic Transitions*. Princeton, N.J.: Princeton University Press.

Institute for Democracy in South Africa. (IDASA). 1997. *Promises, Plans and Priorities*. Cape Town: South Africa Budget Information Services, IDASA.

International Monetary Fund. September 1997. *South Africa—Selected Issues*. IMF Staff Country Report No. 97/82. Washington, D.C.: IMF.

McGrath, M., and A. Whiteford. 1994. "Inequality in the Size Distribution of Income in South Africa." Occasional Paper No. 10. Stellenbosch University, South Africa.

MERG. 1993. *Making Democracy Work: A Framework for Macroeconomic Policy in South Africa*. Capetown, South Africa: Oxford University Press.

Michie, J., and V. Padayachee, eds. 1997. *The Political Economy of South Africa's Transition*. London: Dryden.

Rudin, J. April 1997. *Challenging Apartheid's Foreign Debt*. Cape Town, South Africa: Alternative Information & Development Centre, Woodstock.

Sen, A. 1997. "What's the Point of a Development Strategy?" *Development Economics Research Programme Series DERP*, No. 3. Suntory and Toyota International Centres for Economic and Related Disciplines (STICERD), London School of Economics and Political Science (LSE), London.

South African Reserve Bank Bulletin. 1995. Pretoria, South Africa: SA Reserve Bank.

————. 1996. Pretoria, South Africa: SA Reserve Bank.

World Development Report. 1995. Washington, D.C.: World Bank.

————. 1996. Washington, D.C.: World Bank.

Bibliographical Essay: A Selective Guide to Information Sources

JOHN C. GORMLEY

This guide focuses on the large, persistent government deficits experienced by many countries, with an emphasis on the United States. Materials in languages other than English have been excluded from consideration. Many bibliographies are already available on topics such as accounting, economics, and finance. Their contents will not be repeated here.

BIBLIOGRAPHIES AND LITERATURE GUIDES

Most people understand the word *bibliography* to mean a list of books and articles that were consulted in writing a research paper. The use of the word in the titles below has a different meaning. Librarians use bibliographies to identify sources of information. The words *guide* and *bibliography* are sometimes used interchangeably. Readers with an interest in these topics will want to consult these bibliographies of general interest.

Guides to the Literature of Public Finance

Of literature guides, those relating to public finance are most obviously related.

Marshall, Marion B., and Paul Wasserman. *Public Finance: An Information Sourcebook.* Phoenix, Ariz.: Oryx Press, 1987.
Rabin, Jack. *Public Budgeting and Financial Management: An Annotated Bibliography.* Hamden, Conn.: Garland, 1991.

Guides to Official Publications

Other bibliographies, which do not fit into the above categories, may contain useful information falling outside the scope of this guide.

Bibliographic Guide to Government Publications—Foreign 1994. 2 vols. New York: G. K. Hall, 1995.

Guide to Official Publications of Foreign Countries. Chicago: Government Documents Roundtable, American Library Association, 1990.

Hellebust, Lynn, ed. *State Blue Books, Legislative Manuals and Reference Publications: A Selective Bibliography.* Topeka, Kans.: Government Research Service, 1990.

Hollings, Robert L. *The General Accounting Office: An Annotated Bibliography.* New York: Garland, 1991.

Johansson, Eve. *Official Publications of Western Europe.* Vol. 2, *Austria, Belgium, Federal Republic of Germany, Greece, Norway, Portugal, Sweden, Switzerland, United Kingdom.* London: Mansell Publishing, 1988.

Johnson, Mary E. *International Monetary Fund, 1944–92: A Research Guide.* New York: Garland, 1993.

Salda, Anne C. *International Monetary Fund: A Selected Bibliography.* New Brunswick, N.J.: Transaction Publications, 1992.

Wilson, Carol R. *The World Bank Group: A Guide to Information Sources.* Hamden, Conn.: Garland, 1991.

Guides to Unofficial Publications

Euromonitor Staff. *International Directory of Non-Official Statistics Sources.* Detroit, Mich.: Gale, 1989.

————. *European Directory of Non-Official Statistical Sources,* 2nd ed. Detroit, Mich.: Gale, 1993.

Fildes, Robert, ed. *World Index of Economic Forecasts,* 4th ed. Brookfield, Vt.: Ashgate Publishing Co., 1995.

Kurian, George. *Sourcebook of Global Statistics.* New York: Facts on File, 1986.

Guides to Statistical Information

Statistics vary with regard to detail, frequency of issue, and accuracy. Others have already produced guides that deal with the subject of financial statistics. Interested parties should consider consulting some of the following sources.

Balachandran, M. *A Guide to Statistical Sources in Money, Banking and Finance.* Phoenix, Ariz.: Oryx Press, 1988. The introduction describes this work as a selective and annotated bibliography consisting mainly of serial sources of banking and monetary statistics. International in scope. It was written with the intention of guiding researchers to sources of detailed information. The author aims to fill a gap in the literature for those whose needs are not met by any of the national statistical compendiums.

Sources are grouped into the following categories: state; regional; national; foreign country; international sources, with sections on databases; directory of publishers; and title and subject index.

Barbuto, Domenica M. *The International Financial Statistics Locator: A Research and Information Guide.* Hamden, Conn.: Garland, 1995. Arranged alphabetically by country, with codes showing where statistics appear by topic. The section on government finance under the United States, for instance, shows that statistics on deficit/surplus are regularly reported in periodicals represented by these acronyms: ECI, FSM, FSY, GSY, WDR, and WTA. The key to acronyms in the front of the book reveals that the statistics are found in *Economic Indicators, International Financial Statistics* (Monthly), *International Financial Statistics Yearbook, Government Finance Statistics Yearbook, World Development Report,* and *World Debt Tables.*

Other Bibliographies and Guides of Interest

Listed here are those reference works of interest not fitting into the previous categories.

Daniells, Lorna. *Business Information Sources*, 3rd ed. Berkeley: University of California Press, 1993.
Dicks, G. R., ed. *Sources of World Financial and Banking Information.* Westport, Conn.: Greenwood Press, 1981.
Fildes, Robert, and Thana Chrissanthaki, eds. *World Index of Economic Forecasts*, 4th ed. New York: Stockton Press, 1995.
Holzer, Marc, and Arie Halachmi. *Public Sector Productivity: A Resource Guide.* New York: Garland, 1988.
International Directory of Business Information Sources and Services, 1996, 2nd ed. London: Europa Publications, 1995.
Lester, Ray. *Information Sources in Finance and Banking.* New Providence, N.J.: Bowker-Saur, 1996.
Pagell, Ruth A., and Michael Halperin. *International Business Information: How to Find It, How to Use It.* Phoenix, Ariz.: Oryx Press, 1994.
Slomanson, William R. *International Business Bibliography.* Buffalo, N.Y.: William S. Hein, 1989.

HANDBOOKS, MANUALS, AND DATA COMPILATIONS

Official Statistical Compilations, United States

Nearly every country, and every state of the Union, produces an official statistical compilation. These are commonly referred to as *statistical yearbooks.* For the United States the official compilation bears the title *Statistical Abstract of the United States.* To list the official statistical yearbook for every state would make this guide too lengthy. For most purposes the companion volumes to the *Statistical Abstract* should be sufficient. The title of these compendiums are *County and City Data Book* and *State and Metropolitan Area Data Book.* Those who have an interest in a particular state or county may consult one of the guides to official publications listed above. To use the official publications of another country may require knowledge of a foreign language. These documents are available from the Congressional Information Service and sometimes on the Internet. Fortunately, data compilations exist that show comparative international data on government finances. For most purposes, the compilations listed below should suffice.
Other official sources that contain data on government finances include publications

of the Census and Treasury Departments, as well as the Office of Management and Budget, among others.

Bank of England. Economic Intelligence Department Staff. *Bank of England Statistical Abstract, 1993. Pts. 1 and 2.* Ann Arbor, Mich.: Books on Demand, 1993.

U.S. Department of Commerce. Bureau of Census Staff. *County and City Data Book 1994: A Statistical Abstract Supplement.* Lanham, Md.: Bernan Press, 1994. [Available on CD-ROM as *County and City Plus*, also from Bernan.] A companion volume to the *Statistical Abstract*. The introduction describes this book as providing the most up-to-date statistical information for every state, county, and metropolitan area, congressional district, and all cities in the United States with a 1990 population of 25,000 or more. Data are selected from, among other places, the 1990 census.

————. *Statistical Abstract of the United States, 1996: The National Data Book.* Washington, D.C.: GPO, 1996. http://www.census.gov/stat_abstract/ This is the official statistical compilation for the United States. The preface states that this volume was designed to serve as a summary of government and private statistics for reference and as a guide to other statistical publications. The publications cited as sources at the bottom of each table usually contain more detail and a more comprehensive discussion of definitions and concepts. Of particular interest for this audience are these tables: Summary of the Federal Debt; Federal Budget Summary; All Governments—Revenue, Expenditure and Debt, 1980 to 1993; Federal Receipts by Source, 1980 to 1996; Federal Trust Fund Receipts, Outlays and Balances, 1993 to 1995; Federal Budget Outlay—Defense, Human and Physical Resources, and Net Interest Payments: 1940 to 1996; Federal Budget Outlays in Constant (1987) Dollars: 1980 to 1996; Federal Outlays by Branch and Detailed Function: 1990 to 1996. Also of interest to this audience will be the section on State and Local Finances and Employment.

U.S. Department of Commerce. Bureau of the Census. Economics and Statistics Administration. *Government Finances in* [fiscal year]. Washington, D.C.: GPO. Annual.

Official Statistical Compilations—Intergovernmental Organizations

In addition to the government publications cited, the official publications of intergovernmental organizations furnish statistics on government finances. For purposes of comparison they are probably the most important.

European Communities Staff. *Eurostat "Statistical" Yearbook.* Lanham, Md.: Bernan Associates, 1995.

International Financial Statistics Yearbook. Washington, D.C.: International Monetary Fund, 1979–. Annual.

International Monetary Fund Staff. *Government Finance Statistics Yearbook.* Washington, D.C.: IMF, 1977–. Annual. [Available on 9-track computer tape.] *A Manual on Government Finance Statistics* is a companion volume of this publication. According to the introduction, the information contained herein was obtained primarily from a questionnaire to government finance statistics correspondents.

Of particular interest for this audience will be the definition in the introduction of *deficit/surplus* as the total of revenue and grants minus the total of expenditures and lending minus repayments. Interestingly, deficit/surplus is also equal to net borrowing by the government plus the net change in government cash, deposits, and securities held for liquidity purposes. Also of interest, the section of the introduction on the basis and time of recording of data. Data for the principal aggregates (revenue, grants, expenditures, lending minus repayment, and financing) presented in the yearbook are generally shown on a cash basis.

———. *International Financial Statistics: Supplement on Government Finance*. Ann Arbor, Mich.: Books on Demand, 1982.

National Accounts Statistics: Government Accounts and Tables, 1982. New York: United Nations, 1986.

Organization for Economic Cooperation and Development. *National Accounts*. Vol. 1, *Main Aggregates, 1960–1991*. Paris: OECD, 1993.

———. *National Accounts*. Vol. 2, *Detailed Tables, 1979–1991*. Paris: OECD, 1993.

Statistical Bulletins

In addition to the annual compilations listed above, there are a number of other presentations of statistical materials, published at different intervals.

Board of Governors of the Federal Reserve System. *Federal Reserve Bulletin*. Washington, D.C.: Federal Reserve, 1915–. Monthly.

———. *Balance Sheets for the U.S. Economy*. Washington, D.C.: Federal Reserve, 1929–. Semiannual.

International Financial Statistics. Washington, D.C.: International Monetary Fund, 1947–. Monthly. [Available on CD-ROM and 9-track computer tape.] Updates *Financial Statistics Yearbook*. A standard source of statistics on all aspects of international and domestic finance. Arranged in tables, both for specific countries and world aggregates, this source provides data on exchange rates, international liquidity, international banking, money and banking, interest rates, prices, production, international transactions (including balance of payments), government finance, and national accounts.

Statistical Office of the European Communities. *Eurostatistics: Data for Short-Term Economic Analysis*. Lanham, Md.: UNIPUB. Monthly.

United Nations. *Monthly Bulletin of Statistics*. Lanham, Md.: UNIPUB.

U.S. Bureau of Economic Analysis. Department of Commerce. *Survey of Current Business*. Washington, D.C.: GPO. Monthly.

U.S. Bureau of the Census. *Census of Governments*. Washington, D.C.: GPO. Quinquennial.

U.S. Council of Economic Advisers. *Economic Indicators*. Washington, D.C.: GPO. Monthly.

U.S. Department of Commerce. Bureau of Economic Analysis. *Business Statistics*. Washington, D.C.: GPO. 1929–. Annually.

U.S. Department of the Treasury. *Daily Treasury Statement*. Washington, D.C.: GPO. Daily.

———. *Monthly Statement of the Public Debt of the United States*. Washington, D.C.: GPO. Monthly.

———. *Treasury Bulletin*. Washington, D.C.: GPO. Quarterly. The Bureau of Economic Analysis publishes historical and annual figures on the same subjects covered in current issues. Of possible interest to this audience: Fixed Reproducible Tangible Wealth in the United States, 1925–85.

U.S. Office of Management and Budget. Executive Office of the President. *Budget of the United States Government.* Washington, D.C.: GPO. Annual.

Unofficial Statistical Compilations

Apart from the preceding official sources, statistics on government finance appear in numerous factual compilations, typically referred to as almanacs. There are so many possible sources that I will not attempt to list them all here. While the information contained in these sources may not be as detailed or recent as one would like, they are widely available.

Also, there are a number of significant publications relating to public finance, and the budget deficit in particular, that do not emanate from official sources. These include publications of the Tax Foundation and other public interest groups. Some that may prove helpful are listed here.

All States Tax Handbook 1996. New York: Research Institute of America, 1995.

Almanac of the Fifty States: Basic Data with Comparative Tables. Palo Alto, Calif.: Information Publications, 1996. Arranged into two parts. The first, arranged alphabetically by state, with profiles for each. The second section consists of comparative tables. Of particular interest, table 30, ''Federal Aid to State and Local Government, per capita, 1994.''

Fleenor, Patrick. *Facts & Figures on Government Finance.* Washington, D.C.: Tax Foundation, 1941–. Biennial.

Godin, Seth, ed. *Information Please Almanac and Desk Reference, 1994.* Boston: Houghton Mifflin, 1993.

Reddy, Marlita, ed. *Statistical Abstract of the World.* Detroit, Mich.: Gale, 1994.

Slater, Courtenay M., and George Hall. *County and City Extra: Annual Metro, City and County Data Book 1996.* Lanham, Md.: Bernan Press, 1992. Annual.

Handbooks and Manuals—United States, National

The works cited above consist chiefly of data. Handbooks or manuals offer information on using the information. Some of those listed here are the companion volumes of those listed above.

Collender, Stanley E. *The Guide to the Federal Budget, Fiscal Year 1997.* Lanham, Md.: Rowan & Littlefield Publishers, 1996.

Galbis, Vincente. *IMF's Statistical Systems in the Context of United Nations' ''System of National Accounts.''* Washington, D.C.: International Monetary Fund, 1991.

International Monetary Fund Staff. *A Manual on Government Finance Statistics.* Ann Arbor, Mich.: Books on Demand, 1986.

———. *International Financial Statistics Yearbook 1994.* Washington, D.C.: IMF, 1994.

International Yearbook of Industrial Statistics 1995. Brookfield, Vt.: Ashgate Publishing, 1995.

Lynch, Thomas D., and Lawrence L. Martin, eds. *Handbook of Comparative Public Budgeting and Financial Management*. New York: Marcel Dekker, 1993.

Maltese, G. I., ed. *U.S. Federal Budget Process: An Overview and Glossary of Terms*. Commack, N.Y.: Nova Science Publishers, 1995.

Ott, Attiat F. *Public Sector Budgets—A Comparative Study*. Aldershot, England: Edward Elgar Publishing, 1993.

Schick, Allen. *The Federal Budget: Politics, Policy, Process*. Washington, D.C.: Brookings Institution, 1995.

Statistical Office of the European Communities. *National Accounts Yearbook*. Lanham, Md.: UNIPUB.

———. *Quarterly National Accounts*. Lanham, Md.: UNIPUB.

United Nations. Department of Economic and Social Affairs. Statistical Office. *Handbook of National Accounting: Public Sector Accounts*. New York: United Nations, 1988.

United Nations. Economic and Social Council. *National Accounts and Balances: System of National Accounts (SNA)*. New York: United Nations, 1987. Subtitle: *Links between the System of National Accounts (SNA) and Related Fields of Statistics, with Particular Reference to Balance of Payments Statistics (BOP), Government Finance Statistics (GFS) and Money and Banking Statistics (MBS)*.

United Nations. Industrial Development Organization Staff. *Handbook of Industrial Statistics, 1992*. Brookfield, Vt.: Ashgate Publishing, 1993.

U.S. Congressional Budget Office. *The Economic and Budget Outlook: Fiscal Years 1996–2000*. Washington, D.C.: GPO, 1995.

U.S. Office of Management and Budget. Executive Office of the President. *Budget of the United States: Historical Tables*. New York: Gordon Press, 1995.

———. *Analytical Perspectives: Budget of the United States. FY 1997*. Washington, D.C.: GPO, 1996.

———. *Budget of the U.S. FY 1997*. Washington, D.C.: GPO, 1996.

———. *A Citizen's Guide to the Federal Budget*. Washington, D.C.: GPO, 1996.

World Bank Staff. *World Bank Atlas*. Washington, D.C.: World Bank, 1995.

World Tables 1995. Baltimore, Md.: Johns Hopkins University Press, 1995. [Published annually since 1976.]

ENCYCLOPEDIAS AND DICTIONARIES

Both encyclopedias and dictionaries are convenient sources for finding explanations, although encyclopedias go into greater depth. Their usefulness should be self-evident. There are a number of general business and specialized subject dictionaries that may be of assistance, though no one source stands out as best. Some more recent ones are listed below.

Darnell, Adrian C. *A Dictionary of Econometrics*. Brookfield, Vt.: Ashgate Publishing, 1994.

Downes, John, and Jordan Elliot Goodman. *Dictionary of Finance and Investment Terms*, 4th ed. Hauppauge, N.Y.: Barron's, 1995.

Glossary of Finance and Debt. Washington, D.C.: World Bank, 1991.

Henderson, David R., ed. *The Fortune Encyclopedia of Economics*. New York: Warner Books, 1993.

Kaounides, Lakis C., and Geoffrey Wood. *Debt & Deficits*. 3 vols. Brookfield, Vt.:
    Ashgate Publishing, 1992.

DIRECTORIES

Directories of Products and Services

There are a number of commercial products and services that may prove useful to
those reading this guide. They range from simple screening software to analytical software. No attempt has been made to list them. Interested parties should consult:

Essinger, James, and Joseph Rosen. *The Global Directory of Financial Information Ven-
    dors*. Burr Ridge, Ill.: Irwin, 1994.

Directories of Organizations and Persons

Sciavone, Giuseppe. *International Organizations: A Dictionary and Directory*, 3rd ed.
    New York: St. Martin's Press, 1993.
Who Knows What: A Guide to Experts, 13th ed. Washington, D.C.: Washington Re-
    searchers, 1994.
Who's Who in International Banking, 6th ed. Providence, R. I.: Bowker-Saur, 1992.
    [Published annually since 1984.]

INDEXING AND ABSTRACTING SERVICES

Several indexing and abstracting services are available that help us to identify relevant
journal articles and sometimes books and government reports on the topic of budget
deficits.

Business Index. Belmont, Calif.: Information Access, 1979–. Monthly.
Business Periodicals Index. New York: H. W. Wilson, 1958–. Monthly.
Fed in Print: Economic and Banking Topics. Philadelphia, Pa.: Federal Reserve Bank of
    Philadelphia, 1990–. Semiannual.
International Bibliography of the Social Sciences: Economics. London, England: Rou-
    tledge, 1952–. Annual.
International Bibliography: Publications of Intergovernmental Organizations. Oxford,
    England: Marsten Book Services Ltd., 1973–. Quarterly.
International Current Awareness Services: Economics and Related Disciplines. New
    York: Chapman & Hall, 1989–. Monthly. A monthly update of *International
    Bibliography of the Social Sciences*.
International Social Security Association. *World Bibliography of Social Security*. Geneva,
    Switzerland: International Social Security Association, 1963–. Semiannual.
Sage Public Administration Abstracts. Beverly Hills, Calif.: Sage Publications, 1974–.
    Quarterly.
Statistical Reference Index. Bethesda, Md.: Congressional Information Service, 1980.

ONLINE AND CD-ROM PRODUCTS

The first part of this guide dealt with printed sources of information. The remaining portion relates to computer-readable information. Many of the print publications listed above are also available online or as a CD-ROM product. Some information made available in this form may never appear in print. Even when a print counterpart exists, there may be significant differences. There are too many general sources to list them here. Interested parties may wish to consult:

Business and Legal CD–ROMs in Print. Westport, Conn.: Meckler, 1993–. Annual.
CD-ROM Finder. Medford, N.J.: Learned Information, Inc., 1993–. Annual. Formerly *Optical Publishing Directory*, 1987–1992.
Computer-Readable Data Bases. Compiled by Martha E. Williams. White Plains, N.Y.: Knowledge Industry Publications, 1979–. Annual. Continues earlier *Computer-Readable Bibliographic Data Bases* with a broader scope. Includes numerical databases.

Bibliographic Databases

Computer-searchable versions of Indexing and Abstracting Services are typically called *bibliographic databases*. Many computer-readable databases are available that correspond to the print sources listed under "Data Compilations" and are known as *numeric databases*. These include, notably, publications of the International Monetary Fund.

Grouped here one will find a listing of those that may have some relevance to the problem of budget deficits.

International Bibliography: Publications on Intergovernmental Organizations. Millwood, N.Y.: Kraus, 1972–. Quarterly.
IntlEc CD-ROM: The Index to International Economics, Development and Finance [database]. Washington, D.C.: Joint Bank-Fund Library, 1981–. Quarterly. Available on CD-ROM.
Statistical Masterfile [computer file]. Bethesda, Md.: Congressional Information Service, 1984–. Annual.

Internet Sites of Interest

One should keep in mind that many of the publications listed above are available via the Internet. Similar information may be freely available here that would be expensive elsewhere. For instance, the Bureau of Economic Analysis World Wide Web page offers links to much of the information for which one would have to pay *STAT-USA* (though in less detail).

BudgetNet. http://www.financenet.gov/financenet.fed.budget.budget.htm (June 26, 1998)
Budget of the United States Government Fiscal Year 1997. http://www.doc.gov/BudgetFY97/index.html (February 11, 1997). Includes links for accompanying budget materials such as analytical perspectives, historical tables, and so on.

Bureau of the Public Debt. The Public Debt to the Penny. http://www.publicdebt.treas. gov/opd/opdpenny.htm (February 11, 1997)

Census Bureau: Statistical Agencies (International). http://www.census.gov/main/www/ stat-int.html. Provides links to the statistical agencies of numerous countries.

Census of Governments, Volume 4. No. 5. Government Finances—Compendium of Government Finances. http://www.census.gov/prod/www/abs/msgov05e.html (March 12, 1997)

Congressional Information Service. *Electronic Information Resources.* http:// www.cispubs.com/elecinfo.html (September 20, 1998). Contains links for the Statistical Masterfile, Index to International Statistics, and Current National Statistical Compendiums on Microfiche, as well as others.

Consolidated Financial Statements of the United States Government, 1995 (Prototype). http://www.fms.treas.gov/cfs/

DSBB: Central Government Debt. http://dsbb.imf.org/category/cgdctys.htm (September 14, 1997), links by country.

Economic Issues 3—Confronting Budget Deficits. http://www.imf.org.external/pubs/ft/issues3/index.htm

Eurostat. *European Official Statistics: Sources of Information.* http://europa.eu.int/en/ comm/eurostat/pub/85672en.html (February 11, 1997)

Eurostatistics. http://europa.eu.int/en/comm/eurostat/pub/bj0003a.html

Finance and Development. http://www.worldbank.org/fandd

FinanceNet. http://www.financenet.gov Provides links to the statistical agencies of numerous countries, as well as international financial management associations/organizations.

The Financial Data Finder. http://www.cob.ohio-state.edu:80/dept/fin/osudata.htm Contains a list of links to data providers. Those of interest: Basic Sources of Economic Statistics (from Princeton University); Census Department (U.S.), Central Statistical Office (U.K.).

FinWeb—A Financial Economics WWW Server. http://www.riskweb.com (February 17, 1995) This site aims to list Internet resources offering substantive information on the topics of economics and finance.

Goffe, Bill. *EconData.* http://wueconb.wustl.edu/EconFAQ/node20.html (February 11, 1997)

International Economics Gateway. http://www.access.digex.net/~grimes/gate.html Contains links to, among others, International organizations, data archives, national government pages, and corporate servers.

International Intergovernmental & Non-governmental Resources. http://www.lib. washington.edu/libinfo/libunits/suzzallo/govpubs/intl.html Contains a list of links to international intergovernmental (IGO) and international nongovernmental (NGO) resources, as well as brief abstracts for many sites. Perhaps the most interesting among them for this audience is the G-7 Information Centre.

International Monetary Fund Homepage. http://www.imf.org/external/ (November 15, 1996)

Links to the World—Economics and Government Finance. http://www.leg.state.mn.us/ lrl/links/govern.htm (February 10, 1998)

Monthly Treasury Statement of Receipts and Outlays of the United States Government. http://www.fms.treas.gov/mts/ (May 21, 1998)

1992 Census of Governments. Finance Statistics (Preliminary). http://www.census.gov/ftp/pub/mp/www/rom/msrom9c.html

OECD Electronic Publications on Financial and Fiscal Affairs. http://www.oecdwash.org/PUBS/ELECPUBS/epfin.htm (February 11, 1997)

Office of Management and Budget. http://www.access.gpo.gov/su_docs/budget/index.html

Political Risk Services WWW Index Page. http://www.prsgroup.com

STAT-USA. http://www.stat-usa.gov/ Includes links to Export and International Trade, Domestic Economic News, and Statistical Series.

UN—Statistics Division—Machine Readable Products and Services. http://www.un.org/Depts/unsd/epubls.htm (March 12, 1997)

U.S. Department of Commerce. "President's FY97 Budget." *United States Government Information.* http://www/access.gpo.gov/su_docs/sale/market/97bdgt.html (March 23, 1996). This site provides information on ordering print or CD-ROM versions of the budget of the United States, along with related publications.

The World Bank Homepage. http://www.worldbank.org/

"World-Wide Government Information Sources." *Links to Government Servers and Information.* http://www.eff.org/govt.html

Index

About the Editor and Contributors

SIAMACK SHOJAI is associate professor and former chairman of the Economics and Finance Department at Manhattan College. His papers have appeared in the *Journal of Energy and Development* and the *Journal of Economic Development*. He is the editor of and contributor to two recent volumes in the area of global oil markets. Dr. Shojai is a regular economics and financial commentator on the *Voice of America*. He was on the faculty of Fordham University and Lafayette College prior to joining Manhattan College.

SOHRAB ABIZADEH is professor of economics and former associate dean of Arts and Science at the University of Winnipeg, Canada. He received his doctorate in economics from Oregon State University and has authored over 50 articles in prestigious journals in economics and public finance. He is the coeditor of *Fiscal Systems and Economic Development: A Case Study of Selected Countries* (NOVA Science Publishers, 1996).

ISMAIL ADAMS is the chairperson and senior lecturer at the Department of Economics at the University of the Western Cape, Bellville, Cape Town, South Africa. He has published many articles in public finance journals and is an expert on the fiscal processes in South Africa.

JAMES ALM is a professor of economics at the University of Colorado at Boulder, where he has taught since 1983. He earned his master's degree in economics at the University of Chicago and his doctorate at the University of Wisconsin at Madison. He has also taught at Syracuse University in the Maxwell School of Citizenship and Public Affairs. Professor Alm teaches and conducts research in the area of public economics. Much of his research has examined the responses of individuals and firms to taxation in such areas as tax reform and the tax treatment of the family. He has also worked extensively on fiscal reforms overseas, including projects in Bangladesh, Indonesia, Jamaica, Turkey, Egypt, Hungary, China, the Philippines, and the Russian Federation. He is currently on the editorial boards of the *National Tax Journal* and *Public Finance Review*.

ANTHONY D. APOSTOLIDES has been engaged in research and teaching on public sector economics, including public finance and health care. His research and publications include work on the budget developments of the government in Greece, the bond ratings of cities in midwestern states, and the efficiency of local government in delivering services. He has served with the United Nations, Economic Commission for Europe (Geneva), worked as senior economist with the Medicaid program of the State of Maryland, and has also been associated with The Conference Board, where he engaged in measuring and evaluating research and development expenditures of U.S. transnational corporations. He has taught at Indiana University, Mary Washington College, and Miami University. He received a doctoral degree in economics from the University of Oxford, United Kingdom.

RAUL A. BARRETO is a professor of economics at the University of Adelaide at Boulder, where he earned his doctorate in 1996. Professor Barreto teaches macroeconomics, and his research addresses public sector issues in macroeconomics. In particular, he has examined the effects of public sector corruption on economic growth and development. He is an expert on the Paraguayan's economic history and development.

JAMES R. BARTH is currently the Lowder Eminent Scholar in Finance at Auburn University. Until November 1989, he was the chief economist of the Office of Thrift Supervision and before that the chief economist of the Federal Home Loan Bank Board, from August 1987. He has also been a visiting scholar at the U.S. Congressional Budget Office, Federal Reserve Bank of Atlanta, Office of the Comptroller of the Currency, and associate director of the Economics Program at the National Science Foundation. Mr. Barth received his Ph.D. in economics from Ohio State University with his dissertation supported by a Federal Reserve Bank of Cleveland fellowship. Mr. Barth has published more than 100 articles in professional journals and books and is the author of *The Great Savings and Loan Debacle*, published by the American Enterprise Institute in 1991. He is also included in *Who's Who in Economics: A Biographical Dictionary of Major Economists 1700 to 1995*.

JAMES L. CHAN is professor of accounting and political science at the University of Illinois at Chicago and Emmett Dedmon Visiting Professor in public policy at the University of Chicago. He was the founding editor of *Research in Government and Nonprofit Accounting* and currently serves on the editorial boards of *Public Budgeting and Finance, Public Budgeting and Financial Management, Financial Accounting and Management, Advances in Accounting,* and

The GAO Journal. He has published extensively in the accounting and public finance areas in many nationally reputable journals.

BRUCE COLLINS is associate professor of finance at Western Connecticut State University. He holds a doctorate in economics and has over a decade of experience in financial markets working for The First Boston Corporation, Shearson Lehman Hutton, Morgan Stanley & Company, and Drexel Burnham Lambert, among others. He is the author of numerous journal articles and chapters in books.

JOHN C. GORMLEY is a reference librarian assigned to the Engineering Library at Manhattan College. Prior to his current position, he was an assistant branch manager in the Queens Borough Public Library in New York. He holds a Master of Business Administration degree from Manhattan College

HERSCHEL I. GROSSMAN is Merton P. Stoltz professor in social sciences and professor of economics at Brown University. He is the author of over 60 articles in prestigious journals such as *Journal of Political Economy, Journal of Monetary Economics*, and *American Economics Review*. Currently, he is a research associate at the National Bureau of Economic Research and has served on the editorial boards of the *Journal of Monetary Economics* and *American Economic Review*. Dr. Grossman received his doctorate from John Hopkins University.

HASSAN MOHAMMADI is an associate professor of economics at Illinois State University. His areas of specialty are macroeconomics and monetary economics. His research has focused on empirical examination of the validity of alternative macroeconomic models. His more recent research reexamines the potential adverse macroeconomic effects of government budget deficits.

NEIL T. SKAGGS is professor of economics at Illinois State University. For the past decade his research has centered primarily on the history of monetary economics. He has published widely on nineteenth-century British and American monetary thought. He is the coauthor of a text on the principles of economics.

ROBERT C. A. SORENSEN conducts research on political participation and public policy in Western Europe. He has been on the faculty of the Government Departments of Muhlenberg, Middlebury, and Manhattan Colleges. Currently, he is Assistant Professor at the School of Business, Public Administration, and Information Sciences at Long Island University in Brooklyn, New York.

JAMES M. SUAREZ is professor of economics and finance and dean of the School of Business at Manhattan College. He previously worked as a research economist in government finance at the Federal Reserve Bank of New York and as the director of Economic and Fiscal Analysis at the New York City Finance Department. He has published articles on public finance and public policy.

JOHN M. WELLS is an assistant professor in the Department of Economics at Auburn University and an adjunct scholar with the Ludwig Von Mises Institute. He received his Ph.D. in 1994 from Texas A&M University in the fields of international finance, monetary economics, and econometrics, and was recently awarded a National Science Foundation grant for his work on the economic implications of war and peace.

MAHMOOD YOUSEFI is professor of economics at the University of Northern Iowa. He has authored numerous papers in prestigious journals and many chapters in academic books. He received his doctorate from the University of California at Santa Barbara and was the chairman of the Economics Department at Pahlavi University, Shiraz, Iran from 1975 to 1978.

ISBN 0-275-95712-8

9 780275 957124

HARDCOVER BAR CODE